A TREASURY OF
HUMOROUS POETRY

Field   Riley

Holmes

Lowell   Harte

A Treasury of Humorous Poetry

Being a Compilation of Witty, Facetious, and Satirical Verse Selected from the Writings of British and American Poets

Edited by

FREDERIC LAWRENCE KNOWLES

Illustrated

Granger Index Reprint Series

BOOKS FOR LIBRARIES PRESS

FREEPORT, NEW YORK

First Published 1902
Reprinted 1969

LIBRARY OF CONGRESS CATALOG CARD NUMBER:
71-75713

MANUFACTURED
BY
HALLMARK LITHOGRAPHERS, INC.
IN THE U.S.A.

DEDICATED
BY PERMISSION TO
Samuel Langhorne Clemens
("Mark Twain")

PREFACE

"The great end of comedy," said Doctor Johnson, in speaking of the drama, is "making an audience merry." Whatever else may or may not be true of a humorous compilation, it is certain that unless such a book is amusing, it is a failure.

The aim of this "Treasury" is not that of presenting extracts illustrating the development of humorous poetry in the English language. If that were its purpose, the anthology might have greater value for historical students of literature, but for the average reader it would prove of necessity uninteresting. A sense of relative proportion would have to be observed, which would mean that Chaucer must be liberally represented; that one or more scenes from Shakespeare would have to be transplanted bodily; that the "Rape of the Lock" must needs be included, as well as much of Dryden, Prior, Gay, Samuel Butler, Swift, Southey, and other wits of a former day, and that the jesters who can really amuse a modern audience would have to be represented meagrely or not at all.

The editor's first intention, he confesses, was to produce a book a little after this fashion, but upon examining a number of compilations which aim to preserve a sense of historical perspective, and discovering how uncompromisingly dull they are, viewed in the light of contemporary taste, he abandoned the scheme for one more unpretentious. The selections are almost wholly from nineteenth century writers, but in any anthology which succeeds in interesting a wide audience of readers, this is unavoidable.

And yet the present book has a higher aim than that of collecting ephemeral newspaper rhymes. Although it has been the editor's purpose to include only extracts that are strictly amusing to modern readers, he has given preference to such selections as seem most likely to have something approaching permanent interest. This standard, however, is difficult to preserve, for who shall say that what entertains this generation will succeed in entertaining the next, — or, indeed, that what amuses one reader to-day will be certain to amuse another! At best, any editor's choice must be personal, and all his efforts to determine the tastes of his readers experimental.

The term "humorous" has been interpreted in this compilation very broadly. It has been made to include poems as widely apart as the rollicking ballads of Hood, and the refined, delicately phrased verses of Locker-Lampson, or as the grotesque comicality of Gilbert and the serious irony of Canning, Clough, and Sill. In a word, there has been no attempt to discriminate between humorous poetry in any exact or narrow sense, and society verse, epigram, or satire. The selections vary from broadly comic to merely facetious and lively.

It is interesting to observe how the public taste has changed. In the eighteenth and early nineteenth centuries the dominant influence of Pope led to the substitution of pithy, satirical epigrams for the broader, comic manner which preceded, and which happily has followed. The fondness for epigram persisted well up toward the present time. In Parton's "Humorous Poetry," published fifty years ago, nearly two hundred epigrams are included. The reader of to-day cannot but wonder that many of the supposedly witty couplets and quatrains by Prior, Pope, Swift, Waller, Sheridan, Hook, and others, failed to seem merely flat and vulgar. It would appear that any clever schoolboy could versify the current jests of *Life* or *Puck* with more effective results. Some of these miniature satires were, of course, exceedingly brilliant, but of the majority of the selections in Adams's "English Epigrams," for example, what can one say except that they are either pretty bad, or that our taste has so outgrown the mood which produced them that we are incapable of judging their merits impartially.

But not all the wits, even in the eighteenth century, were busy in making pigmy arrows with poisoned tips. Burns, of course, was a master of humor, and Cowper and Goldsmith also carried on the great tradition begun with Chaucer and continued through Shakespeare and his successors. The early nineteenth century saw a group of real humorists in Barham, the authors of "The Rejected Addresses," and Winthrop Mackworth Praed. In Hood, who lived nearly till the mid-century mark, England produced a man of very high talent almost approaching genius, who could play at will on the keyboard of tears or laughter. For wholesome, exuberant fun, often very extravagant, but never gross, he has had no rival since his too-early death. A new kind of humor, however, has sprung up later, quite different from his own, and in the opinion of many of a superior order. It depends for its effectiveness, not on puns or outrageously comic situations, but on more subtle and pervasive elements. Among English writers, Thackeray, Calverley, Dobson, and Seaman, though each in a different way, represent this deeper mood, and, among Americans, such men as Lowell, Harte, Riley, Leland, and Bunner. Saxe, a very clever poet in his way, belonged to the school of Hood. Doctor Holmes, though from the very first more original than Saxe, showed evidence of the same moulding influence in his earliest humor, but later worked out for himself a much broader style.

It is strange that so few of the most eminent English and American poets have distinguished themselves in the field of humorous composition. Spenser, Milton, Wordsworth, Keats, Shelley, Tennyson, Arnold, Bryant, Longfellow, Emerson, Whittier, Poe, and Whitman — here is surely a formidable list! But it is, perhaps, still more remarkable that among the foremost humorists of the English language so few can be adequately represented in a collection like this. Chaucer and Shakespeare, greatest of English humorous poets, do not lend themselves to quotation, except in very long or else in the briefest and most fragmentary selections. This is also true in a less degree of Pope and of Byron.

The editor has had very free range in the choice of copyrighted material, but it is only fair to add that he would willingly have given larger representation to several American writers, if the number of poems available had not been restricted by their publishers. In the case of one or two American humorists, indeed, he was prevented by copyright difficulties from including them at all. It is a matter of especial regret that the publishers saw fit to forbid the use of Halpine's "Irish Astronomy," and E. S. Martin's "Little Brother of the Rich," — certainly two of the most clever among American humorous poems.

It is possible that among such a large number of selections one or more copyrighted poems may have been included on the supposition that they were common property. For any such unwitting transgression, if such there prove to be, the editor offers sincere apologies, and promises proper acknowledgment in future editions of the book.

The aim of the compiler has been, so far as practicable, to draw directly from original sources. No one can have a greater aversion to the indolent and worse than useless practice of making anthologies from other anthologies. On the other hand, in editing any book like this, it is impossible to disregard the patient labors of one's forerunners. The editor has consulted many humorous collections, of which the following list may serve as examples: Adams's "Comic Poets of the Nineteenth Century," Leigh Hunt's "Wit and Humour," Rossiter Johnson's "Play-day Poems," W. M. Rossetti's "Humorous Poems," Cook's "Anthology of Humorous Verse," Miles's "Poets and Poetry of the Century" (Vol, ix.), Caine's "Humorous Poems of the Century," Parton's "Humorous Poetry of the English Language," Langbridge's "Poets at Play," Locker-Lampson's "Lyra Elegantiarum," Shirley Brooks's "Amusing Poetry," and many others. The editor is also indebted to such compilations as Smeaton's "English Satires," Adams's "English Epigrams," and Hamilton's "Parodies of the Works of English and American Authors." A collection of humorous poems by Irish writers is Graves's "Songs of Irish Wit and Humor," and compilations of American humorous verse are included in "The Canterbury Poets" series of Walter Scott, London, and the "Cap and Gown" series of L. C. Page & Company, Boston. Collections of both prose and verse are Morris's "Half-hours with the Best Humorous Authors," Mason's "Humorous Masterpieces from American Literature," Mark Twain's "Library of Humor," and "The International Humor Series," published by the London house of Walter Scott.

Thanks are due owners of copyright for the use of numerous selections. Poems by the following writers are included by permission of and by special arrangement with *Houghton, Mifflin & Co.*, the publishers of the respective authors:

Ralph Waldo Emerson, James Thomas Fields, Bret Harte, John Hay, Oliver Wendell Holmes, James Russell

Lowell, John Godfrey Saxe, Edward Rowland Sill, Bayard
Taylor, Charles Henry Webb.

Further acknowledgments:

Century Company:
   Irwin Russell.
Dodd, Mead & Co.:
   Paul Laurence Dunbar.
Bowen-Merrill Co.:
   James Whitcomb Riley.
Lee and Shepard:
   Charles Follen Adams; Sam Walter Foss.
Charles Scribner's Sons:
   Henry Cuyler Bunner; Eugene Field.
D. Appleton & Co.:
   Joel Chandler Harris.
Adam and Charles Black:
   Charles Godfrey Leland.
Small, Maynard & Co.:
   Holman F. Day; Charlotte Perkins (Stetson) Gilman.
John Lane:
   Owen Seaman.
Whitaker & Ray Co.:
   Joaquin Miller.
Richard G. Badger & Co.:
   James Jeffrey Roche.
Life Publishing Company:
   J. H. Thacher.
Forbes & Co.:
   Ben King.
Frederick A. Stokes Co.:
   Gelett Burgess; Frank Dempster Sherman.
Kurtz H. Kellam:
   Eugene F. Ware.
R. H. Russell:
   Harry Bache Smith. (The selection quoted is from
   "Stage Lyrics," by Harry B. Smith, copyright 1900,
   by Robert Howard Russell.)

The editor would make personal acknowledgments to
the following authors who have given individual permission to include copyright poems:

Carolyn Wells, Oliver Herford, Charles Edward Carryl,
James Whitcomb Riley, Charles Godfrey Leland, Gelett
Burgess, Eugene F. Ware, Paul Laurence Dunbar, Harrison

Robertson, Samuel Minturn Peck, Joel Chandler Harris, Joaquin Miller, Robert W. Chambers, Albert Bigelow Paine, Charles Henry Webb, Harlan H. Ballard, Nathan Haskell Dole.

F. L. K.

Boston, August 29, 1902.

INDEX OF AUTHORS

List of Illustrations

A TREASURY OF HUMOROUS POETRY

PLAIN LANGUAGE FROM TRUTHFUL JAMES

OR, THE HEATHEN CHINEE

Which I wish to remark —
  And my language is plain —
That for ways that are dark,
  And for tricks that are vain,
The heathen Chinee is peculiar,
  Which the same I would rise to explain.

Ah Sin was his name,
  And I shall not deny
In regard to the same
  What that name might imply;
But his smile it was pensive and childlike,
  As I frequent remarked to Bill Nye.

It was August the third,
  And quite soft was the skies;
Which it might be inferred
  That Ah Sin was likewise;
Yet he played it that day upon William
  And me in a way I despise.

Which we had a small game,
  And Ah Sin took a hand;
It was euchre — the same
  He did not understand;
But he smiled as he sat by the table
  With the smile that was childlike and bland.

1

Yet the cards they were stocked
  In a way that I grieve,
And my feelings were shocked
  At the state of Nye's sleeve,
Which was stuffed full of aces and bowers,
  And the same with intent to deceive.

But the hands that were played
  By that heathen Chinee,
And the points that he made
  Were quite frightful to see,
Till at last he put down a right bower,
  Which the same Nye had dealt unto me.

Then I looked up at Nye,
  And he gazed upon me;
And he rose with a sigh,
  And said, " Can this be?
We are ruined by Chinese cheap labor;"
  And he went for that heathen Chinee.

In the scene that ensued
  I did not take a hand,
But the floor it was strewed
  Like the leaves on the strand
With the cards that Ah Sin had been hiding
  In the game " he did not understand."

In his sleeves, which were long,
  He had twenty-four packs,
Which was coming it strong,
  Yet I state but the facts;
And we found on his nails, which were taper,
  What is frequent in tapers — that's wax.

Which is why I remark —
  And my language is plain —
That for ways that are dark,
  And for tricks that are vain,
The heathen Chinee is peculiar,
  Which the same I am free to maintain.

                              Bret Harte

FAITHLESS NELLY GRAY

Ben Battle was a soldier bold,
    And used to war's alarms;
But a cannon-ball took off his legs,
    So he laid down his arms!

Now, as they bore him off the field,
    Said he, "Let others shoot,
For here I leave my second leg,
    And the Forty-second Foot!"

The army surgeons made him limbs:
    Said he, "They're only pegs:
But there's as wooden members quite
    As represent my legs!"

Now, Ben he loved a pretty maid,
    Her name was Nelly Gray;
So he went to pay her his devours,
    When he devoured his pay!

But when he called on Nelly Gray,
    She made him quite a scoff;
And when she saw his wooden legs,
    Began to take them off!

"O Nelly Gray! O Nelly Gray!
    Is this your love so warm?
The love that loves a scarlet coat
    Should be more uniform!"

Said she, "I loved a soldier once,
    For he was blithe and brave;
But I will never have a man
    With both legs in the grave!

"Before you had those timber toes,
    Your love I did allow,
But then, you know, you stand upon
    Another footing now!"

"O Nelly Gray! O Nelly Gray!
   For all your jeering speeches,
At duty's call I left my legs
   In Badajos's *breaches!* "

"Why, then," said she, "you've lost the feet
   Of legs in war's alarms,
And now you can not wear your shoes
   Upon your feats of arms! "

"O false and fickle Nelly Gray!
   I know why you refuse: —
Though I've no feet — some other man
   Is standing in my shoes!

"I wish I ne'er had seen your face;
   But now, a long farewell!
For you will be my death; — alas,
   You will not be my *Nell!* "

Now, when he went from Nelly Gray,
   His heart so heavy got,
And life was such a burden grown,
   It made him take a knot!

So round his melancholy neck
   A rope he did entwine,
And, for his second time in life,
   Enlisted in the Line!

One end he tied around a beam,
   And then removed his pegs,
And, as his legs were off — of course,
   He soon was off his legs!

And there he hung, till he was dead
   As any nail in town, —
For, though distress had cut him up,
   It could not cut him down!

A dozen men sat on his corpse,
   To find out why he died —
And they buried Ben in four cross-roads,
   With a *stake* in his inside!

Thomas Hood

THE AHKOOND OF SWAT

"The Ahkoond of Swat is dead."— London Papers of Jan. 22, 1878.

What, what, what,
    What's the news from Swat?
  Sad news,
  Bad news,
Comes by the cable led
Through the Indian Ocean's bed,
Through the Persian Gulf, the Red
Sea and the Med-
Iterranean — he's dead;
The Ahkoond is dead!

For the Ahkoond I mourn,
  Who wouldn't?
He strove to disregard the message stern,
  But he Ahkoodn't.
Dead, dead, dead:
  (Sorrow, Swats!)
Swats wha hae wi' Ahkoond bled,
Swats whom he hath often led
Onward to a gory bed,
    Or to victory,
    As the case might be.
      Sorrow, Swats!
Tears shed,
    Shed tears like water.
Your great Ahkoond is dead!
    That Swats the matter!

Mourn, city of Swat,
Your great Ahkoond is not,
But laid 'mid worms to rot.
His mortal part alone, his soul was caught
    (Because he was a good Ahkoond)
    Up to the bosom of Mahound.
Though earthly walls his frame surround
(Forever hallowed by the ground!)

And skeptics mock the lowly mound
And say "He's now of no Ahkoond!"
   His soul is in the skies —
The azure skies that bend above his loved
      Metropolis of Swat.
   He sees with larger, other eyes,
   Athwart all earthly mysteries —
      He knows what's Swat.

Let Swat bury the great Ahkoond
   With a noise of mourning and of
      lamentation!
Let Swat bury the great Ahkoond
   With the noise of the mourning of
      the Swattish nation!
   Fallen is at length
   Its tower of strength;
   Its sun is dimmed ere it had
      nooned;
   Dead lies the great Ahkoond,
   The great Ahkoond of Swat
   Is not!

                              George Thomas Lanigan

THE YARN OF THE "NANCY BELL"

'Twas on the shores that round our coast
   From Deal to Ramsgate span,
That I found alone on a piece of stone
   An elderly naval man.

His hair was weedy, his beard was long,
   And weedy and long was he,
And I heard this wight on the shore recite,
   In a singular minor key:

"Oh, I am a cook and the captain bold,
   And the mate of the *Nancy* brig,
And a bo'sun tight, and a midshipmite,
   And the crew of the captain's gig."

And he shook his fists and he tore his hair,
    Till I really felt afraid,
For I couldn't help thinking the man had been drinking,
    And so I simply said:

" Oh, elderly man, it's little I know
    Of the duties of men of the sea,
And I'll eat my hand if I understand
    How you can possibly be

" At once a cook, and a captain bold,
    And the mate of the *Nancy* brig,
And a bo'sun tight, and a midshipmite,
    And the crew of the captain's gig."

Then he gave a hitch to his trousers, which
    Is a trick all seamen larn,
And having got rid of a thumping quid,
    He spun this painful yarn:

" 'Twas in the good ship *Nancy Bell*
    That we sailed to the Indian Sea,
And there on a reef we come to grief,
    Which has often occurred to me.

" And pretty nigh all the crew was drowned
    (There was seventy-seven o' soul),
And only ten of the *Nancy's* men
    Said 'here' to the muster-roll.

" There was me and the cook and the captain bold,
    And the mate of the *Nancy* brig,
And the bo'sun tight, and a midshipmite,
    And the crew of the captain's gig.

" For a month we'd neither wittles nor drink,
    Till a-hungry we did feel,
So we drawed a lot, and accordin' shot
    The captain for our meal.

" The next lot fell to the *Nancy's* mate,
    And a delicate dish he made;
Then our appetite with the midshipmite
    We seven survivors stayed.

" And then we murdered the bos'un tight,
    And he much resembled pig;
Then we wittled free, did the cook and me,
    On the crew of the captain's gig.

" Then only the cook and me was left,
    And the delicate question, 'Which
Of us two goes to the kettle?' arose,
    And we argued it out as sich.

" For I loved that cook as a brother, I did,
    And the cook he worshipped me;
But we'd both be blowed if we'd either be stowed
    In the other chap's hold, you see.

" ' I'll be eat if you dines off me,' says Tom.
    ' Yes, that,' says I, 'you'll be, —
I'm boiled if I die, my friend,' quoth I.
    And ' Exactly so,' quoth he.

" Says he, ' Dear James, to murder me
    Were a foolish thing to do,
For don't you see that you can't cook *me*,
    While I can — and will — cook *you!*'

" So he boils the water, and takes the salt
    And the pepper in portions true
(Which he never forgot), and some chopped shalot,
    And some sage and parsley too.

" ' Come here,' says he, with a proper pride,
    Which his smiling features tell,
' 'Twill soothing be if I let you see
    How extremely nice you'll smell.'

" And he stirred it round and round and round,
    And he sniffed at the foaming froth;
When I ups with his heels, and smothers his squeals
    In the scum of the boiling broth.

" And I eat that cook in a week or less,
    And — as I eating be

The last of his chops, why, I almost drops,
    For a vessel in sight I see.

.   .   .   .

"And I never larf, and I never smile,
    And I never lark or play,
But sit and croak, and a single joke
    I have, — which is to say:

"Oh, I am a cook and a captain bold,
    And the mate of the *Nancy* brig,
And a bos'un tight, and a midshipmite,
    And the crew of the captain's gig."
                      William S. Gilbert

WIDOW MacSHANE

Near ould Skibbereen, in the gim of the owshun,
    The spaker was born, in a quare-lookin' place,
Where pigs and a cow were in full locomowshun,
    And six other childers were shlapein' in pace.

I cannot say mooch for me father's exthraction,
    Because, do ye see, he was born in the bogs;
But as for me mother, be double transaction,
    She loved the ould chap and the rest of the hogs.

'Twas joost as I enter'd this wurruld of slaughter,
    Me father looked up from his sate be the wall;
Says he, "Me swate Bridget, pray how is our daughter?"
    Says she, "Ye ould fool, it's no daughter at all!"

"Och murther an' turf!" he exclaim'd, in a passion,
    And struck wid his fist on the top of his knee;
His ancient dudheen in the corner went smashin',
    And all on account of perverseness in me!

"Ye red-lookin' thafe!" says the gintle ould sinner,
    Adthressing his illigant languidge to me,
"'Tis a nice-lookin' mout that ye have for a dinner!"
    But I was too spacheless his maneing to see.

"I swore it," says he, "be the sowl of Saint Paythur,
 A nate little daughter should be me next son;
But since ye have chosen a maskelin nayther,
 I'm bound to disown ye, as sure as a gun!

"I hope ye will mate wid the price of transgression,
 Whativer the craytures ye tarry among;
And mark me, me lad! 'tis me private impression
 Ye niver will die 'till the day ye are hoong!"

"Be quiet, me angil," says Bridget, me mother,
 "'Tis aisy to talk when the mischief is done;
Who knows but some day ye may want for a brother,
 And thin ye'll be glad that yere girl is a son!"

(The wimmin are prophets, wheriver ye find 'em;
 For many's the time I have help'd me poor dad
To see the door latchet directly behind him,
 And sometimes to walk — whin the whiskey was bad!)

The way I was bate from the night till the mornin',
 And thin from the mornin' again till to bed,
Should be unto aich sivinth son a sad warnin'
 Against gettin' born till his father is dead.

But batins are said to agree wid some people;
 And sure they were blessin's that caused me to grow
Until I was almost as tall as a staple, —
 And only fell short be an acre or so.

Wan mornin' whin I was ingaged in the gardin,
 Me father came up wid his pipe in his mout;
And "Barney," says he, "I must crave for yere pardin;
 But tell me, ye spalpeen, what *are* ye about?"

"'Tis hoein' the praties," says I, wid affection;
 Says he, "'Tis a mighty big mout ye have got;
And sure ye'd devour, widout frind or connection,
 As mooch as would grow on a tin-acre lot.

"Me farrum, ye know, is not quite so extinsive,
 And, though I'm as fond of ye now as me breath,
I'm fear'd, as yere appetite's so comprehinsive,
 Ye'll stay here to ate till yere starvin' to death."

"Yer servant," said I, like a dignified crayture,
  "And hoe for yersilf in the future," says I;
"For since I am sthrong as yersilf in me stature,
  I don't mind remarkin' to ye that ye lie!

"The wurruld invites me to walk on her bussum,
  And sthrive for a place in the council of state;
And niver has Fortune a low-hangin' blossom,
  But I, like a bee, will extract all its shwate."

"Thin walk on the bussum, me darlin'," he groonted,
  "But mind that ye niver git down in the mout;
Nor go to the land where an Irishman's hoonted
  By oogly know-nothings that's lurkin' about."

I scorn'd to reply to the spacious suggestion;
  But put me wardrobe in the crown of me hat;
And, kissing me mother, to aid me digestion,
  Set out on me thravels as still as a cat.

Ye mind there's a kingdom called Donnybrook famous,
  'Twas there that I wint an adventure to mate:
And whin I arrived I was weary and lame as
  A baste of the plough wid no legs to his fait.

Bad luck to the fortune that carried me in it!
  And sure 'tis the mem'ry that gives me a pain;
For scarce had I been in the tavern a minute
  Whin I fell a victim to Widow MacShane!

'Twas she was the landlord that thrated me dacent,
  And put me to bed wid a brick in me head;
And put some more bricks in a bottle adjacent
  To kape out the cowld whin me arrum was bled.

And be the same token I came for to love her,
  And ask'd her to thry the high-menial line;
She called me "an in-sin-i-*va*-tin' young rover,"
  And put her big mout on a fayture of mine!

Och murther an' ounds! was the divil behind me,
  To blind me affection an' worry me brain?
Or was it the coorse of me father resigned me
  Into the fat arrums of Widow MacShane?

And sure she had childers, the wildest young divils
  That iver disgraced a respictable place;
And wan of me first matrimonial evils
  Was havin' their scratches all over me face!

" Me darlin'," I said to their illigant mother,
  " The childers are rayther too forward," says I;
Whin grabbin' a poker, or somethin' or other,
  She gave me a whack in the small of me thigh!

Because I complain'd of sooch singular tratement,
  She made it appear most uncommonly plain
That I was a baste, whin compared with the statement
  Of all the shwate virtues of Misther MacShane!

Och! sure sooch a life as I led wid the crayture
  Would make the most patient of madmen insane!
And often convaynient I found to my nature
  To invy the ghosht of departed MacShane!

If I didn't wear an ould shirt for a saison,
  And kape it remarkably rigid and clane,
That woman would niver be timpted to raison,
  But talk'd of the nateness of Misther MacShane!

Whiniver the night spread abroad her dark pinions,
  Thim childers would chatter like monkeys in pain;
And thin I was call'd from me drame-land dominions
  To comfort the spalpeens of Misther MacShane!

If coxcombs and guardsmen made love to me woman,
  And I, in me innocence, chose to complain,
She'd intimate sthrongly that I was inhuman,
  And mintion me contrast wid Misther MacShane!

If I took a shillin' to get me some whiskey,
  And didn't remimber to stale it again,
Be all of the Pow'rs but she'd grow mighty frisky,
  And threaten to send me to — Misther MacShane!

I niver went out of the house in the mornin'
  Until it was night of the avening befoor;
Because she would give me a dilicate warnin'
  To manage the childers and scrub up the floor!

And whin I would vinture to spake like an aiqual,
  And tell her she acted confoundedly mane;
She'd tell me a sthory, and tell me the saiquel!
  The life and the *death* of wan Misther MacShane!

I lived like a baste that is kill'd be its master,
  Until I was taken wid prisince of brain;
And thin, niver lightning could thravel mooch faster
  Than I from the relic of Misther MacShane!

I came to this coonthry of freedom and progress;
  And only had been here a couple of hours,
Whin I was elected a mimber of Congress —
  Or daycintly ask'd to be sooch, be the Pow'rs!

But I shall go back to me gim of the owshun
  As soon as me widow is married again,
To give a free vint to me pow'rful emoshun,
  And dance on the grave of ould Misther MacShane!
                              Robert Henry Newell
                              (*" Orpheus C. Kerr"*)

ROBINSON CRUSOE

The night was thick and hazy
When the *Piccadilly Daisy*
Carried down the crew and Captain in the sea;
And I think the water drowned 'em,
For they never, never found 'em,
And I know they didn't come ashore with me.

Oh, 'twas very sad and lonely
When I found myself the only
Population on this cultivated shore;
But I've made a little tavern
In a rocky little cavern,
And I sit and watch for people at the door.

I spent no time in looking
For a girl to do my cooking,
As I'm quite a clever hand at making stews;

But I had that fellow Friday
Just to keep the tavern tidy,
And to put a Sunday polish on my shoes.

I have a little garden
That I'm cultivating lard in,
As the things I eat are rather tough and dry;
For I live on toasted lizards,
Prickly pears, and parrot gizzards,
And I'm really very fond of beetle-pie.

The clothes I had were furry,
And it made me fret and worry
When I found the moths were eating off the hair;
And I had to scrape and sand 'em,
And I boiled 'em and I tanned 'em,
Till I got the fine morocco suit I wear.

I sometimes seek diversion
In a family excursion
With the few domestic animals you see;
And we take along a carrot
As refreshments for the parrot,
And a little cup of jungleberry tea.

Then we gather as we travel
Bits of moss and dirty gravel,
And we chip off little specimens of stone,
And we carry home as prizes
Funny bugs of handy sizes,
Just to give the day a scientific tone.

If the roads are wet and muddy,
We remain at home and study,
For the Goat is very clever at a sum —
And the Dog, instead of fighting,
Studies ornamental writing,
While the cat is taking lessons on the drum.

We retire at eleven,
And we rise again at seven;
And I wish to call attention, as I close,
To the fact that all the scholars
Are correct about their collars,
And particular in turning out their toes.

Charles Edward Carryl

THE BALLAD OF THE OYSTERMAN

It was a tall young oysterman lived by the river-side,
His shop was just upon the bank, his boat was on the tide;
The daughter of a fisherman, that was so straight and slim,
Lived over on the other bank, right opposite to him.

It was the pensive oysterman that saw a lovely maid,
Upon a moonlight evening, a-sitting in the shade;
He saw her wave a handkerchief, as much as if to say,
" I'm wide awake, young oysterman, and all the folks away."

Then up arose the oysterman, and to himself said he,
" I guess I'll leave the skiff at home, for fear that folks
    should see;
I read it in the story-book, that, for to kiss his dear,
Leander swam the Hellespont, and I will swim this here."

And he has leaped into the waves, and crossed the shining
    stream,
And he has clambered up the bank, all in the moonlight
    gleam;
Oh, there are kisses sweet as dew, and words as soft as
    rain —
But they have heard her father's step, and in he leaps again!

Out spoke the ancient fisherman: " Oh, what was that, my
    daughter?"
" 'Twas nothing but a pebble, sir, I threw into the water."
" And what is that, pray tell me, love, that paddles off so
    fast?"
" It's nothing but a porpoise, sir, that's been a-swimming
    past."

Out spoke the ancient fisherman: " Now, bring me my
    harpoon!
I'll get into my fishing-boat, and fix the fellow soon."
Down fell that pretty innocent, as falls a snow-white lamb;
Her hair drooped round her pallid cheeks, like seaweed on
    a clam.

Alas for those two loving ones! she waked not from her
    swound,
And he was taken with the cramp, and in the waves was
    drowned;
But Fate has metamorphosed them, in pity of their woe,
And now they keep an oyster shop for mermaids down
    below.

Oliver Wendell Holmes

ONLY SEVEN

A PASTORAL STORY AFTER WORDSWORTH

I marvell'd why a simple child,
    That lightly draws its breath,
Should utter groans so very wild,
    And look as pale as Death.

Adopting a parental tone,
    I ask'd her why she cried;
The damsel answered with a groan,
    "I've got a pain inside!

"I thought it would have sent me mad
    Last night about eleven."
Said I, "What is it makes you bad?
How many apples have you had?"
    She answered, "Only seven!"

"And are you sure you took no more,
    My little maid?" quoth I;
"Oh, please, sir, mother gave me four,
    But *they* were in a pie!"

"If that's the case," I stammer'd out,
    "Of course you've had eleven."
The maiden answer'd with a pout,
    "I ain't had more nor seven!"

I wonder'd hugely what she meant,
    And said, "I'm bad at riddles;

But I know where little girls are sent
For telling taradiddles.

" Now, if you won't reform," said I,
" You'll never go to Heaven."
But all in vain; each time I try,
That little idiot makes reply,
" I ain't had more nor seven! "

POSTSCRIPT

To borrow Wordsworth's name was wrong,
Or slightly misapplied;
And so I'd better call my song,
" Lines after Ache-Inside."

Henry S. Leigh

THE SOCIETY UPON THE STANISLAUS

I reside at Table Mountain, and my name is Truthful
James;
I am not up to small deceit, or any sinful games;
And I'll tell in simple language what I know about the row
That broke up our Society upon the Stanislow.

But first I would remark, that it is not a proper plan
For any scientific gent to whale his fellow man,
And, if a member don't agree with his peculiar whim,
To lay for that same member for to " put a head " on him.

Now, nothing could be finer or more beautiful to see
Than the first six months' proceedings of that same
society,
Till Brown of Calaveras brought a lot of fossil bones
That he found within a tunnel near the tenement of Jones.

Then Brown he read a paper, and he reconstructed there,
From those same bones, an animal that was extremely rare,
And Jones then asked the chair for a suspension of the
rules,
Till he could prove that those same bones was one of his
lost mules.

Then Brown he smiled a bitter smile, and said he was at
　　fault;
It seemed he had been trespassing on Jones's family vault:
He was a most sarcastic man, this quiet Mr. Brown,
And on several occasions he had cleaned out the town.

Now, I hold it is not decent for a scientific gent
To say another is an ass, — at least, to all intent:
Nor should the individual who happens to be meant
Reply by heaving rocks at him to any great extent.

Then Abner Dean of Angel's raised a point of order —
　　when
A chunk of old red sandstone took him in the abdomen,
And he smiled a kind of sickly smile, and curled up on the
　　floor,
And the subsequent proceedings interested him no more.

For, in less time than I write it, every member did engage
In a warfare with the remnants of a palæozoic age;
And the way they heaved those fossils in their anger was
　　a sin,
Till the skull of an old mammoth caved the head of Thomp-
　　son in.

And this is all I have to say of these improper games,
For I live at Table Mountain, and my name is Truthful
　　James;
And I've told in simple language what I know about the
　　row
That broke up our Society upon the Stanislow.

Bret Harte

AN ACTOR

A shabby fellow chanced one day to meet
The British Roscius in the street,
　　Garrick, of whom our nation justly brags;
　The fellow hugged him with a kind embrace; —
"Good sir, I do not recollect your face,"
　　Quoth Garrick. "No?" replied the man of rags;
"The boards of Drury you and I have trod
　　Full many a time together, I am sure."

"When?" with an oath, cried Garrick, "for, by G—d,
I never saw that face of yours before!
What characters, I pray,
Did you and I together play?"
"Lord!" quoth the fellow, "think not that I mock —
When you played Hamlet, sir, I played the cock!"
John Wolcot ("Peter Pindar")

THE BITER BIT

The sun is in the sky, mother, the flowers are springing
fair,
And the melody of woodland birds is stirring in the air;
The river, smiling to the sky, glides onward to the sea,
And happiness is everywhere, O mother, but with me!

They are going to the church, mother, — I hear the mar-
riage bell;
It booms along the upland, — oh, it haunts me like a knell;
He leads her on his arm, mother, he cheers her faltering
step,
And closely to his side she clings, — she does, the demirep!

They are crossing by the stile, mother, where we so oft
have stood,
The stile beside the shady thorn, at the corner of the wood;
And the boughs, that wont to murmur back the words that
won my ear,
Wave their silver branches o'er him, as he leads his bridal
fere.

He will pass beside the stream, mother, where first my
hand he press'd,
By the meadow where, with quivering lip, his passion he
confess'd;
And down the hedgerows where we've stray'd again and yet
again;
And he will not think of me, mother, his broken-hearted
Jane!

He said that I was proud, mother, that I look'd for rank
    and gold,
He said I did not love him, — he said my words were cold;
He said I'd kept him off and on, in hopes of higher game, —
And it may be that I did, mother; but who hasn't done the
    same?

I did not know my heart, mother, — I know it now too
    late;
I thought that I without a pang could wed some nobler
    mate;
But no nobler suitor sought me, — and he has taken wing,
And my heart is gone, and I am left a lone and blighted
    thing.

You may lay me in my bed, mother, — my head is throbbing
    sore;
And, mother, prithee, let the sheets be duly aired before;
And, if you'd please, my mother dear, your poor despond-
    ing child,
Draw me a pot of beer, mother, and mother, draw it mild!
                                William E. Aytoun
                            In the Bon Gaultier Ballads

ODE TO TOBACCO

Thou who, when fears attack,
Bidst them avaunt, and Black
Care, at the horseman's back
    Perching, unseatest;
Sweet, when the morn is gray;
Sweet, when they've cleared away
Lunch; and at close of day
    Possibly sweetest:

I have a liking old
For thee, though manifold
Stories, I know, are told,
    Not to thy credit;
How one (or two at most)
Drops make a cat a ghost —

Useless, except to roast —
Doctors have said it:

How they who use fusees
All grow by slow degrees
Brainless as chimpanzees,
    Meagre as lizards;
Go mad, and beat their wives;
Plunge (after shocking lives)
Razors and carving knives ·
    Into their gizzards.

Confound such knavish tricks!
Yet know I five or six
Smokers who freely mix
    Still with their neighbors;
Jones — (who, I'm glad to say,
Asked leave of Mrs. J.) —
Daily absorbs a clay
    After his labors.

Cats may have had their goose
Cooked by tobacco-juice;
Still why deny its use
    Thoughtfully taken?
We're not as tabbies are:
Smith, take a fresh cigar!
Jones, the tobacco-jar!
    Here's to thee, Bacon!
                Charles Stuart Calverley

THE SCHOOLMASTER

ABROAD WITH HIS SON

O what harper could worthily harp it,
    Mine Edward! this wide-stretching wold
(Look out *wold*) with its wonderful carpet
    Of emerald, purple, and gold!
Look well at it — also look sharp, it
    Is getting so cold.

The purple is heather (*erica*);
  The yellow, gorse — call'd sometimes " whin."
Cruel boys on its prickles might spike a
  Green beetle as if on a pin.
You may roll in it, if you would like a
    Few holes in your skin.

You wouldn't? Then think of how kind you
  Should be to the insects who crave
Your compassion — and then, look behind you
  At yon barley-ears! Don't they look brave
As they undulate — (*undulate*, mind you,
    From *unda, a wave*).

The noise of those sheep-bells, how faint it
  Sounds here — (on account of our height)!
And this hillock itself — who could paint it,
  With its changes of shadow and light?
Is it not — (never, Eddy, say " ain't it ") —
    A marvelous sight?

Then yon desolate eerie morasses,
  The haunts of the snipe and the hern —
(I shall question the two upper classes
  On *aquatiles,* when we return) —
Why, I see on them absolute masses
    Of *filix* or fern.

How it interests e'en a beginner
  (Or *tiro*) like dear little Ned!
Is he listening? As I am a sinner
  He's asleep — he is wagging his head.
Wake up! I'll go home to my dinner,
    And you to your bed.

The boundless ineffable prairie;
  The splendor of mountain and lake
With their hues that seem ever to vary;
  The mighty pine forests which shake
In the wind, and in which the unwary
    May tread on a snake;

And this wold with its heathery garment —
  Are themes undeniably great.

But — although there is not any harm in't —
It's perhaps little good to dilate
On their charms to a dull little varmint
    Of seven or eight.

                Charles Stuart Calverley

THE DEACON'S MASTERPIECE

OR, THE WONDERFUL "ONE - HOSS SHAY"

A LOGICAL STORY

Have you heard of the wonderful one-hoss shay,
That was built in such a logical way
It ran a hundred years to a day,
And then, of a sudden, it — ah, but stay,
I'll tell you what happened without delay,
Scaring the parson into fits,
Frightening people out of their wits, —
Have you ever heard of that, I say?

Seventeen hundred and fifty-five.
Georgius Secundus was then alive, —
Snuffy old drone from the German hive.
That was the year when Lisbon-town
Saw the earth open and gulp her down,
And Braddock's army was done so brown,
Left without a scalp to its crown.
It was on the terrible Earthquake-day
That the deacon finished the one-hoss shay.

Now in building of chaises, I tell you what,
There is always *somewhere* a weakest spot, —
In hub, tire, felloe, in spring or thill,
In panel, or crossbar, or floor, or sill,
In screw, bolt, thoroughbrace, lurking still,
Find it somewhere you must and will, —
Above or below, or within or without, —
And that's the reason, beyond a doubt,
That a chaise *breaks down*, but doesn't *wear out*.

But the deacon swore (as deacons do,
With an " I dew vum," or an " I tell *yeou* ")
He would build one shay to beat the taown
'N' the keounty 'n' all the kentry raoun';
It should be so built that it *couldn'* break daown:
" Fur," said the deacon, " 't's mighty plain
That the weakes' place mus' stan' the strain;
'N' the way t' fix it, uz I maintain,
Is only jest
T' make that place uz strong uz the rest."

So the deacon inquired of the village folk
Where he could find the strongest oak,
That couldn't be split nor bent nor broke, —
That was for spokes and floor and sills;
He sent for lancewood to make the thills;
The crossbars were ash, from the straightest trees,
The panels of white-wood that cuts like cheese,
But lasts like iron for things like these;
The hubs of logs from the " Settler's Ellum,"
Last of its timber, — they couldn't sell 'em,
Never an axe had seen their chips,
And the wedges flew from between their lips,
Their blunt ends frizzled like celery tips;
Step and prop-iron, bolt and screw,
Spring, tire, axle, and linchpin, too,
Steel of the finest, bright and blue;
Thoroughbrace bison-skin, thick and wide;
Boot, top, dasher, from tough old hide
Found in the pit when the tanner died.
That was the way he " put her through." —
" There," said the deacon, " Naow she'll dew!"

Do! I tell you, I rather guess
She was a wonder, and nothing less!
Colts grew horses, beards turned gray,
Deacon and deaconess dropped away,
Children and grandchildren — where were they?
But there stood the stout old one-hoss shay
As fresh as on Lisbon-Earthquake-day!

EIGHTEEN HUNDRED; — it came and found
The deacon's masterpiece strong and sound.

Eighteen hundred increased by ten; —
" Hahnsum kerridge " they called it then.
Eighteen hundred and twenty came; —
Running as usual; much the same.
Thirty and forty at last arrive,
And then come fifty, and FIFTY-FIVE.

Little of all we value here
Wakes on the morn of its hundredth year
Without both feeling and looking queer.
In fact there's nothing that keeeps its youth,
So far as I know, but a tree and truth.
(This is a moral that runs at large;
Take it. — You're welcome. — No extra charge.).
FIRST OF NOVEMBER —the Earthquake-day —
There are traces of age in the one-hoss shay,
A general flavor of mild decay,
But nothing local, as one may say.
There couldn't be, — for the deacon's art.
Had made it so like in every part
That there wasn't a chance for one to start.
For the wheels were just as strong as the thills,
And the floor was just as strong as the sills,
And the panels were just as strong as the floor,
And the whiffle-tree neither less nor more,
And the back-crossbar as strong as the fore,
And spring and axle and hub *encore.*
And yet *as a whole,* it is past a doubt,
In another hour it will be *worn out!*

First of November, 'Fifty-five!
This morning the parson takes a drive.
Now, small boys, get out of the way!
Here comes the wonderful one-hoss shay,
Drawn by a rat-tailed, ewe-necked bay.
" Huddup ! " said the parson. — Off went they.

The parson was working his Sunday's text —
Had got to *fifthly,* and stopped perplexed
At what the — Moses — was coming next.
All at once the horse stood still,
Close by the meet'n'-house on the hill.
— First a shiver, and then a thrill,

Then something decidedly like a spill, —
And the parson was sitting upon a rock,
At half-past nine by the meet'n'-house clock, —
Just the hour of the Earthquake shock!

— What do you think the parson found,
When he got up and stared around?
The poor old chaise in a heap or mound,
As if it had been to the mill and ground!
You see, of course, if you're not a dunce,
How it went to pieces all at once, —
All at once, and nothing first,
Just as bubbles do when they burst.

End of the wonderful one-hoss shay.
Logic is logic. That's all I say.

Oliver Wendell Holmes

CAPTAIN REECE

Of all the ships upon the blue,
No ship contained a better crew
Than that of worthy Captain Reece,
Commanding of *The Mantelpiece*.

He was adored by all his men,
For worthy Captain Reece, R. N.,
Did all that lay within him to
Promote the comfort of his crew.

If ever they were dull or sad,
Their captain danced to them like mad,
Or told, to make the time pass by,
Droll legends of his infancy.

A feather bed had every man,
Warm· slippers and hot-water can,
Brown Windsor from the captain's store,
A valet, too, to every four.

Did they with thirst in summer burn?
Lo, seltzogenes at every turn,

And on all very sultry days
Cream ices handed round on trays.

Then currant wine and ginger pops
Stood handily on all the " tops ; "
And, also, with amusement rife,
A " Zoetrope, or Wheel of Life."

New volumes came across the sea
From Mister Mudie's library;
The Times and *Saturday Review*
Beguiled the leisure of the crew.

Kind-hearted Captain Reece, R. N.,
Was quite devoted to his men ;
In point of fact, good Captain Reece
Beatified *The Mantelpiece.*

One summer eve, at half-past ten,
He said (addressing all his men) :
" Come, tell me, please, what I can do
To please and gratify my crew.

" By any reasonable plan
I'll make you happy if I can ;
My own convenience count as *nil;*
It is my duty, and I will."

Then up and answered William Lee
(The kindly captain's coxswain he,
A nervous, shy, low-spoken man),
He cleared his throat and thus began :

" You have a daughter, Captain Reece,
Ten female cousins and a niece,
A Ma, if what I'm told is true,
Six sisters, and an aunt or two.

" Now, somehow, sir, it seems to me,
More friendly-like we all should be
If you united of 'em to
Unmarried members of the crew.

" If you'd ameliorate our life,
Let each select from them a wife;
And as for nervous me, old pal,
Give me your own enchanting gal!"

Good Captain Reece, that worthy man,
Debated on his coxswain's plan:
" I quite agree," he said, " O Bill;
It is my duty, and I will.

" My daughter, that enchanting gurl,
Has just been promised to an earl,
And all my other familee
To peers of various degree.

" But what are dukes and viscounts to
The happiness of all my crew?
The word I give you I'll fulfil;
It is my duty, and I will.

" As you desire it shall befall,
I'll settle thousands on you all,
And I shall be, despite my hoard,
The only bachelor on board."

The boatswain of *The Mantelpiece*,
He blushed, and spoke to Captain Reece:
" I beg your honor's leave," he said;
" If you would wish to go and wed,

" I have a widowed mother who
Would be the very thing for you —
She long has loved you from afar:
She washes for you, Captain R."

The captain saw the dame that day —
Addressed her in his playful way —
" And did it want a wedding ring?
It was a tempting ickle sing!

" Well, well, the chaplain I will seek,
We'll all be married this day week
At yonder church upon the hill;
It is my duty, and I will!"

The sisters, cousins, aunts, and niece,
And widowed Ma of Captain Reece
Attended there as they were bid;
It was their duty, and they did.

William S. Gilbert

THE COURTIN'

God makes sech nights, all white an' still
    Fur'z you can look or listen,
Moonshine an' snow on field an' hill,
    All silence an' all glisten.

Zekle crep' up quite unbeknown
    An' peeked in thru' the winder,
An' there sot Huldy all alone,
    'Ith no one nigh to hender.

A fireplace filled the room's one side
    With half a cord o' wood in —
There warn't no stoves (tell comfort died)
    To bake ye to a puddin'.

The wa'nut logs shot sparkles out
    Towards the pootiest, bless her,
An' leetle flames danced all about
    The chiny on the dresser.

Agin the chimbley crook-necks hung,
    An' in amongst 'em rusted
The ole queen's-arm thet gran'ther Young
    Fetched back from Concord busted.

The very room, coz she was in,
    Seemed warm from floor to ceilin',
An' she looked full ez rosy agin
    Ez the apples she was peelin'.

'Twas kin' o' kingdom-come to look
    On sech a blessed cretur,
A dogrose blushin' to a brook
    Ain't modester nor sweeter.

He was six foot o' man, A 1,
  Clear grit an' human natur';
None couldn't quicker pitch a ton
  Nor dror a furrer straighter.

He'd sparked it with full twenty gals,
  Hed squired 'em, danced 'em, druv 'em,
Fust this one, an' then thet, by spells —
  All is, he couldn't love 'em.

But long o' her his veins 'ould run
  All crinkly like curled maple,
The side she breshed felt full o' sun
  Ez a south slope in Ap'il.

She thought no v'ice hed sech a swing
  Ez hisn in the choir;
My! when he made Ole Hunderd ring,
  She *knowed* the Lord was nigher.

An' she'd blush scarlit, right in prayer,
  When her new meetin'-bunnet
Felt somehow thru' its crown a pair
  O' blue eyes sot upon it.

Thet night, I tell ye, she looked *some!*
  She seemed to've gut a new soul,
For she felt sartin-sure he'd come,
  Down to her very shoe-sole.

She heered a foot, an' knowed it tu,
  A-raspin' on the scraper, —
All ways to once her feelin's flew
  Like sparks in burnt-up paper.

He kin' o' l'itered on the mat,
  Some doubtfle o' the sekle,
His heart kep' goin' pity-pat,
  But hern went pity Zekle.

An' yit she gin her cheer a jerk
  Ez though she wished him furder,
An' on her apples kep' to work,
  Parin' away like murder.

"You want to see my Pa, I s'pose?"
  "Wal . . . no . . . I come dasignin'"—
"To see my Ma? She's sprinklin' clo'es
  Agin to-morrer's i'nin'."

To say why gals acts so or so,
  Or don't, 'ould be presumin';
Mebby to mean *yes* an' say *no*
  Comes nateral to women.

He stood a spell on one foot fust,
  Then stood a spell on t'other,
An' on which one he felt the wust
  He couldn't ha' told ye nuther.

Says he, "I'd better call agin;"
  Says she, "Think likely, Mister:"
Thet last word pricked him like a pin,
  An' . . . Wal, he up an' kist her.

When Ma bimeby upon 'em slips,
  Huldy sot pale ez ashes,
All kin' o' smily roun' the lips
  An' teary roun' the lashes.

For she was jes' the quiet kind
  Whose naturs never vary,
Like streams that keep a summer mind
  Snowhid in Jenooary.

The blood clost roun' her heart felt glued
  Too tight for all expressin',
Tell mother see how metters stood,
  An' gin 'em both her blessin'.

Then her red come back like the tide
  Down to the Bay o' Fundy,
An' all I know is they was cried
  In meetin' come nex' Sunday.

                    James Russell Lowell

THE TWINS

In form and feature, face and limb,
  I grew so like my brother,
That folks got taking me for him,
  And each for one another.
It puzzled all our kith and kin,
  It reach'd an awful pitch;
For one of us was born a twin,
  Yet not a soul knew which.

One day (to make the matter worse),
  Before our names were fix'd,
As we were being wash'd by nurse
  We got completely mix'd;
And thus, you see, by Fate's decree,
  (Or rather nurse's whim),
My brother John got christen'd *me*,
  And I got christen'd *him*.

This fatal likeness even dogg'd
  My footsteps when at school,
And I was always getting flogg'd,
  For John turned out a fool.
I put this question hopelessly
  To every one I knew —
What *would* you do, if you were me,
  To prove that you were *you?*

Our close resemblance turn'd the tide
  Of my domestic life;
For somehow my intended bride
  Became my brother's wife.
In short, year after year the same
  Absurd mistakes went on;
And when I died — the neighbors came
  And buried brother John!

                              Henry S. Leigh

LITTLE BREECHES

A PIKE COUNTY VIEW OF SPECIAL PROVIDENCE

I don't go much on religion,
  I never ain't had no show;
But I've got a middlin' tight grip, sir,
  On the handful o' things I know.
I don't pan out on the prophets
  And free-will, and that sort of thing, —
But I b'lieve in God and the angels,
  Ever sence one night last spring.

I come into town with some turnips,
  And my little Gabe come along, —
No four-year-old in the county
  Could beat him for pretty and strong,
Peart and chipper and sassy,
  Always ready to swear and fight, —
And I'd larnt him ter chaw terbacker,
  Jest to keep his milk-teeth white.

The snow come down like a blanket
  As I passed by Taggart's store;
I went in for a jug of molasses
  And left the team at the door.
They scared at something and started, —
  I heard one little squall,
And hell-to-split over the prairie
  Went team, Little Breeches and all.

Hell-to-split over the prairie!
  I was almost froze with skeer;
But we rousted up some torches,
  And sarched for 'em far and near.
At last we struck hosses and wagon,
  Snowed under a soft white mound,
Upsot, dead beat, — but of little Gabe
  No hide nor hair was found.

And here all hope soured on me
  Of my fellow-critters' aid, —
I jest flopped down on my marrow-bones,
  Crotch-deep in the snow, and prayed.

. . . .

By this, the torches was played out,
  And me and Isrul Parr
Went off for some wood to a sheepfold
  That he said was somewhar thar.

We found it at last, and a little shed
  Where they shut up the lambs at night.
We looked in, and seen them huddled thar,
  So warm and sleepy and white;
And *thar* sot Little Breeches and chirped,
  As peart as ever you see,
"I want a chaw of terbacker,
  And that's what's the matter of me."

How did he git thar? Angels.
  He could never have walked in that storm.
They jest scooped down and toted him
  To whâr it was safe and warm.
And I think that saving a little child,
  And fotching him to his own,
Is a derned sight better business
  Than loafing around The Throne.

John Hay

COMPANIONS

A TALE OF A GRANDFATHER

By the Author of "Dewy Memories," etc.

I know not of what we ponder'd
  Or made pretty pretence to talk,
As, her hand within mine, we wander'd
  Tow'rd the pool by the lime-tree walk,
While the dew fell in showers from the passion
    flowers
  And the blush-rose bent on her stalk.

I cannot recall her figure:
  Was it regal as Juno's own?
Or only a trifle bigger
  Than the elves who surround the throne
Of the Faëry Queen, and are seen, I ween,
  By mortals in dreams alone?

What her eyes were like, I know not:
  Perhaps they were blurr'd with tears;
And perhaps in your skies there glow not
  (On the contrary) clearer spheres.
No! as to her eyes I am just as wise
  As you or the cat, my dears.

Her teeth, I presume, were " pearly: "
  But which was she, brunette or blonde?
Her hair, was it quaintly curly,
  Or as straight as a beadle's wand?
That I fail'd to remark; — it was rather dark
  And shadowy round the pond.

Then the hand that reposed so snugly
  In mine, — was it plump or spare?
Was the countenance fair or ugly?
  Nay, children, you have me there!
My eyes were p'raps blurr'd; and besides I'd heard
  That it's horribly rude to stare.

And I — was I brusque and surly?
  Or oppressively bland and fond?
Was I partial to rising early?
  Or why did we twain abscond,
All breakfastless, too, from the public view,
  To prowl by a misty pond?

What pass'd, what was felt or spoken —
  Whether anything pass'd at all —
And whether the heart was broken
  That beat under that shelt'ring shawl —
(If shawl she had on, which I doubt) — has gone,
  Yes, gone from me past recall.

Was I haply the lady's suitor?
  Or her uncle? I can't make out —

Ask your governess, dears, or tutor.
  For myself, I'm in hopeless doubt
As to why we were there, who on earth we were,
  And what this is all about.
                              Charles Stuart Calverley

THE LAWYER'S INVOCATION TO SPRING

Whereas, on certain boughs and sprays
  Now divers birds are heard to sing,
And sundry flowers their heads upraise,
  Hail to the coming on of Spring!

The songs of those said birds arouse
  The memory of our youthful hours,
As green as those said sprays and boughs,
  As fresh and sweet as those said flowers.

The birds aforesaid — happy pairs —
  Love, 'mid the aforesaid boughs, inshrines
In freehold nests; themselves their heirs,
  Administrators, and assigns.

O busiest term of Cupid's Court,
  Where tender plaintiffs actions bring, —
Season of frolic and of sport,
  Hail, as aforesaid, coming Spring!
                              Henry Howard Brownell

NEGRO LULLABY

Bedtime's come fu' little boys,
  Po' little lamb.
Too tiahed out to make a noise,
  Po' little lamb.
You gwine t' have to-morrer sho'?
Yes, you tole me dat befo',
Don't you fool me, chile, no' mo',
  Po' little lamb.

You been bad de livelong day,
Po' little lamb.
Th'owin' stones an' runnin' 'way,
Po' little lamb.
My, but you's a-runnin' wil',
Look jes' lak some po' folks' chile;
Mam' gwine whup you atter while,
Po' little lamb.

Come hyeah! you mos' tiahed to def,
Po' little lamb.
Played yo'se'f clean out o' bref,
Po' little lamb.
See dem han's now — sich a sight!
Would you evah b'lieve dey's white?
Stan' still twell I wash 'em right,
Po' little lamb.

Jes' cain't hol' yo' haid up straight,
Po' little lamb.
Hadn't oughter played so late,
Po' little lamb.
Mammy do' know whut she'd do,
Ef de chillun's all lak you;
You's a caution now fu' true,
Po' little lamb.

Lay yo' haid down in my lap,
Po' little lamb.
Y' ought to have a right good slap,
Po' little lamb.
You been runnin' 'roun' a heap.
Shet dem eyes an' don't you peep,
Dah now, dah now, go to sleep,
Po' little lamb.

Paul Laurence Dunbar

THREE "RHYMES OF IRONQUILL"

CAPERS ET CAPER

From a chimney on the roof
Of the Wilder House hotel,
Did a William goat espy
An old army mule go by;
  Spied those vast and sail-like ears —
And he jeered the mule with jeers.

Then the mule he made a tack,
  Brought his jib round to the wind,
Main and mizzen ears aback,
  And his starboard eye he skinned;
Then he reached that goat a hoof
That dismissed him from the roof.

Soliloquy

Morals two this tale will teach:
  First, there isn't any rule
That will cipher out the reach
  Of an ancient army mule;
Second, there are many dangers
In misestimating strangers.

PASS

A father said unto his hopeful son:
"Who was Leonidas, my cherished one?"
The boy replied, with words of ardent nature:
"He was a member of the Legislature."
"How?" asked the parent; then the youngster saith:
"He got a pass, and held her like grim death."
"Whose pass? What pass?" the anxious father cried;
"'Twas the'r monopoly," the boy replied.

In deference to the public, we must state
That boy has been an orphan since that date.

NÉOPHYTE

Last night a zealous Irishman in town,
Meeting a Jew, squared off and knocked him down.

And when the Jew inquired of such behavior,
Michael replied, " Bedad, ye kilt me Saviour."

The Jew replied: " My friend, that is not so;
It happened eighteen centuries ago."

Mike simply said: " Bedad, ye may be right,
But then — I only heard of it last night!"

And striking out reckless again, and loose,
Becomes a martyr — in the calaboose.

Theology and ignorance combined
Make bigotry, and *that* makes all men blind;
And streams of ruin from this common source
Have swept the world with devastating force.
Eugene F. Ware ("Ironquill")

MY AUNT

My aunt! my dear unmarried aunt!
    Long years have o'er her flown;
Yet still she strains the aching clasp
    That binds her virgin zone;
I know it hurts her, — though she looks
    As cheerful as she can;
Her waist is ampler than her life,
    For life is but a span.

My aunt, my poor deluded aunt!
    Her hair is almost gray;
Why will she train that winter curl
    In such a spring-like way?
How can she lay her glasses down,
    And say she reads as well,
When, through a double convex lens,
    She just makes out to spell?

Her father — grandpapa! forgive
This erring lip its smiles —
Vowed she should make the finest **girl**
Within a hundred miles.
He sent her to a stylish school;
'Twas in her thirteenth June;
And with her, as the rules required,
" Two towels and a spoon."

They braced my aunt against a board,
To make her straight and tall;
They laced her up, they starved her down,
To make her light and small;
They pinched her feet, they singed her hair,
They screwed it up with pins; —
O never mortal suffered more
In penance for her sins.

So, when my precious aunt was done,
My grandsire brought her back;
(By daylight, lest some rabid youth
Might follow on the track;)
" Ah!" said my grandsire, as he shook
Some powder in his pan,
" What could this lovely creature do
Against a desperate man!"

Alas! nor chariot, nor barouche,
Nor bandit cavalcade
Tore from the trembling father's arms
His all-accomplished maid.
For her how happy had it been!
And Heaven had spared to me
To see one sad, ungathered rose
On my ancestral tree.

Oliver Wendell Holmes

THE BABY'S DÉBUT

A BURLESQUE IMITATION OF WORDSWORTH — REJECTED
ADDRESSES

[Spoken in the character of Nancy Lake, a girl eight years of age, who is drawn
upon the stage in a child's chaise by Samuel Hughes, her uncle's porter.]

My brother Jack was nine in May,
And I was eight on New-year's day;
    So in Kate Wilson's shop
Papa (he's my papa and Jack's)
Bought me, last week, a doll of wax,
    And brother Jack a top.

Jack's in the pouts, and this it is —
He thinks mine came to more than his;
    So to my drawer he goes,
Takes out the doll, and, O, my stars!
He pokes her head between the bars,
    And melts off half her nose!

Quite cross, a bit of string I beg,
And tie it to his peg-top's peg,
    And bang, with might and main,
Its head against the parlor-door:
Off flies the head and hits the floor,
    And breaks a window-pane.

This made him cry with rage and spite:
Well, let him cry; it serves him right.
    A pretty thing, forsooth!
If he's to melt, all scalding hot,
Half my doll's nose, and I am not
    To draw his peg-top's tooth!

Aunt Hannah heard the window break,
And cried, "O naughty Nancy Lake,
    Thus to distress your aunt:

No Drury Lane for you to-day!"
And while papa said, " Pooh, she may!"
    Mamma said, " No, she sha'n't!"

Well, after many a sad reproach,
They got into a hackney-coach,
    And trotted down the street.
I saw them go; one horse was blind,
The tails of both hung down behind,
    Their shoes were on their feet.

The chaise in which poor Brother Bill
Used to be drawn to Pentonville,
    Stood in the lumber-room:
I wiped the dust from off the top,
While Molly mopped it with a mop,
    And brushed it with a broom.

My uncle's porter, Samuel Hughes,
Came in at six to black the shoes
    (I always talk to Sam),
So what does he, but takes, and drags
Me in the chaise along the flags,
    And leaves me where I am.

My father's walls are made of brick,
But not so tall and not so thick
    As these; and, goodness me!
My father's beams are made of wood,
But never, never half so good
    As those that now I see.

What a large floor! 'tis like a town!
The carpet, when they lay it down,
    Won't hide it, I'll be bound;
And there's a row of lamps! — my eye!
How they do blaze! I wonder why
    They keep them on the ground.

At first I caught hold of the wing,
And kept away; but Mr. Thing-
    umbob, the prompter-man,

Gave with his hand my chaise a shove,
And said, " Go on, my pretty love;
    Speak to 'em, little Nan.

" You've only got to curtsey, whisp-
er, hold you're chin up, laugh and lisp,
    And then you're sure to take:
I've known the day when brats, not quite
Thirteen, got fifty pounds a night;
    Then why not Nancy Lake? "

But while I'm speaking, where's papa?
And where's my aunt? and where's mamma?
    Where's Jack? O there they sit!
They smile, they nod; I'll go my ways,
And order round poor Billy's chaise,
    To join them in the pit.

And now, good gentlefolks, I go
To join mamma, and see the show;
    So, bidding you adieu,
I curtsey like a pretty miss,
And if you'll blow to me a kiss,
    I'll blow a kiss to you.

[Blows a kiss, and exit.]

James Smith

LARRIE O'DEE

Now the Widow McGee,
And Larrie O'Dee,
Had two little cottages out on the green,
With just room enough for two pig-pens between.
The widow was young and the widow was fair,
With the brightest of eyes and the brownest of hair,
And it frequently chanced, when she came in the morn,
With the swill for her pig, Larrie came with the corn,
And some of the ears that he tossed from his hand
In the pen of the widow were certain to land.

One morning said he:
"Och! Misthress McGee,
It's a waste of good lumber, this runnin' two rigs,
Wid a fancy purtition betwane our two pigs!"
"Indade, sur, it is!" answered Widow McGee,
With the sweetest of smiles upon Larrie O'Dee.
"And thin, it looks kind o' hard-hearted and mane,
Kapin' two friendly pigs so exsaidenly near
That whiniver one grunts the other can hear,
And yit kape a cruel purtition betwane."

"Shwate Widow McGee,"
Answered Larrie O'Dee,
"If ye fale in your heart we are mane to the pigs,
Ain't we mane to ourselves to be runnin' two rigs?
Och! it made me heart ache when I paped through the
        cracks
Of me shanty, lasht March, at yez shwingin' yer axe;
An' a-bobbin' yer head an' a-shtompin' yer fate,
Wid yer purty white hands jisht as red as a bate,
A-shplittin' yer kindlin'-wood out in the shtorm,
When one little shtove it would kape us both warm!"

"Now, piggy," says she,
"Larrie's courtin' o' me,
Wid his dilicate tinder allusions to you;
So now yez must tell me jisht what I must do:
For, if I'm to say yes, shtir the swill wid yer snout;
But if I'm to say no, ye must kape yer nose out.
Now Larrie, for shame! to be bribin' a pig
By a-tossin' a handful of corn in its shwig!"
"Me darlint, the piggy says yes," answered he.
And that was the courtship of Larrie O'Dee.

William W. Fink

TIM TURPIN

Tim Turpin he was gravel blind,
    And ne'er had seen the skies:
For Nature, when his head was made,
    Forgot to dot his eyes.

So, like a Christmas pedagogue,
    Poor Tim was forced to do, —
Look out for pupils, for he had
    A vacancy for two.

There's some have specs to help their sight
    Of objects dim and small;
But Tim had *specks* within his eyes,
    And could not see at all.

Now Tim he wooed a servant maid,
    And took her to his arms;
For he, like Pyramus, had cast
    A wall-eye on her charms.

By day she led him up and down
    Where'er he wished to jog,
A happy wife, although she led
    The life of any dog.

But just when Tim had lived a month
    In honey with his wife,
A surgeon oped his Milton eyes,
    Like oysters, with a knife.

But when his eyes were opened thus,
    He wished them dark again;
For when he looked upon his wife,
    He saw her very plain.

Her face was bad, her figure worse,
    He couldn't bear to eat;
For she was anything but like
    A Grace before his meat.

Now Tim he was a feeling man:
    For when his sight was thick,
It made him feel for everything, —
    But that was with a stick.

So, with a cudgel in his hand, —
    It was not light or slim, —
He knocked at his wife's head until
    It opened unto him.

And when the corpse was stiff and cold,
　He took his slaughtered spouse,
And laid her in a heap with all
　The ashes of her house.

But, like a wicked murderer,
　He lived in constant fear
From day to day, and so he cut
　His throat from ear to ear.

The neighbors fetched a doctor in:
　Said he, " This wound I dread
Can hardly be sewed up, — his life
　Is hanging on a thread."

But when another week was gone,
　He gave him stronger hope, —
Instead of hanging on a thread,
　Of hanging on a rope.

Ah! when he hid his bloody work,
　In ashes round about,
How little he supposed the truth
　Would soon be sifted out!

But when the parish dustman came,
　His rubbish to withdraw,
He found more dust within the heap
　Than he contracted for!

A dozen men to try the fact,
　Were sworn that very day;
But though they all were jurors, yet
　No conjurors were they.

Said Tim unto those jurymen,
　" You need not waste your breath,
For I confess myself, at once,
　The author of her death.

" And O, when I reflect upon
　The blood that I have spilt,
Just like a button is my soul,
　Inscribed with double *guilt!* "

Then turning round his head again
He saw before his eyes
A great judge, and a little judge,
The judges of a-size!

The great judge took his judgment-cap,
And put it on his head,
And sentenced Tim by law to hang
Till he was three times dead.

So he was tried, and he was hung
(Fit punishment for such)
On Horsham drop, and none can say
It was a drop too much.

Thomas Hood

THE ELF - CHILD

Little Orphant Annie's come to our house to stay,
An' wash the cups and saucers up, an' brush the crumbs
away,
An' shoo the chickens off the porch, an' dust the hearth an'
sweep
An' make the fire, an' bake the bread, an' earn her board
an' keep;
An' all us other children, when the supper things is done,
We set around the kitchen fire an' has the mostest fun
A-list'nin' to the witch tales 'at Annie tells about,
An' the Gobble-uns 'at gits you
                    Ef you
                        Don't
                            Watch
                                Out!

Onc't they was a little boy who wouldn't say his prayers —
An' when he went to bed at night, away up-stairs,
His mammy heerd him holler an' his daddy heerd him
bawl,
An' when they turn't the kivvers down he wasn't there
at all!

An' they seeked him in the rafter room an' cubby-hole
    an' press,
An' seeked him up the chimbly-flue, an' everywheres, I
    guess,
But all they ever found was thist his pants an' round-
    about! —
An' the Gobble-uns 'll git you
              Ef you
            Don't
                Watch
                  Out!

An' one time a little girl 'ud allus laugh an' grin,
An' make fun of ever' one an' all her blood-an'-kin,
An' onc't when they was "company," an' old folks was
    there,
She mocked 'em, an' shocked 'em, an' said she didn't care;
An' thist as she kicked her heels, an' turn't to run an' hide,
They was two great big Black Things a-standin' by her
    side,
An' they snatched her through the ceilin' 'fore she knowed
    what she's about!
An' the Gobble-uns 'll git you
              Ef you
            Don't
                Watch
                  Out!

An' little Orphant Annie says, when the blaze is blue,
An' the lampwick sputters, an' the wind goes woo-oo!
An' you hear the crickets quit, an' the moon is gray,
An' the lightnin'-bugs in dew is all squenched away —
You better mind yer parents, an' yer teachers fond an' dear,
An' churish them 'at loves you, an' dry the orphant's tear
An' he'p the pore an' needy ones 'at clusters all about,
Er the Gobble-uns 'll git you
              Ef you
            Don't
                Watch
                  Out!
                    James Whitcomb Riley

THE PERILS OF INVISIBILITY

Old Peter led a wretched life —
Old Peter had a furious wife;
Old Peter, too, was truly stout,
He measured several yards about.

The little fairy Picklekin
One summer afternoon looked in,
And said, " Old Peter, how de do?
Can I do anything for you?

" I have three gifts — the first will give
Unbounded riches while you live;
The second, health where'er you be;
The third, invisibility."

" O little fairy Picklekin,"
Old Peter answered with a grin,
" To hesitate would be absurd —
Undoubtedly I choose the third."

" 'Tis yours," the fairy said; " be quite
Invisible to mortal sight
Whene'er you please. Remember me
Most kindly, pray, to Mrs. P."

Old Mrs. Peter overheard
Wee Picklekin's concluding word,
And, jealous of her girlhood's choice,
Said, " That was some young woman's voice! "

Old Peter let her scold and swear —
Old Peter, bless him, didn't care.
" My dear, your rage is wasted quite —
Observe, I disappear from sight! "

A well-bred fairy (so I've heard)
Is always faithful to her word:
Old Peter vanished like a shot,
But then — *his suit of clothes did not.*

For when conferred the fairy slim
Invisibility on *him,*
She popped away on fairy wings,
Without referring to his " things."

So there remained a coat of blue,
A vest and double eyeglass too,
His tail, his shoes, his socks as well,
His pair of — no, I must not tell.

Old Mrs. Peter soon began
To see the failure of his plan,
And then resolved (I quote the Bard)
To "Hoist him with his own petard."

Old Peter woke next day and dressed,
Put on his coat, and shoes, and vest,
His shirt and stock — *but could not find
His only pair of* — never mind!

Old Peter was a decent man,
And though he twigged his lady's plan,
Yet, hearing her approaching, he
Resumed invisibility.

"Dear Mrs. P., my only joy,"
Exclaimed the horrified old boy,
" Now give them up, I beg of you —
You know what I'm referring to!"

But no; the cross old lady swore
She'd keep his — what I said before —
To make him publicly absurd;
And Mrs. Peter kept her word.

The poor old fellow had no rest;
His coat, his stock, his shoes, his vest,
Were all that now met mortal eye —
The rest, invisibility!

"Now, madam, give them up, I beg —
I've had rheumatics in my leg;
Besides, until you do, it's plain,
I cannot come to sight again!

" For though some mirth it might afford
To see my clothes without their lord,
Yet there would rise indignant oaths
If he were seen without his clothes ! "

But no; resolved to have her quiz,
The lady held her own — and his —
And Peter left his humble cot
To find a pair of — you know what.

But — here's the worst of this affair —
Whene'er he came across a pair
Already placed for him to don,
He was too stout to get them on !

So he resolved at once to train,
And walked and walked with all his main ;
For years he paced this mortal earth,
To bring himself to decent girth.

At night, when all around is still,
You'll find him pounding up a hill ;
And shrieking peasants whom he meets,
Fall down in terror on the peats !

Old Peter walks through wind and rain,
Resolved to train, and train, and train,
Until he weighs twelve stone or so —
And when he does, I'll let you know.

William S. Gilbert

HANS BREITMANN'S PARTY

Hans Breitmann gife a barty;
  Dey had biano-blayin':
I felled in lofe mit a Merican frau,
  Her name was Madilda Yane.
She hat haar as prown ash a pretzel,
  Her eyes vas himmel-plue,
Und ven dey looket indo mine,
  Dey shplit mine heart in two.

Hans Breitmann gife a barty:
 I vent dere, you'll pe pound.
I valtzet mit Madilda Yane
 Und vent shpinnen round und round.
De pootiest Fräulein in de house,
 She vayed 'pout dwo hoondred pound,
Und efery dime she gife a shoomp
 She make de vindows sound.

Hans Breitmann gife a barty:
 I dells you it cost him dear.
Dey rolled in more ash sefen kecks
 Of foost-rate Lager Beer,
Und venefer dey knocks de shpicket in
 De Deutschers gifes a cheer.
I dinks dat so vine a barty
 Nefer coom to a het dis year.

Hans Breitmann gife a barty:
 Dere all vas Souse und Brouse;
Ven de sooper comed in, de gompany
 Did make demselfs to house.
Dey ate das Brot und Gensy broost,
 De Bratwurst und Braten fine,
Und vash der Abendessen down
 Mit four parrels of Neckarwein.

Hans Breitmann gife a barty.
 We all cot troonk ash bigs.
I poot mine mout to a parrel of bier,
 Und emptied it oop mit a schwigs.
Und denn I gissed Madilda Yane
 Und she shlog me on de kop,
Und de gompany fited mit daple-lecks
 Dill de coonshtable made oos shtop.

Hans Breitmann gife a barty —
 Where ish dat barty now!
Where ish de lofely golden cloud
 Dat float on de moundain's prow?
Where ish de himmelstrahlende Stern —
 De shtar of de shpirit's light?
All goned afay mit de Lager Beer —
 Afay in de Ewigkeit!

Charles Godfrey Leland

"*I valtzet mit Madilda Yane
Und vent shpinnen round und round.*"

SALAD

O cool in the summer is salad,
And warm in the winter is love;
And a poet shall sing you a ballad
Delicious thereon and thereof.
A singer am I, if no sinner,
My muse has a marvellous wing,
And I willingly worship at dinner
The Sirens of Spring.

Take endive — like love it is bitter,
Take beet — for like love it is red;
Crisp leaf of the lettuce shall glitter,
And cress from the rivulet's bed;
Anchovies, foam-born, like the lady
Whose beauty has maddened this bard;
And olives, from groves that are shady;
And eggs — boil 'em hard.

Mortimer Collins

THE ORIGIN OF THE BANJO

FROM "CHRISTMAS NIGHT IN THE QUARTERS"

Go 'way, fiddle! Folks is tired o' hearin' you a-squawkin',
Keep silence fur yo' betters! — don't you heah de banjo
     talkin'?
About de 'possum's tail she's gwine to lecter — ladies, lis-
     ten —
About de ha'r whut isn't dar, an' why de ha'r is missin'.

"Dar's gwine to be a' oberflow," said Noah, lookin' sol-
     emn —
Fur Noah tuk the "Herald," an' he read de ribber column —
An' so he sot his hands to wuk a-cl'arin' timber patches,
An' 'lowed he's gwine to build a boat to beat the steamah
Natchez.

Ol' Noah kep' a-nailin', an' a-chippin', an' a-sawin';
An' all de wicked neighbors kep' a-laughin' an' a-pshawin',
But Noah didn't min' 'em, knowin' whut wuz gwine to hap-
    pen,
An' forty days an' forty nights de rain it kep' a-drappin'.

Now, Noah had done catched a lot ob ebry sort o' beas'es,
Ob all de shows a-trabbelin', it beat 'em all to pieces!
He had a Morgan colt an' sebral head o' Jarsey cattle —
An' druv 'em board de Ark as soon's he heered de thunder
    rattle.

Den sech anoder fall ob rain! It come so awful hebby
De ribber riz immejitly, an' busted troo de lebbee;
De people all wuz drownded out — 'cep' Noah an' de
    critters
An' men he'd hired to work de boat, an' one to mix de
    bitters.

De Ark she kep' a-sailin' an' a-sailin' *an'* a-sailin';
De lion got his dander up, an' like to bruk de palin';
De sarpints hissed; de painters yelled; tell whut wid all
    de fussin'
You c'u'dn't hardly heah de mate a-bossin' 'roun' an'
    cussin'.

Now Ham, de only nigger whut wuz runnin' on de packet,
Got lonesome in de barber-shop an c'u'dn't stan' de racket;
An' so, fur to amuse hisse'f, he steamed some wood an'
    bent it,
An' soon he had a banjo made — de fust dat was invented.

He wet de ledder, stretched it on; made bridge an' screws
    an' aprin,
An' fitted in a proper neck — 'twuz berry long an' tap'rin'.
He tuk some tin, an' twisted him a thimble fur to ring it;
An' den de mighty question riz: how wuz he gwine to
    string it?

De 'possum had as fine a tail as dis dat I's a-singin';
De ha'rs so long an' thick an' strong — des fit fur banjo-
    stringin';

Dat nigger shaved 'em off as short as washday-dinner
 graces;
An' sorted ob 'em by de size, f'om little E's to bases.

He strung her, tuned her, struck a jig — 'twuz " Nebber
 min' de wedder " —
She soun' like forty-leben bands a-playin' all togedder.
Some went to pattin'; some to dancin'; Noah called de
 figgers,
An' Ham he sot an' knocked de tune, de happiest ob
 niggers!

Now, sence dat time — it's mighty strange — dere's not de
 slightes' showin'
Ob any ha'r at all upon de 'possum's tail a-growin';
An' curi's, too, dat nigger's ways: his people nebber los'
 'em —
Fur whar you finds de nigger — dar's de banjo an' de
 'possum.

Irwin Russell

WANDERERS

As o'er the hill we roam'd at will,
 My dog and I together,
We mark'd a chaise, by two bright bays
 Slow-moved along the heather:

Two bays arch-neck'd, with tails erect,
 And gold upon their blinkers;
And by their side an ass I spied;
 It was a travelling tinker's.

The chaise went by, nor aught cared I;
 Such things are not in my way:
I turned me to the tinker, who
 Was loafing down a byway:

I ask'd him where he lived — a stare
 Was all I got in answer,
And on he trudged; I rightly judged
 The stare said, " Where I can, sir."

I ask'd him if he'd take a whiff
    Of 'bacco; he acceded;
He grew communicative, too,
    (A pipe was all he needed),
Till of the tinker's life, I think,
    I knew as much as he did.

> " I loiter down by thorp and town ;
>   For any job I'm willing ;
> Take here and there a dusty brown,
>   And here and there a shilling.

> " I deal in every ware in turn,
>   I've rings for buddin' Sally,
> That sparkle like those eyes of her'n ;
>   I've liquor for the valet.

> " I steal from th' parson's strawberry-plots,
>   I hide by th' squire's covers ;
> I teach the sweet young housemaids what's
>   The art of trapping lovers.

> " The things I've done 'neath moon and stars
>   Have got me into messes :
> I've seen the sky through prison bars,
>   I've torn up prison dresses :

> " I've sat, I've sigh'd, I've gloom'd, I've glanced
>   With envy at the swallows
> That through the window slid, and danced
>   (Quite happy) round the gallows.

> " But out again I come, and show
>   My face, nor care a stiver,
> For trades are brisk and trades are slow,
>   But mine goes on forever."

Thus on he prattled like a babbling brook.
Then I, " The sun hath slipped behind the hill,
And my Aunt Vivian dines at half-past six."
So in all love we parted ; I to the Hall,
They to the village. It was noised next noon
That chickens had been miss'd at Syllabub Farm.
                    Charles Stuart Calverley

FERDINANDO AND ELVIRA

OR, THE GENTLE PIEMAN

PART I.

At a pleasant evening party I had taken down to supper
One whom I will call Elvira, and we talked of love and
    Tupper.

Mr. Tupper and the Poets, very lightly with them dealing,
For I've always been distinguished for a strong poetic
    feeling.

Then we let off paper crackers, each of which contained a
    motto,
And she listened while I read them, till her mother told
    her not to.

Then she whispered, " To the ballroom we had better, dear,
    be walking;
If we stop down here much longer, really people will be
    talking."

There were noblemen in coronets, and military cousins,
There were captains by the hundred, there were baronets by
    dozens.

Yet she heeded not their offers, but dismissed them with a
    blessing;
Then she let down all her back hair, which had taken long
    in dressing.

Then she had convulsive sobbings in her agitated throttle,
Then she wiped her pretty eyes and smelt her pretty smell-
    ing, bottle.

So I whispered, "Dear Elvira, say, — what can the matter
    be with you?
Does anything you've eaten, darling Popsy, disagree with
    you?"

But spite of all I said, her sobs grew more and more distressing,
And she tore her pretty back hair, which had taken long
in dressing.

Then she gazed upon the carpet, at the ceiling, then above
me,
And she whispered, " Ferdinando, do you really, *really* love
me? "

" Love you? " said I, then I sighed, and then I gazed upon
her sweetly —
For I think I do this sort of thing particularly neatly.

" Send me to the Arctic regions, or illimitable azure,
On a scientific goose-chase, with my Coxwell or my
Glaisher!

" Tell me whither I may hie me — tell me, dear one, that I
may know —
Is it up the highest Andes? down a horrible volcano? "

But she said, " It isn't polar bears, or hot volcanic grottoes;
Only find out who it is that writes those lovely cracker
mottoes! "

PART II.

" Tell me, Henry Wadsworth, Alfred, Poet Close, or Mister
Tupper,
Do you write the bon-bon mottoes my Elvira pulls at sup-
per? "

But Henry Wadsworth smiled, and said he had not had
that honor;
And Alfred, too, disclaimed the words that told so much
upon her.

" Mister Martin Tupper, Poet Close, I beg of you inform
us; "
But my question seemed to throw them both into a rage
enormous.

Mister Close expressed a wish that he could only get anigh
    to me;
And Mister Martin Tupper sent the following reply to me:

"A fool is bent upon a twig, but wise men dread a
    bandit," —
Which I know was very clever; but I didn't understand it.

Seven weary years I wandered — Patagonia, China, Nor-
    way,
Till at last I sank exhausted at a pastrycook his doorway.

There were fuchsias and geraniums, and daffodils and
    myrtle;
So I entered, and I ordered half a basin of mock turtle.

He was plump and he was chubby, he was smooth and he
    was rosy,
And his little wife was pretty and particularly cosy.

And he chirped and sang, and skipped about, and laughed
    with laughter hearty —
He was wonderfully active for so very stout a party.

And I said, "O gentle pieman, why so very, very merry?
Is it purity of conscience, or your one-and-seven sherry?"

But he answered, "I'm so happy — no profession could be
    dearer —
If I am not humming 'Tra la la' I'm singing 'Tirer, lirer!'

"First I go and make the patties, and the puddings, and
    the jellies,
Then I make a sugar bird-cage, which upon a table swell is:

"Then I polish all the silver, which a supper-table lacquers:
Then I write the pretty mottoes which you find inside the
    crackers — "

"Found at last!" I madly shouted. "Gentle pieman, you
    astound me!"
Then I waved the turtle soup enthusiastically round me.

And I shouted and I danced until he'd quite a crowd
    around him,
And I rushed away, exclaiming, "I have found him! I
    have found him!"

And I heard the gentle pieman in the road behind me trill-
    ing,
"'Tira! lira!' stop him, stop him! 'Tra! la! la!' the
    soup's a shilling!"

But until I reached Elvira's home, I never, never waited,
And Elvira to her Ferdinand's irrevocably mated!

William S. Gilbert

THE ROMANCE OF THE CARPET

Basking in peace in the warm spring sun,
South Hill smiled upon Burlington.

The breath of May! and the day was fair,
And the bright motes danced in the balmy air.

And the sunlight gleamed where the restless breeze
Kissed the fragrant blooms on the apple-trees.

His beardless cheek with a smile was spanned,
As he stood with a carriage whip in his hand.

And he laughed as he doffed his bobtail coat,
And the echoing folds of the carpet smote.

And she smiled as she leaned on her busy mop,
And said she'd tell him when to stop.

So he pounded away till the dinner-bell
Gave him a little breathing spell.

But he sighed when the kitchen clock struck one,
And she said the carpet wasn't done.

But he lovingly put in his biggest licks,
And he pounded like mad till the clock struck six.

And she said, in a dubious sort of way,
That she guessed he could finish it up next day.

Then all that day, and the next day, too,
That fuzz from the dirtless carpet flew.

And she'd give it a look at eventide,
And say, " Now beat on the other side."

And the new days came as the old days went,
And the landlord came for his regular rent.

And the neighbors laughed at the tireless broom,
And his face was shadowed with clouds of gloom.

Till at last, one cheerless winter day,
He kicked at the carpet and slid away.

Over the fence and down the street,
Speeding away with footsteps fleet.

And never again the morning sun
Smiled on him beating his carpet-drum.

And South Hill often said with a yawn,
" Where's the carpet-martyr gone? "

Years twice twenty had come and passed
And the carpet swayed in the autumn blast.

For never yet, since that bright spring-time,
Had it ever been taken down from the line.

Over the fence a gray-haired man
Cautiously clim, clome, clem, clum, clamb.

He found him a stick in the old woodpile,
And he gathered it up with a sad, grim smile.

A flush passed over his face forlorn
As he gazed at the carpet, tattered and torn.

And he hit it a most resounding thwack,
Till the startled air gave his echoes back.

And out of the window a white face leaned,
And a palsied hand the pale face screened.

She knew his face; she gasped, and sighed,
" A little more on the other side."

Right down on the ground his stick he throwed,
And he shivered and said, " Well, I am blowed! "

And he turned away, with a heart full sore,
And he never was seen not more, not more.

Robert Jones Burdette

THE FRIEND OF HUMANITY AND THE KNIFE - GRINDER

FRIEND OF HUMANITY

" Needy Knife-grinder! whither are you going?
Rough is the road, your wheel is out of order, —
Bleak blows the blast; your hat has got a hole in't,
      So have your breeches!

" Weary Knife-grinder! little think the proud ones,
Who in their coaches roll along the turnpike-
Road, what hard work 'tis crying all day, ' Knives and
      Scissors to grind O!'

" Tell me, Knife-grinder, how came you to grind knives?
Did some rich man tyrannically use you?
Was it the squire? or parson of the parish?
      Or the attorney?

" Was it the squire, for killing of his game? or
Covetous parson, for his tithes distraining?
Or roguish lawyer, made you lose your little
      All in a lawsuit?

" (Have you not read the 'Rights of Man,' by Tom
  Paine?)
Drops of compassion tremble on my eyelids,
Ready to fall, as soon as you have told your
      Pitiful story."

KNIFE - GRINDER

" Story! God bless you! I have none to tell, sir,
Only last night, a-drinking at the Chequers,
This poor old hat and breeches, as you see, were
    Torn in a scuffle.

" Constables came up, for to take me into
Custody; they took me before the justice;
Justice Oldmixon put me in the parish-
    Stocks for a vagrant.

" I should be glad to drink your Honor's health in
A pot of beer, if you will give me sixpence;
But for my part, I never love to meddle
    With politics, sir."

FRIEND OF HUMANITY

" I give thee sixpence! I will see thee damned first —
Wretch! whom no sense of wrongs can rouse to ven-
    geance, —
Sordid, unfeeling, reprobate, degraded,
    Spiritless outcast! "

[Kicks the Knife-grinder, overturns his wheel, and exit in a trans-
port of Republican enthusiasm and universal philanthropy.

George Canning

LEEDLE YAWCOB STRAUSS

I haf von funny leedle poy,
    Vot comes schust to mine knee;
Der queerest schap, der createst rogue,
    As efer you dit see.
He runs, und schumps, und schmashes dings
    In all barts off der house:
But vot off dot? He vas mine son,
    Mine leedle Yawcob Strauss.

He get der measles und der mumbs
    Und eferyding dot's oudt;

He sbills mine glass off lager bier,
  Poots schnuff indo mine kraut.
He fills mine pipe mit Limburg cheese —
  Dot vas der roughest chouse;
I'd dake dot vrom no oder poy
  But leedle Yawcob Strauss.

He dakes der milk-ban for a dhrum,
  Und cuts mine cane in dwo,
To make der schticks to beat it mit —
  Mine cracious, dot vas drue!
I dinks mine hed vas schplit abart,
  He kicks oup sooch a touse:
But nefer mind; der poys vas few
  Like dot young Yawcob Strauss.

He asks me questions sooch as dese:
  Who baints mine nose so red?
Who vas it cuts dot schmoodth blace oudt
  Vrom der hair ubon mine hed?
Und vere dere plaze goes vrom der lamp
  Vene'er der glim I douse.
How gan I all dose dings eggsblain
  To dot schmall Yawcob Strauss?

I somedimes dink I schall go vild
  Mit sooch a grazy poy,
Und vish vonce more I gould haf rest,
  Und beaceful dimes enshoy;
But ven he vas aschleep in ped
  So guiet as a mouse,
I prays der Lord, "Dake anyding,
  But leaf dot Yawcob Strauss."

                                Charles Follen Adams

JONES AT THE BARBER SHOP

SCENE. — *A Barber's Shop. Barber's men engaged in cutting hair, making wigs and other barberesque operations.*

Enter JONES, *meeting* OILY *the barber*

Jones. I wish my hair cut.
Oily. Pray, sir, take a seat.

[OILY puts a chair for JONES, who sits. During the following
dialogue OILY continues cutting JONES's hair.

Oily. We've had much wet, sir.
Jones. Very much, indeed.
Oily. And yet November's early days were fine.
Jones. They were.
Oily. I hoped fair weather might have lasted us
Until the end.
Jones. At one time — so did I.
Oily. But we have had it very wet.
Jones. We have.

[A pause of some minutes.

Oily. I know not, sir, who cut your hair last time;
But this I say, sir, it was badly cut:
No doubt 'twas in the country.
Jones. No! in town!
Oily. Indeed! I should have fancied otherwise.
Jones. 'Twas cut in town — and in this very room.
Oily. Amazement! — but I now remember well.
We had an awkward, new provincial hand,
A fellow from the country. Sir, he did
More damage to my business in a week
Than all my skill can in a year repair.
He must have cut your hair.
Jones (looking at him). No — 'twas yourself.
Oily. Myself! Impossible! You must mistake.
Jones. I don't mistake — 'twas you that cut my hair.

[A long pause, interrupted only by the clipping of the scissors.

Oily. Your hair is very dry, sir.
Jones. Oh! indeed.
Oily. Our Vegetable Extract moistens it.
Jones. I like it dry.

Oily. But, sir, the hair when dry
Turns quickly gray.
Jones. That color I prefer.
Oily. But hair, when gray, will rapidly fall off,
And baldness will ensue.
Jones. I would be bald.
Oily. Perhaps you mean to say you'd like a wig. —
We've wigs so natural they can't be told
From real hair.
Jones. Deception I detest.

[Another pause ensues, during which OILY blows down JONES's neck and relieves him from the linen wrapper in which he has been enveloped during the process of hair-cutting.

Oily. We've brushes, soaps, and scent, of every kind.
Jones. I see you have. (*Pays 6d.*) I think you'll find
that right.
Oily. If there is nothing I can show you, sir.
Jones. No: nothing. Yet — there may be something, too,
That you may show me.
Oily. Name it, sir.
Jones. The door.

[*Exit* JONES.

Oily (*to his man*). That's a rum customer, at any rate.
Had I cut him as short as he cut me,
How little hair upon his head would be!
But if kind friends will all our pains requite,
We'll hope for better luck another night.

[Shop-bell rings and curtain falls.

Punch

WEDDED BLISS

"O come and be my mate!" said the Eagle to the Hen;
"I love to soar, but then
I want my mate to rest
Forever in the nest!"
Said the Hen, "I cannot fly,
I have no wish to try,
But I joy to see my mate careering through the sky!"
They wed, and cried, "Ah, this is Love, my own!"
And the Hen sat, the Eagle soared, alone.

"O come and be my mate!" said the Lion to the Sheep;
  "My love for you is deep!
  I slay, a Lion should,
  But you are mild and good!"
  Said the Sheep, "I do no ill —
  Could not, had I the will —
But I joy to see my mate pursue, devour, and kill."
They wed, and cried, "Ah, this is Love, my own!"
And the Sheep browsed, the Lion prowled, alone.

"O come and be my mate!" said the Salmon to the Clam;
  "You are not wise, but I am.
  I know sea and stream as well;
  You know nothing but your shell."
  Said the Clam, "I'm slow of motion,
  But my love is all devotion,
And I joy to have my mate traverse lake and stream and
    ocean!"
They wed, and cried, "Ah, this is Love, my own!"
And the Clam sucked, the Salmon swam, alone.

                    Charlotte Perkins (Stetson) Gilman

THE HEIGHT OF THE RIDICULOUS

I wrote some lines once on a time,
  In wondrous merry mood,
And thought, as usual, men would say
  They were exceeding good.

They were so queer, so very queer,
  I laughed as I would die;
Albeit, in the general way,
  A sober man am I.

I called my servant, and he came;
  How kind it was of him,
To mind a slender man like me,
  He of the mighty limb!

"These to the printer," I exclaimed,
  And, in my humorous way,

I added (as a trifling jest),
  " There'll be the devil to pay."

He took the paper, and I watched,
  And saw him peep within;
At the first line he read, his face
  Was all upon the grin.

He read the next; the grin grew broad,
  And shot from ear to ear;
He read the third; a chuckling noise
  I now began to hear.

The fourth; he broke into a roar;
  The fifth; his waistband split;
The sixth; he burst five buttons off,
  And tumbled in a fit.

Ten days and nights, with sleepless eye,
  I watched that wretched man,
And since, I never dare to write
  As funny as I can.

                                Oliver Wendell Holmes

ADDRESS TO THE TOOTHACHE

My curse upon your venom'd stang,
That shoots my tortur'd gooms alang;
An' thro' my lug gies monie a twang,
              Wi' gnawing vengeance;
Tearing my nerves wi' bitter pang,
              Like racking engines!

A' down my beard the slavers trickle!
I throw the wee stools o'er the mickle,
While round the fire the giglets keckle
              To see me loup;
An', raving mad, I wish a heckle
              Were i' their doup!

When fevers burn, or ague freezes,
Rheumatics gnaw, or colic squeezes,

"*My curse upon your venom'd stang,*
That shoots my tortur'd gooms alang."

Our neebors sympathize to ease us
      Wi' pitying moan;
But thee! — thou hell o' a' diseases,
      They mock our groan!

Of a' the num'rous human dools,
Ill-hairsts, daft bargains, cutty-stools,
Or worthy frien's laid i' the mools,
      Sad sight to see!
The tricks o' knaves, or fash o' fools,
      Thou bear'st the gree!

Whare'er that place be priests ca' hell,
Whare a' the tones o' misery yell,
An' rankèd plagues their numbers tell
      In dreadfu' raw,
Thou, Toothache, surely bear'st the bell
      Amang them a'!

O thou grim, mischief-making chiel,
That gars the notes o' discord squeel,
'Till humankind aft dance a reel
      In gore a shoe-thick; —
Gie a' the faes o' Scotland's weal
      A towmond's toothache!

                Robert Burns

PRIOR TO MISS BELLE'S APPEARANCE

What makes you come *here* fer, Mister,
    So much to *our* house? — *Say?*
Come to see our big sister! —
An' Charley he says 'at you kissed her
    An' he ketched you, thuther day! —
Didn' you, Charley? — But we p'omised Belle
And crossed our heart to never to tell —
'Cause *she* gived us some o' them-er
Chawk'lut-drops 'at you bringed to her!

Charley he's my little b'uther —
    An' we has a-mostest fun,

Don't we, Charley? — Our Muther,
Whenever we whips one-anuther,
　　Tries to whip *us* — an' we *run* —
Don't we, Charley? — An' nen, bime-by,
Nen she gives us cake — an' pie —
Don't she, Charley? — when we come in
An' p'omise never to do it agin!

He's named Charley. — I'm *Willie* —
　　An' I'm got the purtiest name!
But Uncle Bob *he* calls me "Billy" —
Don't he, Charley? — 'Nour filly
　　We named "Billy," the same
Ist like me! An' our Ma said
'At "Bob put foolishnuss into our head!" —
Didn' she, Charley? — An' *she* don't know
Much about *boys!* — 'Cause Bob said so!

Baby's a funniest feller!
　　Naint no hair on his head —
Is they, Charley? It's meller
Wite up there! An' ef Belle er
　　Us ask wuz *we* that way, Ma said, —
"Yes; an' yer *Pa's* head wuz soft as that,
An' it's that way yet!" — An' Pa grabs his hat
An' says, "Yes, childern, she's right abcut Pa —
'Cause that's the reason he married yer Ma!"

An' our Ma says 'at "Belle couldn'
　　Ketch nothin' at all but ist '*bows!*'"
An' *Pa* says 'at "you're soft as puddun!" —
An' *Uncle Bob* says "you're a good-un —
　　'Cause he can tell by yer nose!" —
Didn' he, Charley? And when Belle'll play
In the poller on th' pianer, some day,
Bob makes up funny songs about you,
Till she gits mad — like he wants her to!

Our sister *Fanny,* she's '*leven*
　　Years old. 'At's mucher 'an *I* —
Ain't it, Charley? . . . I'm seven! —
But our sister Fanny's in *Heaven!*
　　Nere's where you go ef you die! —

Don't you, Charley? Nen you has *wings* —
Ist like Fanny! — an' *purtiest things!* —
Don't you, Charley? An' nen you can *fly* —
Ist fly —an' *ever*'thing! . . . Wisht *I'd* die!
James Whitcomb Riley

FAITHLESS SALLY BROWN

Young Ben he was a nice young man,
   A carpenter by trade;
And he fell in love with Sally Brown,
   That was a lady's maid.

But as they fetched a walk one day,
   They met a press-gang crew;
And Sally she did faint away,
   Whilst Ben he was brought to.

The boatswain swore with wicked words,
   Enough to shock a saint,
That though she did seem in a fit,
   'Twas nothing but a feint.

"Come, girl," said he, "hold up your head,
   He'll be as good as me;
For when your swain is in our boat,
   A boatswain he will be."

So when they'd made their game of her,
   And taken off her elf,
She roused, and found she only was
   A coming to herself.

"And is he gone, and is he gone?"
   She cried, and wept outright:
"Then I will to the water side,
   And see him out of sight."

A waterman came up to her, —
   "Now, young woman," said he,
"If you weep on so, you will make
   Eye-water in the sea."

Alas! they've taken my beau, Ben,
  To sail with old Benbow;"
And her woe began to run afresh,
  As if she'd said, "Gee woe!"

Says he, "They've only taken him
  To the Tender-ship, you see;"
"The Tender-ship," cried Sally Brown,
  "What a hard-ship that must be!

"O! would I were a mermaid now,
  For then I'd follow him;
But, O!—I'm not a fish-woman,
  And so I cannot swim.

"Alas! I was not born beneath
  The virgin and the scales,
So I must curse my cruel stars,
  And walk about in Wales."

Now Ben had sailed to many a place
  That's underneath the world;
But in two years the ship came home,
  And all her sails were furled.

But when he called on Sally Brown,
  To see how she got on,
He found she'd got another Ben,
  Whose Christian name was John.

"O, Sally Brown, O, Sally Brown,
  How could you serve me so?
I've met with many a breeze before,
  But never such a blow!"

Then reading on his 'bacco-box,
  He heaved a heavy sigh,
And then began to eye his pipe,
  And then to pipe his eye.

And then he tried to sing "All's Well,"
  But could not, though he tried;
His head was turned, and so he chewed
  His pigtail till he died.

His death, which happened in his berth,
  At forty-odd befell:
They went and told the sexton, and
  The sexton tolled the bell.

Thomas Hood

FIRST LOVE

O my earliest love, who, ere I number'd
  Ten sweet summers, made my bosom thrill!
Will a swallow — or a swift, or some bird —
  Fly to her and say, I love her still?

Say my life's a desert drear and arid,
  To its one green spot I aye recur:
Never, never — although three times married —
  Have I cared a jot for aught but her.

No, mine own! though early forced to leave you,
  Still my heart was there where first we met;
In those "Lodgings with an ample sea-view,"
  Which were, forty years ago, " To Let."

There I saw her first, our landlord's oldest
  Little daughter. On a thing so fair
Thou, O Sun, — who (so they say) beholdest
  Everything, — hast gazed, I tell thee, ne'er.

There she sat — so near me, yet remoter
  Than a star — a blue-eyed, bashful imp:
On her lap she held a happy bloater,
  'Twixt her lips a yet more happy shrimp.

And I loved her, and our troth we plighted
  On the morrow by the shingly shore:
In a fortnight to be disunited
  By a bitter fate forevermore.

O my own, my beautiful, my blue-eyed!
  To be young once more, and bite my thumb
At the world and all its cares with you, I'd
  Give no inconsiderable sum.

Hand in hand we tramp'd the golden seaweed,
  Soon as o'er the gray cliff peep'd the dawn:
Side by side, when came the hour for tea, we'd
  Crunch the mottled shrimp and hairy prawn: —

Has she wedded some gigantic shrimper,
  That sweet mite with whom I loved to play?
Is she girt with babes that whine and whimper,
  That bright being who was always gay?

Yes — she has at least a dozen wee things!
  Yes — I see her darning corduroys,
Scouring floors, and setting out the tea-things,
  For a howling herd of hungry boys,

In a home that reeks of tar and sperm-oil!
  But at intervals she thinks, I know,
Of those days which we, afar from turmoil,
  Spent together forty years ago.

O my earliest love, still unforgotten,
  With your downcast eyes of dreamy blue!
Never, somehow, could I seem to cotton
  To another as I did to you!
                    Charles Stuart Calverley

A DIALOGUE FROM PLATO

"Le temps le mieux employé est celui qu' on perd."
                    — *Claude Tillier.*

I'd read three hours. Both notes and text
  Were fast a mist becoming;
In bounced a vagrant bee, perplexed,
  And filled the room with humming,

Then out. The casement's leafage sways,
  And, .parted light, discloses
Miss Di., with hat and book, — a maze
  Of muslin mixed with roses.

"You're reading Greek?" "I am — and you?"
  "O, mine's a mere romancer!"

"So Plato is." "Then read him — do;
  And I'll read mine in answer."

I read. "My Plato (Plato, too, —
  That wisdom thus should harden!)
Declares 'blue eyes look doubly blue
  Beneath a Dolly Varden.'"

She smiled. "My book in turn avers
  (No author's name is stated)
That sometimes those Philosophers
  Are sadly mis-translated."

"But hear, — the next's in stronger style:
  The Cynic School asserted
That two red lips which part and smile
  May not be controverted!"

She smiled once more — "My book, I find,
  Observes some modern doctors
Would make the Cynics out a kind
  Of album-verse concoctors."

Then I — "Why not? 'Ephesian law,
  No less than time's tradition,
Enjoined fair speech on all who saw
  Diana's apparition.'"

She blushed — this time. "If Plato's page
  No wiser precept teaches,
Then I'd renounce that doubtful sage,
  And walk to Burnham-beeches."

"Agreed," I said. "For Socrates
  (I find he too is talking)
Thinks Learning can't remain at ease
  While Beauty goes a-walking."

She read no more. I leapt the sill:
  The sequel's scarce essential —
Nay, more than this, I hold it still
  Profoundly confidential.

                              Austin Dobson

THE LEARNED NEGRO

There was a negro preacher, I have heard,
In Southern parts before rebellion stirred,
Who did not spend his strength in empty sound;
His was a mind deep-reaching and profound.
Others might beat the air, and make a noise,
And help to amuse the silly girls and boys;
But as for him, he was a man of thought,
Deep in theology, although untaught.
He could not read or write, but he was wise,
And knew right smart how to extemporize.
One Sunday morn, when hymns and prayers were
        said,
The preacher rose, and rubbing up his head,
" Bredren and sisterin, and companions dear,
Our preachment for to-day, as you shall hear,
Will be ob de creation, — ob de plan
On which God fashioned Adam, de fust man.
When God made Adam, in de ancient day,
He made his body out ob earth and clay,
He shape him all out right, den by and by,
He set him up agin de fence to dry."
" Stop," said a voice; and straightway there arose
An ancient negro in his master's clothes.
" Tell me," said he, " before you farder go,
One little thing which I should like to know.
It does not quite get through dis niggar's har.
How came dat fence so nice and handy dar? "
Like one who in the mud is tightly stuck,
Or one nonplussed, astonished, thunderstruck,
The preacher looked severely on the pews,
And rubbed his hair to know what words to use.
" Bredren," said he, " dis word I hab to say;
De preacher can't be bothered in dis way;
For, if he is, it's jest as like as not,
Our whole theology will be upsot."

                                    Anonymous

"A noble savage lady, of a color rather shady."

TRUE TO POLL

I'll sing you a song, not very long,
  But the story somewhat new,
Of William Kidd, who, whatever he did,
  To his Poll was always true.
He sailed away in a galliant ship
  From the port of old Bris*tol,*
    And the last words he uttered,
    As his hankercher he fluttered,
  Were, " My heart is true to Poll."

      His heart was true to Poll,
      His heart was true to Poll.
        It's no matter what you do
        If your heart be only true :
      And his heart *was* true to Poll.

'Twas a wreck. Willi*am,* on shore he swam,
  And looked about for an inn ;
When a noble savage lady, of a color rather
    shady,
  Came up with a kind of grin :
" Oh, marry *me,* and a king you'll be,
  And in a palace loll ;
    Or we'll eat you willy-nilly."
    So he gave his *hand,* did Billy,
  But his *heart* was true to Poll.

Away a twelvemonth sped, and a happy life
    he led
  As the King of the Kikeryboos ;
His paint was red and yellar, and he used a
    big umbrella,
  And he wore a pair of over-*shoes;*
He'd corals and knives, and twenty-six wives,
  Whose beauties I cannot here extol ;
    One day they all revolted,
    So he back to Bristol bolted,
  For his *heart* was true to Poll.

His heart was true to Poll,
His heart was true to Poll,
It's no matter what you do
If your heart be only true:
And his heart *was* true to Poll.

Frank C. Burnand

THE WIDOW MALONE

Did you hear of the Widow Malone
            O hone!
Who lived in the town of Athlone
            Alone?
O, she melted the hearts
Of the swains in them parts;
So lovely the Widow Malone,
            O hone!
So lovely the Widow Malone.

Of lovers she had a full score
            Or more;
And fortunes they all had galore
            In store;
From the minister down
To the clerk of the Crown,
All were courting the Widow Malone
            O hone!
All were courting the Widow Malone.

But so modest was Mrs. Malone,
            'Twas known,
That no one could see her alone,
            O hone!
Let them ogle and sigh,
They could ne'er catch her eye;
So bashful the Widow Malone,
            O hone!
So bashful the Widow Malone.

Till one Mister O'Brien from Clare,
            How quare!

'Tis little for blushing they care
    Down there;
Put his arm round her waist,
Gave ten kisses at laste,
And says he, " You're my Molly Malone,
    My own."
Says he, " You're my Molly Malone."

And the widow they all thought so shy —
    My eye!
Never thought of a simper or sigh;
    For why?
" O Lucius," said she,
" Since you've now made so free,
You may marry your Mary Malone,
    Your own;
You may marry your Mary Malone."

There's a moral contained in my song,
    Not wrong;
And one comfort it's not very long,
    But strong: —
If for widows you die,
Learn to kiss — not to sigh,
For they're all like sweet Mistress Malone!
    O hone!
O they're all like sweet Mistress Malone!

Charles Lever

AN INVITATION TO THE ZOOLOGICAL GARDENS

BY A STUTTERING LOVER

I have found out a gig-gig-gift for my fuf-fuf-fair,
  I have found where the rattlesnakes bub-bub-breed;
Will you co-co-come, and I'll show you the bub-bub-bear,
  And the lions and tit-tit-tigers at fuf-fuf-feed.

I know where the co-co-cockatoo's song
  Makes mum-mum-melody through the sweet vale;
Where the mum-monkeys gig-gig-grin all the day long,
  Or gracefully swing by the tit-tit-tit-tail.

You shall pip-play, dear, some did-did-delicate joke
  With the bub-bub-bear on the tit-tit-top of his pip-pip-pip-
    pole;
But observe, 'tis forbidden to pip-pip-poke
  At the bub-bub-bear with your pip-pip-pink pip-pip-pip-
    pip-parasol!

You shall see the huge elephant pip-pip-play,
  You shall gig-gig-gaze on the stit-stit-stately raccoon;
And then, did-did-dear, together we'll stray,
  To the cage of the bub-bub-blue-faced bab-bab-boon.

You wished (I r-r-remember it well,
  And I lul-lul-loved you the m-m-more for the wish)
To witness the bub-bub-beautiful pip-pip-pel-
  ican swallow the l-l-live little fuf-fuf-fish!

                                        Punch

EARLY RISING

"God bless the man who first invented sleep!"
    So Sancho Panza said, and so say I:
And bless him, also, that he didn't keep
    His great discovery to himself; nor try
To make it — as the lucky fellow might —
A close monopoly by patent-right!

Yes — bless the man who first invented sleep,
    (I really can't avoid the iteration;)
But blast the man, with curses loud and deep,
    Whate'er the rascal's name, or age, or station,
Who first invented, and went round advising,
That artificial cut-off — Early Rising!

"Rise with the lark, and with the lark to bed,"
    Observes some solemn, sentimental owl;
Maxims like these are very cheaply said;
    But, ere you make yourself a fool or fowl,
Pray just inquire about his rise and fall,
And whether larks have any beds at all!

The time for honest folks to be a-bed
    Is in the morning, if I reason right;

And he who cannot keep his precious head
  Upon his pillow till it's fairly light,
And so enjoy his forty morning winks,
Is up to knavery; or else — he drinks!

Thompson, who sung about the " Seasons," said
  It was a glorious thing to *rise* in season;
But then he said it — lying — in his bed,
  At ten o'clock A. M., — the very reason
He wrote so charmingly. The simple fact is
His preaching wasn't sanctioned by his practice.

'Tis, doubtless, well to be sometimes awake, —.
  Awake to duty, and awake to truth, —
But when, alas! a nice review we take
  Of our best deeds and days, we find, in sooth,
The hours that leave the slightest cause to weep
Are those we passed in childhood or asleep!

'Tis beautiful to leave the world awhile
  For the soft visions of the gentle night;
And free, at last, from mortal care or guile,
  To live as only in the angels' sight,
In sleep's sweet realm so cosily shut in,
Where, at the worst, we only *dream* of sin!

So let us sleep, and give the Maker praise.
  I like the lad who, when his father thought
To clip his morning nap by hackneyed phrase
  Of vagrant worm by early songster caught,
Cried, " Served him right! — it's not at all surprising;
The worm was punished, sir, for early rising!"
                    John Godfrey Saxe

THE FARMER AND THE COUNSELLOR

A Counsel in the Common Pleas,
  Who was esteemed a mighty wit,
  Upon the strength of a chance hit
Amid a thousand flippancies,
And his occasional bad jokes
  In bullying, bantering, browbeating,
  Ridiculing, and maltreating

Women, or other timid folks,
In a late cause resolved to hoax
A clownish Yorkshire farmer — one
Who, by his uncouth look and gait,
Appeared expressly meant by Fate
For being quizzed and played upon:
So having tipped the wink to those
In the back rows,
Who kept the laughter bottled down,
Until our wag should draw the cork,
He smiled jocosely on the clown,
And went to work.
"Well, Farmer Numscull, how go calves at York?"
"Why — not, sir, as they do wi' you,
But on four legs, instead of two."
"Officer!" cried the legal elf,
Piqued at the laugh against himself,
"So pray keep silence down below there.
Now look at me, clown, and attend;
Have I not seen you somewhere, friend?"
"Yees — very like — I often go there."
"Our rustic's waggish — quite laconic,"
The counsel cried, with grin sardonic;
"I wish I'd known this prodigy,
This genius of the clods, when I
On circuit was at York residing.
Now, Farmer, do for once speak true —
Mind, you're on oath, so tell me, you,
Who doubtless think yourself so clever,
Are there as many fools as ever
In the West Riding?"
"Why — no, sir, no; we've got our share,
But not so many as when *you* were there!"

Horace Smith

BALLAD

The auld wife sat at her ivied door,
    (*Butter and eggs and a pound of cheese*)
A thing she had frequently done before;
    And her spectacles lay on her apron'd knees.

The piper he piped on the hilltop high,
　(*Butter and eggs and a pound of cheese*)
Till the cow said " I die," and the goose asked
　" Why? "
　And the dog said nothing, but search'd for fleas.

The farmer he strode through the square farmyard;
　(*Butter and eggs and a pound of cheese*)
His last brew of ale was a trifle hard —
　The connection of which with the plot one sees.

The farmer's daughter hath frank blue eyes;
　(*Butter and eggs and a pound of cheese*)
She hears the rooks caw in the windy skies,
　As she sits at her lattice and shells her peas.

The farmer's daughter hath ripe red lips;
　(*Butter and eggs and a pound of cheese*)
If you try to approach her, away she skips
　Over tables and chairs with apparent ease.

The farmer's daughter hath soft brown hair;
　(*Butter and eggs and a pound of cheese*)
And I met with a ballad, I can't say where,
　Which wholly consisted of lines like these.

PART II.

She sat with her hands 'neath her dimpled cheeks,
　(*Butter and eggs and a pound of cheese*)
And spake not a word. While a lady speaks
　There is hope, but she didn't even sneeze.

She sat, with her hands 'neath her crimson cheeks;
　(*Butter and eggs and a pound of cheese*)
She gave up mending her father's breeks,
　And let the cat roll in her new chemise.

She sat with her hands 'neath her burning cheeks,
　(*Butter and eggs and a pound of cheese*)
And gazed at the piper for thirteen weeks;
　Then she follow'd him o'er the misty leas.

Her sheep follow'd her, as their tails did them,
  (*Butter and eggs and a pound of cheese*)
And this song is consider'd a perfect gem,
  And as to the meaning, it's what you please.
Charles Stuart Calverley

THE GOUTY MERCHANT AND THE STRANGER

In Broad Street Buildings on a winter night,
Snug by his parlor-fire, a gouty wight
Sat all alone, with one hand rubbing
His feet, rolled up in fleecy hose:
While t'other held beneath his nose
The *Public Ledger,* in whose columns grubbing,
  He noted all the sales of hops,
    Ships, shops, and slops;
Gum, galls, and groceries; ginger, gin,
Tar, tallow, turmeric, turpentine, and tin;
When lo! a decent personage in black
Entered and most politely said:
" Your footman, sir, has gone his nightly track
  To the King's Head,
And left your door ajar; which I
Observed in passing by,
  And thought it neighborly to give you notice."
" Ten thousand thanks; how very few get,
In time of danger,
Such kind attentions from a stranger!
Assuredly, that fellow's throat is
Doomed to a final drop at Newgate:
He knows, too (the unconscionable elf!),
That there's no soul at home except myself."
" Indeed," replied the stranger (looking grave),
" Then he's a double knave;
He knows that rogues and thieves by scores
Nightly beset unguarded doors:
And see, how easily might one
  Of these domestic foes,
  Even beneath your very nose,
Perform his knavish tricks;
Enter your room, as I have done,
Blow out your candles — *thus* — and *thus* —

Pocket your silver candlesticks,
   And — walk off — *thus!* " —
So said, so done; he made no more remark
   Nor waited for replies,
   But marched off with his prize,
Leaving the gouty merchant in the dark.
                              Horace Smith

THE TRUTH ABOUT HORACE[1]

It is very aggravating
To hear the solemn prating
Of the fossils who are stating
   That old Horace was a prude;
When we know that with the ladies
He was always raising Hades,
And with many an escapade his
   Best productions are imbued.

There's really not much harm in a
Large number of his carmina,
But these people find alarm in a
   Few records of his acts;
So they'd squelch the muse caloric,
And to students sophomoric
They'd present as metaphoric
   What old Horace meant for facts.

We have always thought 'em lazy;
Now we adjudge 'em crazy!
Why, Horace was a daisy
   That was very much alive!
And the wisest of us know him
As his Lydia verses show him, —
Go, read that virile poem, —
   It is No. 25.

He was a very owl, sir,
And starting out to prowl, sir,

1 From "A Little Book of Western Verse." Copyright, 1889, by Eugene Field, and published by Charles Scribner's Sons.

You bet he made Rome howl, sir,
   Until he filled his date;
With a massic-laden ditty
And a classic maiden pretty,
He painted up the city,
   And Mæcenas paid the freight!

Eugene Field

SALLY SIMPKIN'S LAMENT

"Oh! what is that comes gliding in,
   And quite in middling haste?
It is the picture of my Jones,
   And painted to the waist.

"It is not painted to the life,
   For where's the trousers blue?
O Jones, my dear! — Oh, dear! my Jones,
   What is become of you?"

"O Sally, dear, it is too true, —
   The half that you remark
Is come to say my other half
   Is bit off by a shark!

"O Sally, sharks do things by halves,
   Yet most completely do!
A bite in one place seems enough,
   But I've been bit in two.

"You know I once was all your own,
   But now a shark must share!
But let that pass — for now to you
   I'm neither here nor there.

"Alas! death has a strange divorce
   Effected in the sea,
It has divided me from you,
   And even me from me!

"Don't fear my ghost will walk o' nights
   To haunt, as people say;

My ghost *can't* walk, for, oh! my legs
  Are many leagues away!

"Lord! think when I am swimming round,
  And looking where the boat is,
A shark just snaps away a *half,*
  Without 'a *quarter's notice.'*

"One half is here, the other half
  Is near Columbia placed;
O Sally, I have got the whole
  Atlantic for my waist.

"But now, adieu — a long adieu!
  I've solved death's awful riddle,
And would say more, but I am doomed
  To break off in the middle!"

Thomas Hood

THE V - A - S - E

From the madding crowd they stand apart,
The maidens four and the Work of Art;

And none might tell from sight alone
In which had culture ripest grown, —

The Gotham Millions fair to see,
The Philadelphia Pedigree,

The Boston Mind of azure hue,
Or the Soulful Soul from Kalamazoo, —

For all loved Art in a seemly way,
With an earnest soul and a capital A.

. . . . o

Long they worshipped; but no one broke
The sacred stillness, until up spoke

The Western one from the nameless place,
Who blushing said, "What a lovely vace!"

Over three faces a sad smile flew,
And they edged away from Kalamazoo.

But Gotham's haughty soul was stirred
To crush the stranger with one small word;

Deftly hiding reproof in praise,
She cries, " 'Tis, indeed, a lovely vaze!"

But brief her unworthy triumph when
The lofty one from the home of Penn,

With the consciousness of two grandpapas,
Exclaims, "It is quite a lovely vahs!"

And glances round with an anxious thrill,
Awaiting the word of Beacon Hill.

But the Boston maid smiles courteouslee,
And gently murmurs, "Oh, pardon me!

"I did not catch your remark, because
I was so entranced with that charming vaws!"

Dies erit prægelida
Sinistra quum Bostonia.
James Jeffrey Roche

THE RABBINICAL ORIGIN OF WOMAN

They tell us that Woman was made of a rib,
 Just picked from a corner, so snug, in the side,
But the Rabbins swear to you that this is a fib,
 And 'twas not so at all that the sex was supplied.

For old Adam was fashion'd, the first of his kind,
 With a tail like a monkey, full a yard and a span;
And when Nature cut off this appendage behind,
 Why then woman was made of the tail of the man.

If such is the tie between women and men,
The ninny who weds is a pitiful elf;
For he takes to his tail, like an idiot, again,
And makes a most horrible ape of himself.

Yet, if we may judge, as the fashions prevail,
Every husband remembers th' original plan;
And, knowing his wife is no more than his tail,
Why — he leaves her behind him as much as he can.

Thomas Moore

FATHER MOLLOY

OR, THE CONFESSION

Paddy McCabe was dying one day,
    And Father Molloy he came to confess him;
Paddy pray'd hard he would make no delay,
    But forgive him his sins and make haste for to bless
        him.
" First tell me your sins," says Father Molloy,
" For I'm thinking you've not been a very good boy."
" Oh," says Paddy, " so late in the evenin', I fear,
'Twould throuble you such a long story to hear,
For you've ten long miles o'er the mountains to go,
While the road *I've* to travel's much longer, you know.
So give us your blessin' and get in the saddle,
To tell all my sins my poor brain it would addle;
And the docther gave ordhers to keep me so quiet —
'Twould disturb me to tell all my sins, if I'd thry it,
And your Reverence has towld us, unless we tell *all*,
'Tis worse than not makin' confession at all.
So I'll say in a word I'm no very good boy —
And, therefore, your blessin', sweet Father Molloy."

" Well, I'll read from a book," says Father Molloy,
    " The manifold sins that humanity's heir to;
And when you hear those that your conscience annoy,
    You'll just squeeze my hand, as acknowledging
        thereto."
Then the father began the dark roll of iniquity,
And Paddy, thereat, felt his conscience grow rickety,

And he gave such a squeeze that the priest gave a
    roar —
"Oh, murdher," says Paddy, "don't read any more,
For, if you keep readin', by all that is thrue,
Your Reverence's fist will be soon black and blue;
Besides, to be throubled my conscience begins,
That your Reverence should have any hand in my sins,
So you'd betther suppose I committed them all,
For whether they're great ones, or whether they're small,
Or if they're a dozen, or if they're fourscore,
'Tis your Reverence knows how to absolve them, astore;
So I'll say in a word, I'm no very good boy —
And, therefore, your blessin', sweet Father Molloy."

"Well," says Father Molloy, "if your sins I forgive,
    So you must forgive all your enemies truly;
And promise me also that, if you should live,
    You'll leave off your old tricks, and begin to live
    newly."
"I forgive ev'rybody," says Pat, with a groan,
    "Except that big vagabone Micky Malone;
And him I will murdher if ever I can —"
    "Tut, tut," says the priest, "you're a very bad man;
For without your forgiveness, and also repentance,
You'll ne'er go to Heaven, and that is my sentence."
    "Poo!" says Paddy McCabe, "that's a very hard case —
With your Reverence and Heaven I'm content to make
    pace;
But with Heaven and your Reverence I wondher —
    Och hone —
You would think of comparin' that blackguard Malone —
But since I'm hard press'd and that I *must* forgive,
I forgive — if I die — but as sure as I live
That ugly blackguard I will surely desthroy! —
So, *now* for your blessin', sweet Father Molloy!"
                                        Samuel Lover

MISS BIDDY'S EPISTLE

(*An extract from "The Fudge Family in Paris"*)

Where *shall* I begin with the endless delights
Of this Eden of milliners, monkeys, and sights —
This dear, busy place, where there's nothing transacting
But dressing and dinnering, dancing and acting?

Imprimis, the Opera — mercy, my ears!
Brother Bobby's remark t'other night was a true one;
"This *must* be music," said he, "of the *spears,*
For I'm cursed if each note of it doesn't run through
one!"
No — never was known in this riotous sphere
Such a breach of the peace as their singing, my dear,
So bad, too, you'd swear that the god of both arts,
Of Music and Physic, had taken a frolic
For setting a loud fit of asthma in parts,
And composing a fine rumbling base to a colic!

But the dancing — *ah, parlez-moi,* Dolly, *de ça* —
There, indeed, is a treat that charms all but Papa.
Such beauty — such grace — oh, ye sylphs of romance!
Fly, fly to Titania, and ask her if *she* has
One light-footed nymph in her train, that can dance
Like divine Bigottini and sweet Fanny Bias!
Fanny Bias in Flora — dear creature! — you'd swear
When her delicate feet in the dance twinkle round,
That her steps are of light, that her home is the air,
And she only *par complaisance* touches the ground.

And when Bigottini in Psyche dishevels
Her black flowing hair, and by demons is driven,
Oh! who does not envy those rude little devils,
That hold her, and hug her, and keep her from Heaven?
Then the music — so softly its cadences die,
So divinely — oh, Dolly! between you and I,
It's as well for my peace that there's nobody nigh
To make love to me then — *you've* a soul and can judge
What a crisis 'twould be for your friend Biddy Fudge!

The next place (which Bobby has near lost his heart in),
They call it the playhouse — I think — of Saint Martin;
Quite charming — and *very* religious — what folly
To say that the French are not pious, dear Dolly,
When here one beholds, so correctly and rightly,
The Testament turn'd into melo-drames nightly;
And, doubtless, so fond they're of Scriptural facts,
They will soon get the Pentateuch up in five acts.
Here Daniel, in pantomime, bids bold defiance
To Nebuchadnezzar and all his stuff'd lions,
While pretty young Israelites dance round the Prophet,
In very thin clothing, and *but* little of it; —
Here Bégrand, who shines in this Scriptural path
   As the lovely Susanna, without even a relic
Of drapery round her, comes out of the bath
   In a manner that Bob says is quite *Eve-angelic!*
But, in short, dear, 'twould take me a month to recite
All the exquisite places we're at, day and night.

                                          Thomas Moore

CURE FOR HOMESICKNESS

She wrote to her daddy in Portland, Maine, from out in
   Denver, Col.,
And she wrote, alas, despondently that life had commenced
   to pall;
And this was a woful, woful case, for she was a six month's
   bride,
Who was won and wed in the State of Maine by the side
   of the bounding tide.
And ah, alack, she was writing back, that she longed for
   Portland, Maine,
Till oh, her feelings had been that wrenched she could
   hardly stand the strain!
Though her hubby dear was still sincere, she sighed the
   livelong day
For a good old sniff of the sewers and salt from the breast
   of Casco Bay.
And she wrote she sighed, and she said she'd cried, and
   her appetite fell off,
And she'd grown as thin's a belaying-pin, with a terrible
   hacking cough;

And she sort of hinted that pretty soon she'd start on a
reckless scoot
And hook for her home in Portland, Maine, by the very
shortest route.
But her daddy dear was a man of sense, and he handles
fish wholesale,
And he sat and fanned himself awhile with a big broad
codfish tail;
And he recollected the way he felt when he dwelt in the
World's Fair whirl,
He slapped his head. "By hake," he said, "I know what
ails that girl."
And he went to a ten-cord pile of cod and he pulled the
biggest out,
A jib-shaped critter, broad's a sail, — three feet from tail to
snout.
And he pasted a sheet of postage stamps from snout clear
down to tail,
Put on a quick delivery stamp, and sent the cod by mail.
She smelled it a-coming two blocks off on the top of the
postman's pack;
She rushed to meet him, and scared him blind by climbing
the poor man's back.
But she got the fish, bit out a hunk, ate postage stamps
and all,
And a happy wife in a happy home lives out in Denver,
Col.

Holman F. Day

THE LITTLE PEACH [1]

A little peach in the orchard grew, —
A little peach of emerald hue;
Warmed by the sun and wet by the dew,
        It grew.

One day, passing that orchard through,
That little peach dawned on the view
Of Johnny Jones and his sister Sue —
        Them two.

[1] From "A Little Book of Western Verse," published by Charles Scribner's
Sons.

Up at that peach a club they threw —
Down from the stem on which it grew
Fell that peach of emerald hue.
    Mon Dieu!

John took a bite and Sue a chew,
And then the trouble began to brew, —
Trouble the doctor couldn't subdue.
    Too true!

Under the turf where the daisies grew
They planted John and his sister Sue,
And their little souls to the angels flew, —
    Boo hoo!

What of that peach of the emerald hue,
Warmed by the sun and wet by the dew?
Ah, well, its mission on earth is through.
    Adieu!

Eugene Field

TO THE LORD OF POTSDAM

ON SENDING A CERTAIN TELEGRAM

Majestic Monarch! whom the other gods,
  For fear of their immediate removal,
Consulting hourly, seek your awful nod's
    Approval;

Lift but your little finger up to strike,
  And lo! "the massy earth is riven" (Shelley),
The habitable globe is shaken like
    A jelly.

By your express permission for the last
  Eight years the sun has regularly risen;
And editors, that questioned this, have passed
    To prison.

In Art you simply have to say, " I shall! "
Beethoven's fame is rendered transitory;
And Titian cloys beside your clever all-
egory.

We hailed you Admiral; your eagle sight
Foresaw Her Majesty's benign intentions;
A uniform was ready of the right
Dimensions.

Your wardrobe shines with all the shapes and shades,
That genius can fix in fancy suitings;
For *levées,* false alarums, full parades
And shootings.

But save the habit marks the man of gore
Your spurs are yet to win, my callow Kaiser!
Of fighting in the field you know no more
Than I, Sir!

When Grandpapa was thanking God with hymns
For gallant Frenchmen dying in the ditches,
Your nurse had barely braced your little limbs
In breeches.

And, doubtless, where he roosts beside his bock,
The Game Old Bird that played the leading fiddle
Smiles grimly as he hears your perky cock-
-a-diddle.

Be well advised, my youthful friend, abjure
These tricks that smack of Cleon and the tanners;
And let the Dutch instruct a German Boor
In manners.

Nor were you meant to solve the nation's knots,
Or be the Earth's Protector, willy-nilly;
You only make yourself and royal Pots-
-dam silly.

Our racing yachts are not at present dressed
In bravery of bunting to amuse you,
Nor can the license of an honored guest
Excuse you.

But if your words are more than wanton play,
  And you would like to meet the old sea-rover,
Name any course from Delagoa Bay
    To Dover.

Meanwhile observe a proper reticence;
  We ask no more; there never was a rumor
Of asking Hohenzollerns for a sense
    Of humor!

                                    Owen Seaman

TO JULIA UNDER LOCK AND KEY

" A form of betrothal gift in America is an anklet secured by a padlock, of
which the other party keeps the key."

When like a bud my Julia blows
In lattice-work of silken hose,
Pleasant I deem it is to note
How, 'neath the nimble petticoat,
Above her fairy shoe is set
The circumvolving zonulet.
And soothly for the lover's ear
A perfect bliss it is to hear
About her limb so lithe and lank
My Julia's ankle-bangle clank.
Not rudely tight, for 'twere a sin
To corrugate her dainty skin;
Nor yet so large that it might fare
Over her foot at unaware;
But fashioned nicely with a view
To let her airy stocking through:
So as, when Julia goes to bed,
Of all her gear disburdenèd,
This ring at least she shall not doff,
Because she cannot take it off.
And since thereof I hold the key,
She may not taste of liberty,
Not though she suffer from the gout,
Unless I choose to let her out.

                                    Owen Seaman

REVIVAL HYMN[1]

A SONG OF "UNCLE REMUS"

Oh, whar shill we go w'en de great day comes,
Wid de blowin' er de trumpits en de bangin' er de drums?
How many po' sinners'll be kotched out late
En fine no latch ter de golden gate?
    No use fer ter wait twel ter-morrer!
    De sun mustn't set on yo' sorrer,
    Sin's ez sharp ez a bamboo-brier —
    Oh, Lord! fetch de mo'ners up higher!

W'en de nashuns er de earf is a-stan'in' all aroun',
Who's a gwine ter be choosen fer ter w'ar de glory-crown?
Who's a gwine fer ter stan' stiff-kneed en bol',
En answer to der name at de callin' er de roll?
    You better come now ef you comin' —
    Ole Satun is loose en a bummin' —
    De wheels er distruckshun is a hummin' —
    Oh, come 'long, sinner, ef you comin'!

De song er salvashun is a mighty sweet song,
En de Pairidise win' blow fur en blow strong,
En Aberham's bosom, hit's saft en hit's wide,
En right dar's de place whar de sinners oughter hide!
    Oh, you nee'nter be a stoppin' en a lookin';
    Ef you fool wid ole Satun you'll git took in;
    You'll hang on de aidge en get shook in,
    Ef you keep on a stoppin' en a lookin'.

De time is right now, en dish yer's de place —
Let de sun er salvashun shine squar' in yo' face;
Fight de battles er de Lord, fight soon en fight late,
En you'll allers fine a latch ter de golden gate.
    No use fer ter wait twel ter-morrer,
    De sun mustn't set on yo' sorrer —
    Sin's ez sharp ez a bamboo-brier,
    Ax de Lord fer ter fetch you up higher!
                 Joel Chandler Harris

THE COLD - WATER MAN

It was an honest fisherman,
   I knew him passing well, —
And he lived by a little pond,
   Within a little dell.

A grave and quiet man was he,
   Who loved his book and rod, —
So even ran his line of life,
   His neighbors thought it odd.

For science and for books, he said,
   He never had a wish, —
No school to him was worth a fig,
   Except a school of fish.

He ne'er aspired to rank or wealth,
   Nor cared about a name, —
For though much famed for fish was he,
   He never fished for fame.

Let others bend their necks at sight
   Of Fashion's gilded wheels,
He ne'er had learned the art to "bob"
   For anything but eels.

A cunning fisherman was he,
   His angles all were right;
The smallest nibble at his bait
   Was sure to prove "a bite."

All day this fisherman would sit
   Upon an ancient log,
And gaze into the water, like
   Some sedentary frog;

With all the seeming innocence,
   And that unconscious look,
That other people often wear
   When they intend to "hook."

To charm the fish he never spoke, —
  Although his voice was fine,
He found the most convenient way
  Was just to drop a line.

And many a gudgeon of the pond,
  If they could speak to-day,
Would own, with grief, this angler had
  A mighty taking way.

Alas! one day this fisherman
  Had taken too much grog,
And being but a landsman, too,
  He couldn't keep the log.

'Twas all in vain with might and main
  He strove to reach the shore;
Down — down he went, to feed the fish
  He'd baited oft before.

The jury gave their verdict that
  'Twas nothing else but gin
Had caused the fisherman to be
  So sadly taken in;

Though one stood out upon a whim,
  And said the angler's slaughter,
To be exact about the fact,
  Was, clearly, gin-and-*water!*

The moral of this mournful tale,
  To all is plain and clear, —
That drinking habits bring a man
  Too often to his bier;

And he who scorns to " take the pledge,"
  And keep the promise fast,
May be, in spite of fate, a *stiff*
  Cold-water man at last!

                            John Godfrey Saxe

DIBDIN'S GHOST [1]

Dear wife, last midnight, whilst I read
 The tomes you so despise,
A spectre rose beside the bed,
 And spake in this true wise:
"From Canaan's beatific coast
 I've come to visit thee,
For I am Frognall Dibdin's ghost,"
 Says Dibdin's ghost to me.

I bade him welcome, and we twain
 Discussed with buoyant hearts
The various things that appertain
 To bibliomaniac arts.
"Since you are fresh from t'other side,
 Pray tell me of that host
That treasured books before they died,"
 Says I to Dibdin's ghost.

"They've entered into perfect rest;
 For in the life they've won
There are no auctions to molest,
 No creditors to dun.
Their heavenly rapture has no bounds,
 Beside that jasper sea;
It is a joy unknown to Lowndes,"
 Says Dibdin's ghost to me.

Much I rejoiced to hear him speak
 Of biblio-bliss above,
For I am one of those who seek
 What bibliomaniacs love.
"But tell me, for I long to hear
 What doth concern me most,
Are wives admitted to that sphere?
 Says I to Dibdin's ghost.

"The women folk are few up there;
 For 'twere not fair, you know,

[1] From " Second Book of Verse," published by Charles Scribner's Sons.

That they our heavenly joy should share
 Who vex us here below.
The few are those who have been kind
 To husbands such as we;
They knew our fads, and didn't mind,"
 Says Dibdin's ghost to me.

"But what of thòse who scold at us
 When we would read in bed?
Or, wanting victuals, make a fuss
 If we buy books instead?
And what of those who've dusted not
 Our motley pride and boast,—
Shall they profane that sacred spot?"
 Says I to Dibdin's ghost.

"Oh, no! they tread that other path,
 Which leads where torments roll,
And worms, yes, bookworms, vent their wrath
 Upon the guilty soul.
Untouched of bibliomaniac grace,
 That saveth such as we,
They wallow in that dreadful place,"
 Says Dibdin's ghost to me.

"To my dear wife will I recite
 What things I've heard you say;
She'll let me read the books by night,
 She's let me buy by day.
For we together by and by
 Would join that heavenly host;
She's earned a rest as well as I,"
 Says I to Dibdin's ghost.

Eugene Field

THE VICAR

Some years ago, ere Time and Taste
 Had turned our parish topsy-turvy,
When Darnel Park was Darnel Waste,
 And roads as little known as scurvy,
The man who lost his way between
 St. Mary's Hill and Sandy Thicket,

Was always shown across the green,
And guided to the Parson's wicket.

Back flew the bolt of lissom lath;
Fair Margaret, in her tidy kirtle,
Led the lorn traveller up the path,
Through clean-clipp'd rows of box and myrtle:
And Don and Sancho, Tramp and Tray,
Upon the parlor steps collected,
Wagged all their tails, and seemed to say,
"Our master knows you; you're expected!"

Up rose the Reverend Doctor Brown,
Up rose the doctor's "winsome marrow;"
The lady lay her knitting down,
Her husband clasped his ponderous Barrow;
Whate'er the stranger's caste or creed,
Pundit or papist, saint or sinner,
He found a stable for his steed,
And welcome for himself, and dinner.

If, when he reach'd his journey's end,
And warm'd himself in court or college,
He had not gain'd an honest friend,
And twenty curious scraps of knowledge: —
If he departed as he came,
With no new light on love or liquor, —
Good sooth, the traveller was to blame,
And not the Vicarage, or the Vicar.

His talk was like a stream which runs
With rapid change from rocks to roses;
It slipp'd from politics to puns:
It pass'd from Mahomet to Moses:
Beginning with the laws which keep
The planets in their radiant courses,
And ending with some precept deep
For dressing eels, or shoeing horses.

He was a shrewd and sound divine,
Of loud Dissent the mortal terror;
And when, by dint of page and line,
He 'stablish'd Truth, or startled Error,

The Baptist found him far too deep;
  The Deist sigh'd with saving sorrow;
And the lean Levite went to sleep,
  And dream'd of tasting pork to-morrow.

His sermon never said or show'd
  That Earth is foul, that Heaven is gracious,
Without refreshment on the road
  From Jerome, or from Athanasius;
And sure a righteous zeal inspired
  The hand and head that penn'd and plann'd them,
For all who understood, admired,
  And some who did not understand them.

He wrote, too, in a quiet way,
  Small treatises and smaller verses;
And sage remarks on chalk and clay,
  And hints to noble lords — and nurses;
True histories of last year's ghost,
  Lines to a ringlet or a turban;
And trifles for the *Morning Post*,
  And nothings for Sylvanus Urban.

He did not think all mischief fair,
  Although he had a knack of joking;
He did not make himself a bear,
  Although he had a taste for smoking;
And when religious sects ran mad,
  He held, in spite of all his learning,
That if a man's belief is bad,
  It will not be improved by burning.

And he was kind, and loved to sit
  In the low hut or garnish'd cottage,
And praise the farmer's homely wit,
  And share the widow's homelier pottage:
At his approach complaint grew mild,
  And when his hand unbarr'd the shutter,
The clammy lips of fever smiled
  The welcome which they could not utter.

He always had a tale for me
  Of Julius Cæsar, or of Venus:

From him I learn'd the rule of three,
    Cat's cradle, leap-frog, and *Quæ genus;*
I used to singe his powdered wig,
    To steal the staff he put such trust in;
And make the puppy dance a jig
    When he began to quote Augustine.

Alack the change! in vain I look
    For haunts in which my boyhood trifled;
The level lawn, the trickling brook,
    The trees I climb'd, the beds I rifled:
The church is larger than before:
    You reach it by a carriage entry:
It holds three hundred people more:
    And pews are fitted up for gentry.

Sit in the Vicar's seat: you'll hear
    The doctrine of a gentle Johnian,
Whose hand is white, whose tone is clear,
    Whose phrase is very Ciceronian.
Where is the old man laid? — look down,
    And construe on the slab before you,
Hic jacet GVLIELMVS BROWN,
    Vir nullâ non donandus lauru.
                Winthrop Mackworth Praed

MY OTHER CHINEE COOK

Yes, I got another Johnny; but he was to Number One
As a Satyr to Hyperion, as a rushlight to the sun;
He was lazy, he was cheeky, he was dirty, he was sly,
But he had a single virtue, and its name was " rabbit-pie."

We had fixed one day to sack him, and agreed to moot the
    point,
When my lad should bring our usual regale of cindered
    joint,
But instead of cindered joint we saw and smelt, my wife
    and I,
Such a lovely, such a beautiful, oh! such a rabbit-pie!

There was quite a new expression on his lemon-colored
    face,
And the unexpected odor won him temporary grace,
For we tacitly postponed the sacking point till by and by,
And we tacitly said nothing save the one word "rabbit-
    pie."

I had learned that pleasant mystery should simply be en-
    dured,
And forebore to ask of Johnny where the rabbits were pro-
    cured!
I had learned from Number One to stand aloof from how
    and why,
And I threw myself upon the simple fact of rabbit-pie.

And when the pie was opened, what a picture did we see!
"They lay in beauty side by side, they filled our home with
    glee!"
How excellent, how succulent, back, neck, and leg and
    thigh;
What a noble gift is manhood! what a trust is rabbit-pie!

For a week the thing continued, rabbit-pie from day to day;
Though where he got the rabbits John would ne'er vouch-
    safe to say;
But we never seemed to tire of them, and daily could de-
    scry
Subtle shades of new delight in each successive rabbit-pie.

Sunday came; by rabbit reckoning, the seventh day of the
    week;
We had dined; we sat in silence, both our hearts (?) too
    full to speak;
When in walks Cousin George, and, with a sniff, says he,
    "Oh, my!
What a savory suggestion! what a smell of rabbit-pie!"

"Oh, why so late, George?" says my wife, "the rabbit-pie
    is gone;
But you *must* have one for tea, though. Ring the bell, my
    dear, for John.
So I rang the bell for John, to whom my wife did signify,
"Let us have an early tea, John, and another rabbit-pie."

But John seemed taken quite aback, and shook his funny
    head,
And uttered words I comprehended no more than the dead;
" Go, do as you are bid," I cried, " we wait for no reply;
Go! let us have tea early, and another rabbit-pie!"

Oh, that I had stopped his answer! But it came out with
    a run:
"Last-a week-a plenty puppy; this-a week-a puppy done!"
Just then my wife, my love, my life, the apple of mine eye,
Was seized with what seemed "mal-de-mer"—"sick tran-
    sit" rabbit-pie!

And George! By George, he laughed, and then he howled
    like any bear!
The while my wife contorted like a mad convulsionnaire;
And I—I rushed on Johnny, and I smote him hip and
    thigh,
And I never saw him more, nor tasted more of rabbit-pie.

And the childless mothers met me, as I kicked him from
    the door,
With loud maternal wailings, and anathemas galore;
I must part with pretty Tiny, I must part with little Fly,
For I'm sure they know the story of the so-called "rabbit-
    pie."

James Brunton Stephens

PREHISTORIC SMITH

QUATERNARY EPOCH — POST-PLIOCENE PERIOD

A man sat on a rock and sought
    Refreshment from his thumb;
A dinotherium wandered by
    And scared him some.

His name was Smith. The kind of rock
    He sat upon was shale.
One feature quite distinguished him—
    He had a tail.

The danger past, he fell into
A revery austere;
While with his tail he whisked a fly
From off his ear.

" Mankind deteriorates," he said,
" Grows weak and incomplete;
And each new generation seems
Yet more effete.

" Nature abhors imperfect work,
And on it lays her ban;
And all creation must despise
A tailless man.

" But fashion's dictates rule supreme,
Ignoring common sense;
And fashion says, to dock your tail
Is just immense.

" And children now come in the world
With half a tail or less;
Too stumpy to convey a thought,
And meaningless.

" It kills expression. How can one
Set forth, in words that drag,
The best emotions of the soul,
Without a wag? "

Sadly he mused upon the world,
Its follies and its woes;
Then wiped the moisture from his eyes,
And blew his nose.

But clothed in earrings, Mrs. Smith
Came wandering down the dale;
And, smiling, Mr. Smith arose,
And wagged his tail.

David Law Proudfit

NO!

No sun — no moon!
No morn — no noon —
No dawn — no dusk — no proper time of day —
No sky — no earthly view —
No distance looking blue —
No road — no street — no "t'other side the way" —
No end to any Row —
No indications where the Crescents go —
No top to any steeple —
No recognitions of familiar people —
No courtesies for showing 'em —
No knowing 'em!
No travelling at all — no locomotion,
No inkling of the way — no notion —
"No go" — by land or ocean —
No mail — no post —
No news from any foreign coast —
No park — no ring — no afternoon gentility —
No company — no nobility —·
No warmth, no cheerfulness, no healthful ease,
No comfortable feel in any member —
No shade, no shine, no butterflies, no bees,
No fruits, no flowers, no leaves, no birds,
November!

Thomas Hood

THE IRISH SCHOOLMASTER

"Come here, my boy; hould up your head,
And look like a jintlemàn, Sir;
Jist tell me who King David was —
Now tell me if you can, Sir."
"King David was a mighty man,
And he was King of Spain, Sir;
His eldest daughter 'Jessie' was
The 'Flower of Dunblane,' Sir."

" Come here, my boy ; hould up your head."

"You're right, my boy; hould up your head,
  And look like a jintlemàn, Sir;
Sir Isaac Newton — who was he?
  Now tell me if you can, Sir."
"Sir Isaac Newton was the boy
  That climbed the apple-tree, Sir;
He then fell down and broke his crown,
  And lost his gravity, Sir."

"You're right, my boy; hould up your head,
  And look like a jintlemàn, Sir;
Jist tell me who ould Marmion was —
  Now tell me if you can, Sir."
"Ould Marmion was a soldier bold,
  But he went all to pot, Sir;
He was hanged upon the gallows tree,
  For killing Sir Walter Scott, Sir."

"You're right, my boy; hould up your head,
  And look like a jintlemàn, Sir;
Jist tell me who Sir Rob Roy was;
  Now tell me if you can, Sir."
"Sir Rob Roy was a tailor to
  The King of the Cannibal Islands;
He spoiled a pair of breeches, and
  Was banished to the Highlands."

"You're right, my boy; hould up your head,
  And look like a jintlemàn, Sir;
Then, Bonaparte — say, who was he?
  Now tell me if you can, Sir."
"Ould Bonaparte was King of France
  Before the Revolution;
But he was kilt at Waterloo,
  Which ruined his constitution."

"You're right, my boy; hould up your head,
  And look like a jintlemàn, Sir;
Jist tell me who King Jonah was;
  Now tell me if you can, Sir."
"King Jonah was the strangest man
  That ever wore a crown, Sir;
For though the whale did swallow him,
  It couldn't keep him down, Sir."

"You're right, my boy; hould up your head,
  And look like a jintlemàn, Sir;
Jist tell me who that Moses was;
  Now tell me if you can, Sir."
"Shure Moses was the Christian name
  Of good King Pharaoh's daughter;
She was a milkmaid, and she took
  A *profit* from the water."

"You're right, my boy; hould up your head,
  And look like a jintlemàn, Sir;
Jist tell me now where Dublin is;
  Now tell me if you can, Sir."
"Och, Dublin is a town in Cork,
  And built on the equator;
It's close to Mount Vesuvius,
  And watered by the 'craythur.'"

"You're right, my boy; hould up your head,
  And look like a jintlemàn, Sir;
Jist tell me now where London is;
  Now tell me if you can, Sir."
"Och, London is a town in Spain;
  'Twas lost in the earthquake, Sir;
The cockneys murther English there,
  Whenever they do spake, Sir."

"You're right, my boy; hould up your head,
  Ye're now a jintlemàn, Sir;
For in history and geography
  I've taught you all I can, Sir.
And if any one should ask you now,
  Where you got all your knowledge,
Jist tell them 'twas from Paddy Blake,
  Of Bally Blarney College."

                                        James A. Sidey

THE OWL - CRITIC

"Who stuffed that white owl?" No one spoke in the shop,
The barber was busy, and he couldn't stop;
The customers, waiting their turns, were all reading
The *Daily,* the *Herald,* the *Post,* little heeding
The young man who blurted out such a blunt question;
Not one raised a head, or even made a suggestion;
   And the barber kept on shaving.

"Don't you see, Mr. Brown,"
Cried the youth, with a frown,
"How wrong the whole thing is,
How preposterous each wing is,
How flattened the head is, how jammed down the neck is —
In short, the whole owl, what an ignorant wreck 'tis!
I make no apology;
I've learned owl-eology.
I've passed days and nights in a hundred collections,
And cannot be blinded to any deflections
Arising from unskilful fingers that fail
To stuff a bird right, from his beak to his tail.
Mister Brown! Mister Brown!
Do take that bird down,
Or you'll soon be the laughing-stock all over town!"
   And the barber kept on shaving.

"I've *studied* owls,
And other night fowls,
And I tell you
What I know to be true;
An owl cannot roost
With his limbs so unloosed;
No owl in this world
Ever had his claws curled,
Ever had his legs slanted,
Ever had his bill canted,
Ever had his neck screwed
Into that attitude.
He can't *do* it, because
'Tis against all bird laws.

Anatomy teaches,
Ornithology preaches
An owl has a toe
That *can't* turn out so!
I've made the white owl my study for years,
And to see such a job almost moves me to tears!
Mister Brown, I'm amazed
You should be so gone crazed
As to put up a bird
In that posture absurd!
To *look* at that owl really brings on a dizziness;
The man who stuffed *him* don't half know his business!
       And the barber kept on shaving.

" Examine those eyes.
I'm filled with surprise
Taxidermists should pass
Off on you such poor glass;
So unnatural they seem
They'd make Audubon scream,
And John Burroughs laugh
To encounter such chaff.
Do take that bird down;
Have him stuffed again, Brown!"
       And the barber kept on shaving.

"With some sawdust and bark
I could stuff in the dark
An owl better than that.
I could make an old hat
Look more like an owl
Than that horrid fowl,
Stuck up there so stiff like a side of coarse leather.
In fact, about *him* there's not one natural feather."

Just then, with a wink and a sly normal lurch,
The owl, very gravely, got down from his perch,
Walked round, and regarded his faultfinding critic
(Who thought he was stuffed) with a glance analytic,
And then fairly hooted, as if he should say:
" Your learning's at fault *this* time, anyway;
Don't waste it again on a live bird, I pray.
I'm an owl; you're another. Sir Critic, good day!"
       And the barber kept on shaving.
             James Thomas Fields

" The owl, very gravely, got down from his perch."

MR. BARNEY MAGUIRE'S ACCOUNT OF THE CORONATION

Och! the Coronation! what celebration
    For emulation can with it compare?
When to Westminster the Royal Spinster
    And the Duke of Leinster, all in order did repair!
'Twas there you'd see the new Polishemen
    Make a scrimmage at half after four;
And the Lords and Ladies, and the Miss O'Gradys,
    All standing round before the Abbey door.

Their pillows scorning, that self-same morning
    Themselves adorning, all by the candle-light,
With roses and lilies, and daffy-down-dillies,
    And gould and jewels, and rich di'monds bright.
And then approaches five hundred coaches,
    With Gineral Dullbeak. — Och! 'twas mighty fine
To see how asy bould Corporal Casey,
    With his sword drawn, prancing, made them kape the
    line.

Then the guns' alarums, and the King of Arums,
    All in his Garters and his Clarence shoes,
Opening the massy doors to the bould Ambassydors,
    The Prince of Potboys, and great haythen Jews;
'Twould have made you crazy to see Esterhazy
    All jools from his jasey to his di'mond boots.
With Alderman Harmer, and that swate charmer,
    The famale heiress, Miss Anjä-ly Coutts.

And Wellington, walking with his swoord drawn, talking
    To Hill and Hardinge, haroes of great fame;
And Sir De Lacy, and the Duke Dalmasey
    (They call'd him Sowlt afore he changed his name),
Themselves presading, Lord Melbourne lading
    The Queen, the darling, to her royal chair,
And that fine ould fellow, the Duke of Pell-Mello,
    The Queen of Portingal's Chargy-de-fair.

Then the noble Prussians, likewise the Russians,
  In fine laced jackets with their goulden cuffs,
And the Bavarians, and the proud Hungarians,
  And Everythingarians all in furs and muffs.
Then Misther Spaker, with Misther Pays the Quaker,
  All in the gallery you might persave;
But Lord Brougham was missing, and gone a-fishing,
  Ounly crass Lord Essex would not give him lave.

There was Baron Alten himself exalting,
  And Prince Von Schwartzenburg, and many more;
Och! I'd be bother'd, and entirely smother'd,
  To tell the half of 'em was to the fore;
With the swate Peeresses, in their crowns and dresses,
  And Aldermanesses, and the Boord of Works;
But Mehemet Ali said, quite gintaly,
  " I'd be proud to see the likes among the Turks! "

Then the Queen, Heaven bless her! och! they did dress her
  In her purple garaments and her goulden crown,
Like Venus, or Hebe, or the Queen of Sheby,
  With eight young ladies houlding up her gown;
Sure 'twas grand to see her, also for to he-ar
  The big drums bating, and the trumpets blow;
And Sir George Smart, oh! he played a Consarto,
  With his four-and-twenty fiddlers all on a row!

Then the Lord Archbishop held a goulden dish up
  For to resave her bounty and great wealth,
Saying, " Plase your Glory, great Queen Vic-tory!
  Ye'll give the Clargy lave to dhrink your health! "
Then his Riverence, retrating, discoorsed the mating: —
  " Boys, here's your Queen! deny it if you can!
And if any bould traitor, or infarior craythur,
  Sneezes at that, I'd like to see the man! "

Then the Nobles kneeling, to the Pow'rs appealing —
  " Heaven send your Majesty a glorious reign! "
And Sir Claudius Hunter, he did confront her,
  All in his scarlet gown and goulden chain.
The great Lord May'r, too, sat in his chair too,
  But mighty sarious, looking fit to cry,
For the Earl of Surrey, all in his hurry,
  Throwing the thirteens, hit him in his eye.

Then there was preaching, and good store of speeching,
   With Dukes and Marquises on bended knee;
And they did splash her with raal Macasshur,
   And the Queen said, " Ah! then thank ye all for me!"
Then the trumpets braying, and the organ playing,
   And the swate trombones, with their silver tones;
But Lord Rolle was rolling, — 'twas mighty consoling
   To think his Lordship did not break his bones!

Then the crames and custard, and the beef and mustard,
   All on the tombstones like a poultherer's shop;
With lobsters and white-bait, and other swate-meats,
   And wine and nagus, and Imparial Pop!
There was cakes and apples in all the Chapels,
   With fine polonies, and rich mellow pears, —
Och! the Count Von Strogonoff, sure he got prog enough,
   The sly ould Divil, undernathe the stairs.

Then the cannons thunder'd, and the people wonder'd,
   Crying, " God save Victoria, our Royal Queen!"
Och! if myself should live to be a hundred,
   Sure it's the proudest day that I'll have seen!
And now, I've ended, what I pretended,
   This narration splendid in swate poe-thry.
Ye dear bewitcher, just hand the pitcher,
   Faith, it's myself that's getting mighty dhry.
                              Richard Harris Barham

BECAUSE

Sweet Nea! — for your lovely sake
   I weave these rambling numbers,
Because I've lain an hour awake,
   And can't compose my slumbers;
Because your beauty's gentle light
   Is round my pillow beaming,
And flings, I know not why, to-night,
   Some witchery o'er my dreaming!

Because we've pass'd some joyous days,
   And danced some merry dances;
Because we love old Beaumont's plays,
   And old Froissart's romances!

Because whene'er I hear your words
  Some pleasant feeling lingers;
Because I think your heart has cords
  That vibrate to your fingers!

Because you've got those long, soft curls,
  I've sworn should deck my goddess;
Because you're not, like other girls,
  All bustle, blush, and bodice;
Because your eyes are deep and blue,
  Your fingers long and rosy;
Because a little child and you
  Would make one's home so cozy!

Because your little tiny nose
  Turns up so pert and funny;
Because I know you choose your beaux
  More for their mirth than money;
Because I think you'd rather twirl
  A waltz, with me to guide you,
Than talk small nonsense with an earl,
  And a coronet beside you!

Because you don't object to walk,
  And are not given to fainting;
Because you have not learnt to talk
  Of flowers, and Poonah-painting;
Because I think you'd scarce refuse
  To sew one on a button;
Because I know you'd sometimes choose
  To dine on simple mutton!

Because I think I'm just so weak
  As, some of those fine morrows,
To ask you if you'll let me speak
  My story — and *my* sorrows;
Because the rest's a simple thing,
  A matter quickly over,
A church — a priest — a sigh — a ring —
  And a chaise and four to Dover.

                                        Edward Fitzgerald

FEMININE ARITHMETIC

LAURA

On me he shall ne'er put a ring,
    So, mamma, 'tis in vain to take trouble —
For I was but eighteen in spring,
    While his age exactly is double.

MAMMA

He's but in his thirty-sixth year,
    Tall, handsome, good-natured and witty,
And should you refuse him, my dear,
    May you die an old maid without pity!

LAURA

His figure, I grant you, will pass,
    And at present he's young enough plenty;
But when I am sixty, alas!
    Will not he be a hundred and twenty?
              Charles Graham Halpine

SKY - MAKING

(TO PROFESSOR TYNDALL)

Just take a trifling handful, O philosopher!
Of magic matter: give it a slight toss over
    The ambient æther — and I don't see why
    You shouldn't make a sky.

O hours Utopian which we may anticipate!
Thick London fog how easy 'tis to dissipate,
    And make the most pea-soupy day as clear
    As Bass's brightest beer!

Poet-professor! Now my brain thou kindlest:
I am become a most determined Tyndallist.
If it is known a fellow can make skies,
    Why not make bright blue eyes?

This to deny, the folly of a dunce it is:
Surely a girl as easy as a sunset is.
If you can make a halo or eclipse,
    Why not two laughing lips?

The creed of Archimedes, erst of Sicily,
And of D'Israeli . . . *forti nil difficile*,
    Is likewise mine. Pygmalion was a fool
    Who should have gone to school.

Why should an author scribble rhymes or articles?
Bring me a dozen tiny Tyndall particles;
    Therefrom I'll coin a dinner, Nash's wine,
    And a nice girl to dine.

                Mortimer Collins

MRS. SMITH

Last year I trod these fields with Di,
Fields fresh with clover and with rye;
    They now seem arid!
Then Di was fair and single; how
Unfair it seems on me, for now
    Di's fair — and married!

A blissful swain — I scorn'd the song
Which says that though young Love is strong,
    The Fates are stronger;
Breezes then blew a boon to men,
The buttercups were bright, and then
    This grass was longer.

That day I saw and much esteem'd
Di's ankles, which the clover seem'd
    Inclined to smother;
It twitch'd, and soon untied (for fun)
The ribbon of her shoes, first one,
    And then the other.

I'm told that virgins augur some
Misfortune if their shoe-strings come
    To grief on Friday:
And so did Di, and then her pride
Decreed that shoe-strings so untied
    Are " so untidy! "

Of course I knelt; with fingers deft
I tied the right, and then the left;
    Says Di, " The stubble
Is very stupid! — as I live,
I'm quite ashamed! — I'm shock'd to give
    You so much trouble! "

For answer I was fain to sink
To what we all would say and think
    Were Beauty present:
" Don't mention such a simple act —
A trouble? not the least! in fact
    It's rather pleasant! "

I trust that Love will never tease
Poor little Di, or prove that he's
    A graceless rover.
She's happy now as *Mrs. Smith* —
And less polite when walking with
    Her chosen lover!

Heigh-ho! Although no moral clings
To Di's blue eyes, and sandal strings,
    We've had our quarrels! —
I think that Smith is thought an ass;
I know that when they walk in grass
    She wears *balmorals.*

Frederick Locker-Lampson

THE LOST HEIR

One day, as I was going by
That part of Holborn christened High,
I heard a loud and sudden cry
That chilled my very blood;

And lo! from out a dirty alley,
Where pigs and Irish wont to rally,
I saw a crazy woman sally,
Bedaubed with grease and mud.
She turned her East, she turned her West,
Staring like Pythoness possest,
With streaming hair and heaving breast
As one stark mad with grief.
This way and that she wildly ran,
Jostling with woman and with man —
Her right hand held a frying-pan,
The left a lump of beef.
At last her frenzy seemed to reach
A point just capable of speech,
And with a tone almost a screech,
As wild as ocean birds,
Or female Ranter moved to preach,
She gave her "sorrow words."

"O Lord! O dear, my heart will break, I shall go stick
    stark staring wild!
Has ever a one seen anything about the streets like a cry-
    ing lost-looking child?
Lawk help me, I don't know where to look, or to run, if
    I only knew which way —
A Child as is lost about London streets, and especially
    Seven Dials, is a needle in a bottle of hay.
I am all in a quiver — get out of my sight, do, you wretch,
    you little Kitty M'Nab!
You promised to have half an eye on him, you know you
    did, you dirty deceitful young drab.
The last time as ever I see him, poor thing, was with my
    own blessed Motherly eyes,
Sitting as good as gold in the gutter, a playing at making
    little dirt pies.
I wonder he left the court where he was better off than
    all the other young boys,
With two bricks, an old shoe, nine oyster-shells, and a dead
    kitten by way of toys.
When his Father comes home, and he always comes home
    as sure as ever the clock strikes one,
He'll be rampant, he will, at his child being lost; and the
    beef and the inguns not done!

La bless you, good folks, mind your own consarns, and don't
    be making a mob in the street;
O Sergeant M'Farlane! you have not come across my poor
    little boy, have you, in your beat?
Do, good people, move on! don't stand staring at me like
    a parcel of stupid stuck pigs;
Saints forbid! but he's p'r'aps been inviggled away up a
    court for the sake of his clothes by the prigs;
He'd a very good jacket, for certain, for I bought it myself
    for a shilling one day in Rag Fair;
And his trousers considering not very much patched, and
    red plush, they was once his Father's best pair.
His shirt, it's very lucky I'd got washing in the tub, or that
    might have gone with the rest;
But he'd got on a very good pinafore with only two slits
    and a burn on the breast.
He'd a goodish sort of hat, if the crown was sewed in,
    and not quite so much jagg'd at the brim.
With one shoe on, and the other shoe is a boot, and not a
    fit, and you'll know by that if it's him.
Except being so well dressed, my mind would misgive, some
    old beggar woman in want of an orphan,
Had borrowed the child to go a-begging with, but I'd
    rather see him laid out in his coffin!
Do, good people, move on, such a rabble of boys! I'll
    break every bone of 'em I come near,
Go home — you're spilling the porter — go home — Tommy
    Jones, go along home with your beer.
This day is the sorrowfullest day of my life, ever since my
    name was Betty Morgan,
Them vile Savoyards! they lost him once before all along
    of following a Monkey and an Organ.
O my Billy — my head will turn right round — if he's got
    kiddynapped with them Italians,
They'll make him a plaster parish image boy, they will, the
    outlandish tatterdemalions.
Billy — where are you, Billy? — I'm as hoarse as a crow,
    with screaming for ye, you young sorrow!
And sha'n't have half a voice, no more I sha'n't, for crying
    fresh herrings to-morrow.
O Billy, you're bursting my heart in two, and my life won't
    be of no more vally,
If I'm to see other folk's darlin's, and none of mine, playing
    like angels in our alley,

And what shall I do but cry out my eyes, when I looks
    at the old three-legged chair
As Billy used to make coach and horses of, and there a'n't
    no Billy there!
I would run all the wide world over to find him, if I only
    know'd where to run;
Little Murphy, now I remember, was once lost for a month
    through stealing a penny bun, —
The Lord forbid of any child of mine! I think it would
    kill me raily,
To find my Bill holdin' up his little innocent hand at the
    Old Bailey.
For though I say it as oughtn't, yet I will say, you may
    search for miles and mileses
And not find one better brought up, and more pretty be-
    haved, from one end to t'other of St. Giles's.
And if I called him a beauty, it's no lie, but only as a
    Mother ought to speak;
You never set eyes on a more handsomer face, only it
    hasn't been washed for a week;
As for hair, tho' it's red, it's the most nicest hair when I've
    time to just show it the comb;
I'll owe 'em five pounds, and a blessing besides, as will only
    bring him safe and sound home.
He's blue eyes, and not to be called a squint, though a little
    cast he's certainly got;
And his nose is still a good un, tho' the bridge is broke,
    by his falling on a pewter pint pot;
He's got the most elegant wide mouth in the world, and
    very large teeth for his age;
And quite as fit as Mrs. Murdockson's child to play Cupid
    on the Drury Lane Stage.
And then he has got such dear winning ways — but O I
    never, never shall see him no more!
O dear! to think of losing him just after nussing him back
    from death's door!
Only the very last month when the windfalls, hang 'em, was
    at twenty a penny!
And the threepence he'd got by grottoing was spent in
    plums, and sixty for a child is too many.
And the Cholera man came and whitewashed us all and,
    drat him, made a seize of our hog. —
It's no use to send the Crier to cry him about, he's such a
    blunderin' drunken old dog;

The last time he was fetched to find a lost child, he was
  guzzling with his bell at the Crown,
And went and cried a boy instead of a girl, for a distracted
  Mother and Father about Town.
Billy — where are you, Billy, I say? come, Billy, come
  home, to your best of Mothers!
I'm scared when I think of them Cabroleys, they drive so,
  they'd run over their own Sisters and Brothers.
Or may be he's stole by some chimbly sweeping wretch, to
  stick fast in narrow flues and what not,
And be poked up behind with a picked pointed pole, when
  the soot has ketched, and the chimbly's red hot.
Oh, I'd give the whole wide world, if the world was mine,
  to clap my two longin' eyes on his face.
For he's my darlin' of darlin's, and if he don't soon come
  back, you'll see me drop stone dead on the place.
I only wish I'd got him safe in these two Motherly arms,
  and wouldn't I hug him and kiss him!
Lawk! I never knew what a precious he was — but a child
  don't not feel like a child till you miss him.
Why, there he is! Punch and Judy hunting, the young
  wretch, it's that Billy as sartin as sin!
But let me get him home, with a good grip of his hair, and
  I'm blest if he shall have a whole bone in his skin!

Thomas Hood

A PIAZZA TRAGEDY

The beauteous Ethel's father has a
Newly painted front piazza —
    He has a
    Piazza;
When with tobacco juice 'twas tainted
They had the front piazza painted —
    That tainted
    Piazza painted.

Algernon called that night, perchance,
Arrayed in comely sealskin pants —
    That night, perchance,
    In gorgeous pants;

Engaging Ethel in a chat
On that piazza down he sat —
　　In chat,
　　They sat.

And when an hour or two had pass'd,
He tried to rise, but oh! stuck fast —
　　At last
　　Stuck fast!
Fair Ethel shrieked, "It is the paint!"
And fainted in a deadly faint —
　　This saint
　　Did faint.

Algernon sits there till this day —
He cannot tear himself away, —
　　Away?
　　Nay, nay!
His pants are firm, the paint is dry —
He's nothing else to do but die —
　　To die!
　　O my!

Eugene Field

MISADVENTURES AT MARGATE

MR. SIMPKINSON (*loquitur*)

I was in Margate last July, I walk'd upon the pier,
I saw a little vulgar Boy, — I said, "What make you
　　here? —
The gloom upon your youthful cheek speaks anything but
　　joy;"
Again I said, "What make you here, you little vulgar
　　Boy?"

He frown'd, that little vulgar Boy, — he deem'd I meant to
　　scoff, —
And when the little heart is big, a little "sets it off;"
He put his finger in his mouth, his little bosom rose, —
He had no little handkerchief to wipe his little nose!

"Hark! don't you hear, my little man? — it's striking nine,"
I said,
"An hour when all good little boys and girls should be in
bed.
Run home and get your supper, else your Ma will scold, —
O fie! —
It's very wrong indeed for little boys to stand and cry!"

The tear-drop in his little eye again began to spring,
His bosom throbb'd with agony, — he cried like anything!
I stoop'd, and thus amidst his sobs I heard him murmur,—
"Ah!
I haven't got no supper! and I haven't got no Ma!

"My father, he is on the seas, — my mother's dead and
gone!
And I am here, on this here pier, to roam the world alone;
I have not had, this livelong day, one drop to cheer my
heart,
Nor '*brown*' to buy a bit of bread with, — let alone a tart.

"If there's a soul will give me food, or find me in employ,
By day or night, then blow me tight!" (he was a vulgar
Boy;)
"And now I'm here, from this here pier it is my fixed
intent
To jump, as Mr. Levi did from off the Monu-ment!"

"Cheer up! cheer up! my little man — cheer up!" I kindly
said,
"You are a naughty boy to take such things into your head;
If you should jump from off the pier, you'd surely break
your legs,
Perhaps your neck, — then Bogey'd have you, sure as eggs
are eggs!

"Come home with me, my little man, come home with me
and sup;
My landlady is Mrs. Jones, — we must not keep her up, —
There's roast potatoes at the fire, — enough for me and
you, —
Come home, — you little vulgar Boy, — I lodge at Number 2."

I took him home to Number 2, the house beside "The
      Foy,"
I bade him wipe his dirty shoes, — that little vulgar Boy, —
And then I said to Mistress Jones, the kindest of her sex,
" Pray be so good as go and fetch a pint of double X!"

But Mrs. Jones was rather cross, she made a little noise,
She said she "did not like to wait on little vulgar Boys."
She with her apron wiped the plates, and, as she rubb'd the
      delf,
Said I might "go to Jericho, and fetch my beer myself!"

I did not go to Jericho, — I went to Mr. Cobb, —
I changed a shilling — (which in town the people call " a
      Bob"), —
It was not so much for myself as for that vulgar child, —
And I said, "A pint of double X, and please to draw it
      mild!"

When I came back I gazed about, — I gazed on stool and
      chair, —
I could not see my little friend, — because he was not there!
I peep'd beneath the table-cloth, — beneath the sofa, too, —
I said, "You little vulgar Boy! why, what's become of
      you?"

I could not see my table-spoons, — I look'd, but could not
      see
The little fiddle-pattern'd ones I use when I'm at tea;
— I could not see my sugar-tongs — my silver watch — oh,
      dear!
I know 'twas on the mantelpiece when I went out for beer.

I could not see my mackintosh! — it was not to be seen!
Nor yet my best white beaver hat, broad-brimm'd and lined
      with green;
My carpet-bag, — my cruet-stand, that holds my sauce and
      soy, —
My roast potatoes! — all are gone! — and so's that vulgar
      Boy!

I rang the bell for Mrs. Jones, for she was down below,
" — Oh, Mrs. Jones! what *do* you think? — ain't this a
pretty go?
— That horrid little vulgar Boy whom I brought here to-
night,
— He's stolen my things and run away!" — Says she,
"And sarve you right!"

Next morning I was up betimes, — I sent the Crier round,
All with his bell and gold-laced hat, to say I'd give a
pound
To find that little vulgar Boy, who'd gone and used me so;
But when the Crier cried "O Yes!" the people cried "O
No!"

I went to "Jarvis' Landing-place," the glory of the town,
There was a common sailor-man a-walking up and down;
I told my tale — he seemed to think I'd not been treated
well,
And called me "Poor old Buffer!" — what that means I
cannot tell.

That sailor-man, he said he'd seen that morning on the
shore,
A son of — something — 'twas a name I'd never heard before,
A little "gallows-looking chap," — dear me, what could he
mean?
With a "carpet-swab," and "mucking-togs," and a hat
turned up with green.

He spoke about his "precious eyes," and said he'd seen him
"sheer,"
— It's very odd that sailor-men should talk so very queer, —
And then he hitch'd his trousers up, as is, I'm told, their
use,
— It's very odd that sailor-men should wear those things
so loose.

I did not understand him well, but think he meant to say,
He'd seen that little vulgar Boy that morning swim away
In Captain Large's *Royal George,* about an hour before,
And they were now, as he supposed, "some*wheres*" about
the Nore.

A landsman said, " I *twig* the chap — he's been upon the
    Mill, —
And 'cause he *gammons* so the *flats,* ve calls him Veeping
    Bill ! "
He said " he'd done me werry brown," and " nicely *stow'd*
    the *swag.*"
— That's French, I fancy, for a hat — or else a carpet-bag.

I went and told the constable my property to track;
He asked me if " I did not wish that I might get it back? "
I answered, " To be sure I do! — it's what I'm come
    about."
He smiled and said, " Sir, does your mother know that you
    are out? "

Not knowing what to do, I thought I'd hasten back to
    town,
And beg our own Lord Mayor to catch the Boy who'd
    " done me brown."
His Lordship very kindly said he'd try and find him out,
But he " rather thought that there were several vulgar boys
    about."

He sent for Mr. Whithair then, and I described " the swag,"
My Mackintosh, my sugar-tongs, my spoons, and carpet-
    bag;
He promised that the New Police should all their powers
    employ;
But never to this hour have I beheld that vulgar Boy!

MORAL

Remember, then, what when a boy I've heard my Grandma
    tell,
" *Be warn'd in time by others' harm, and you shall do full
    well!* "
Don't link yourself with vulgar folks, who've got no fix'd
    abode,
Tell lies, use naughty words, and say they " wish they may
    be blow'd! "

Don't take too much of double X! and don't at night go
  out
To fetch your beer yourself, but make the pot-boy bring
  your stout!
And when you go to Margate next, just stop and ring the
  bell,
Give my respects to Mrs. Jones, and say I'm pretty well!
                                    Richard Harris Barham

FABLE

The mountain and the squirrel
Had a quarrel,
And the former called the latter " Little Prig; "
Bun replied,
" You are doubtless very big;
But all sorts of things and weather
Must be taken in together,
To make up a year
And a sphere.
And I think it no disgrace
To occupy my place.
If I'm not so large as you,
You are not so small as I,
And not half so spry.
I'll not deny you make
A very pretty squirrel track;
Talents differ; all is well and wisely put;
If I cannot carry forests on my back,
Neither can you crack a nut."
                                    Ralph Waldo Emerson

A KISS IN THE RAIN

One stormy morn I chanced to meet
  A lassie in the town;
Her locks were like the ripened wheat,
  Her laughing eyes were brown.
I watched her as she tripped along
  Till madness filled my brain,

And then — and then — I know 'twas wrong —
  I,kissed her in the rain!

With rain-drops shining on her cheek,
  Like dew-drops on a rose,
The little lassie strove to speak
  My boldness to oppose;
She strove in vain, and quivering
  Her fingers stole in mine;
And then the birds began to sing,
  The sun began to shine.

Oh, let the clouds grow dark above,
  My heart is light below;
'Tis always summer when we love,
  However winds may blow;
And I'm as proud as any prince,
  All honors I disdain:
She says I am her *rain beau* since
  I kissed her in the rain.

                    Samuel Minturn Peck

JACK AT THE OPERA

At Wapping I landed, and called to hail Mog;
  She had just shaped her course to the play:
Of two rums and one water I ordered my grog,
  And to speak her soon stood under weigh.
But the Haymarket I for old Drury mistook,
  Like a lubber so raw and so soft;
Half a George handed out, at the change did not look,
  Manned the ratlins, and went up aloft.

As I mounted to one of the uppermost tiers,
  With many a coxcomb and flirt,
Such a damnable squalling saluted my ears
  I thought there'd been somebody hurt;
But the devil a bit — 'twas your outlandish rips
  Singing out with their lanterns of jaws;
You'd ha' swored you'd been taking of one of they trips
  'Mongst the Caffres or wild Catabaws.

"What's the play, Ma'am?" says I, to a good-natured tit.
"The play! 'tis the *uproar,* you quiz."
"My timbers," cried I, "the right name on't you've hit,
For the devil an uproar it is."
For they pipe and they squeal, now alow, now aloft;
If it wa'nt for the petticoat gear,
With their squeaking so mollyish, tender, and soft,
One should scarcely know ma'am from mounseer.

Next at kicking and dancing they took a long spell,
All springing and bounding so neat,
And spessiously one curious Madamaselle, —
Oh, she daintily handled her feet!
But she hopped, and she sprawled, and she spun round so
queer,
'Twas, you see, rather oddish to me;
And so I sung out, " Pray be decent, my dear;
Consider I'm just come from the sea.

" 'Taint an Englishman's taste to have none of these goes;
So away to the playhouse I'll jog,
Leaving all your fine Bantums and Ma'am Parisoes,
For old Billy Shakespeare and Mog."
So I made for the theatre, and hailed my dear spouse;
She smiled as she sawed me approach;
And, when I'd shook hands and saluted her bows,
We to Wapping set sail in a coach.

Charles Dibdin

VAT YOU PLEASE

Some years ago, when civil faction
Raged like a fury through the fields of Gaul,
And children, in the general distraction,
Were taught to curse as soon as they could squall;
When common sense in common folks was dead,
And murder show'd a love of nationality,
And France, determined not to have a head,
Decapitated all the higher class,
To put folks more on an equality;
When coronets were not worth half a crown,

And liberty, in *bonnet-rouge,* might pass
For Mother Redcap up at Camden Town;
Full many a Frenchman then took wing
Bidding *soupe-maigre* an abrupt farewell,
   And hither came, *pell-mell,*
Sans cash, *sans* clothes, almost *sans* everything!

Two Messieurs who about this time came over,
Half-starved, but *toujours-gai*
(No weasels e'er were thinner),
Trudged up to town from Dover;
Their slender store exhausted on the way,
Extremely puzzled how to get a dinner,
From morn till noon, from noon to dewy eve,
Our Frenchmen wander'd on their expedition;
Great was their need, and sorely did they grieve.
Stomach and pocket in the same condition!
At length by mutual consent they parted,
And different ways on the same errand started.

This happened on a day most dear
To epicures, when general use
Sanctions the roasting of the sav'ry goose.
To'ards night, one Frenchman, at a tavern near,
Stopp'd, and beheld the glorious cheer;
While greedily he snuff'd the luscious gale in,
That from the kitchen window was exhaling.
He instant set to work his busy brain,
And snuff'd and long'd, and long'd and snuff'd again.
Necessity's the mother of invention
(A proverb I've heard many mention);
So now one moment saw his plan completed,
And our sly Frenchman at a table seated;
The ready waiter at his elbow stands —
"Sir, will you favor me with your commands?
We've roast and boil'd, sir; choose you those or these?"
"Sare! you are very good, sare! *Vat you please.*"

Quick at the word,
Upon the table smokes the wish'd-for bird.
No time in talking did he waste,
But pounced pell-mell upon it;
Drum-sticks and merry-thought he pick'd in haste,
Exulting in the merry thought that won it.

Pie follows goose, and after pie comes cheese —
"Stilton or Cheshire, sir?" — "Ah! *vat you please.*"
And now our Frenchman, having ta'en his fill,
Prepares to go, when — "Sir, your little *bill!* "
"Ah, vat you're Bill! Vell, Mr. Bill, good day!
Bon jour, good Villiam." — "No, sir, stay;
My name is Tom, sir — you've this bill to pay."
"Pay, pay, *ma foi!*
I call for noting, sare — *pardonnez moi!*
You bring me vat you call your goose, your cheese,
You ask-a-me to eat; I tell you, *Vat you please!* "
Down came the master, each explain'd the case,
The one with cursing, t'other with grimace!
But Boniface, who dearly loved a jest
(Although sometimes he dearly paid for it),
And finding nothing could be done (you know,
That when a man has got no money,
To make him pay some would be rather funny),
Of a bad bargain made the best,
Acknowledged much was to be said for it;
Took pity on the Frenchman's meagre face,
And, Briton-like, forgave a fallen foe,
Laugh'd heartily, and let him go.
Our Frenchman's hunger thus subdued,
Away he trotted in a merry mood;
When turning round the corner of a street,
Who but his countryman he chanced to meet!
To him, with many a shrug and many a grin,
He told him how he'd taken *Jean Bull* in!
Fired with the tale, the other licks his chops,
Makes his congee, and seeks the shop of shops.
Entering, he seats himself, just at his ease,
"What will you take, sir?" — "*Vat you please.*"

The waiter turned as pale as Paris plaster,
And up-stairs running, thus address'd his master:
"These vile *mounseers* come over sure in pairs;
Sir, there's another '*Vat you please!*' down-stairs."
This made the landlord rather crusty,
Too much of one thing — the proverb's somewhat musty.
Once to be *done,* his anger didn't touch,
But when a *second* time they tried the treason,
It made him *crusty,* sir, and with good reason,
You would be *crusty* were you *done* so much.

There is a kind of instrument
Which greatly helps a serious argument,
And which, when properly applied, occasions
Some most unpleasant tickling sensations!
'Twould make more clumsy folks than Frenchmen skip,
'Twill strike you presently — a stout horsewhip.
This instrument our *Maître l'Hôte*
Most carefully concealed beneath his coat;
And seeking instantly the Frenchman's station,
Addressed him with the usual salutation.

Our Frenchman, bowing to his threadbare knees,
Determined whilst the iron's hot to strike it,
Pat with his lesson, answers — "*Vat you please!*"
But scarcely had he let the sentence slip,
Than round his shoulders twines the pliant whip!
"Sare, sare! ah, *misericorde, parbleu!*
Oh, dear, Monsieur, vat make you use me so?
Vat you call dis?" "Oh, don't you know?
That's what I please," says Bonny, "how d'ye like it?
Your friend, though I paid dearly for his funning,
Deserved the goose he gained, sir, for his cunning;
But you, Monsieur, or else my time I'm wasting,
Are *goose* enough, and only wanted *basting*."
James Robinson Planché

TAM O'SHANTER: A TALE

When chapman billies leave the street,
And drouthy neebors neebors meet;
As market-days are wearin' late,
An' folk begin to tak the gate;
While we sit bousing at the nappy,
An' gettin' fou and unco happy,
We think na on the lang Scots miles,
The mosses, waters, slaps, and styles,
That lie between us and our hame,
Whare sits our sulky sullen dame,
Gathering her brows like gathering storm,
Nursing her wrath to keep it warm.

This truth fand honest Tam O'Shanter,
As he frae Ayr ae night did canter,
(Auld Ayr, wham ne'er a town surpasses
For honest men and bonnie lassies).

O Tam! hadst thou but been sae wise
As ta'en thy ain wife Kate's advice!
She tauld thee weel thou wast a skellum,
A blethering, blustering, drunken blellum;
That frae November till October,
Ae market-day thou was nae sober;
That ilka melder, wi' the miller,
Thou sat as long as thou had siller;
That every naig was ca'd a shoe on,
The smith and thee gat roaring fou on;
That at the Lord's house, even on Sunday,
Thou drank wi' Kirkton Jean till Monday.
She prophesied that, late or soon,
Thou would be found deep drown'd in Doon!
Or catch'd wi' warlocks in the mirk,
By Alloway's auld haunted kirk.

Ah, gentle dames! it gars me greet
To think how monie counsels sweet,
How monie lengthen'd, sage advices,
The husband frae the wife despises!

But to our tale: — Ae market-night,
Tam had got planted unco right,
Fast by an ingle, bleezing finely,
Wi' reaming swats, that drank divinely;
And at his elbow, Souter Johnie,
His ancient, trusty, drouthy cronie:
Tam lo'ed him like a very brither —
They had been fou for weeks thegither!
The night drave on wi' sangs and clatter,
And aye the ale was growing better:
The landlady and Tam grew gracious,
Wi' secret favors, sweet and precious;
The Souter tauld his queerest stories;
The landlord's laugh was ready chorus:
The storm without might rair and rustle —
Tam did na mind the storm a whistle.

Care, mad to see a man sae happy,
E'en drown'd himsel amang the nappy!
As bees flee hame wi' lades o' treasure,
The minutes wing'd their way wi' pleasure:
Kings may be blest, but Tam was glorious,
O'er a' the ills o' life victorious!

But pleasures are like poppies spread,
You seize the flow'r, it's bloom is shed!
Or like the snow falls in the river,
A moment white — then melts forever;
Or like the borealis race,
That flit ere you can point their place;
Or like the rainbow's lovely form,
Evanishing amid the storm.
Nae man can tether time or tide;
The hour approaches Tam maun ride;
That hour, o' night's black arch the keystane,
That dreary hour Tam mounts his beast in;
And sic a night he taks the road in
As ne'er poor sinner was abroad in.

The wind blew as 'twad blawn its last;
The rattling showers rose on the blast;
The speedy gleams the darkness swallow'd;
Loud, deep, and lang, the thunder bellow'd:
That night, a child might understand,
The Deil had business on his hand.

Weel mounted on his gray mare Meg,
A better never lifted leg,
Tam skelpit on thro' dub and mire,
Despising wind, and rain, and fire;
Whiles holding fast his guid blue bonnet,
Whiles crooning o'er some auld Scots sonnet;
Whiles glow'ring round wi' prudent cares,
Lest bogles catch him unawares:
Kirk-Alloway was drawing nigh,
Whare ghaists and houlets nightly cry.

By this time he was 'cross the ford,
Whare in the snaw the chapman smoor'd;
And past the birks and meikle stane
Whare drunken Charlie brak's neck-bane:

And through the whins, and by the cairn,
Whare hunters fand the murder'd bairn;
And near the thorn, aboon the well,
Whare Mungo's mither hang'd hersel.
Before him Doon pours a' his floods;
The doubling storm roars thro' the woods;
The lightnings flash frae pole to pole;
Near and more near the thunders roll;
When, glimmering thro' the groaning trees,
Kirk-Alloway seem'd in a bleeze;
Thro' ilka bore the beams were glancing,
And loud resounded mirth and dancing.

Inspiring bold John Barleycorn!
What dangers thou canst mak us scorn!
Wi' tippenny, we fear nae evil;
Wi' usquabae, we'll face the Devil! —
The swats sae ream'd in Tammie's noddle,
Fair play, he cared na deils a boddle.
But Maggie stood, right sair astonish'd,
Till, by the heel and hand admonish'd,
She ventur'd forward on the light;
And, vow! Tam saw an unco sight!

Warlocks and witches in a dance;
Nae cotillion, brent-new frae France,
But hornpipes, jigs, strathspeys, and reels,
Put life and mettle in their heels:
A winnock-bunker, in the east,
There sat Auld Nick, in shape o' beast;
A tousie tyke, black, grim, and large,
To gie them music was his charge;
He screw'd the pipes, and gart them skirl,
Till roof and rafters a' did dirl.
Coffins stood round, like open presses,
That shaw'd the dead in their last dresses;
And by some devilish cantraip sleight
Each in its cauld hand held a light, —
By which heroic Tam was able
To note upon the haly table,
A murderer's banes in gibbet-airns;
Twa span-lang, wee, unchristen'd bairns;
A thief new-cutted frae a rape,
Wi' his last gasp his gab did gape;

Five tomahawks, wi' bluid red-rusted;
Five scymitars, wi' murder crusted;
A garter, which a babe had strangled;
A knife, a father's throat had mangled,
Whom his ain son o' life bereft,
The gray hairs yet stack to the heft:
Wi' mair o' horrible and awfu',
Which even to name wad be unlawfu'.

As Tammie glowr'd, amaz'd and curious,
The mirth and fun grew fast and furious:
The piper loud and louder blew,
The dancers quick and quicker flew;
They reel'd, they set, they cross'd, they cleekit,
Till ilka carlin swat and reekit,
And coost her duddies to the wark,
And linket at it in her sark.

Now Tam! O Tam! had thae been queans,
A' plump and strappin' in their teens!
Their sarks, instead o' creeshie flannen,
Been snaw-white seventeen-hunder linen!
Thir breeks o' mine, my only pair,
That ance were plush, o' guid blue hair,
I wad hae gi'en them aff my hurdies,
For ae blink o' the bonnie burdies!

But wither'd beldams, auld and droll,
Rigwoodie hags, wad spean a foal,
Lowpin and flingin' on a crummock,
I wonder did na turn thy stomach!

But Tam kend what was what fu' brawlie,
There was ae winsome wench and wawlie,
That night enlisted in the core,
Lang after kend on Carrick shore;
(For monie a beast to dead she shot,
An' perish'd monie a bonnie boat,
And shook baith meikle corn and bear,
And kept the country-side in fear).
Her cutty sark, o' Paisley harn,
That, while a lassie, she had worn,
In longitude though sorely scanty,
It was her best, and she was vauntie.

Ah! little kend thy reverend grannie,
That sark she coft for her wee Nannie,
Wi' twa pund Scots ('twas a' her riches),
Wad ever grac'd a dance o' witches!

But here my Muse her wing maun cour,
Sic flights are far beyond her power;
To sing how Nannie lap and flang
(A souple jade she was, and strang),
And how Tam stood, like ane bewitch'd,
And thought his very een enrich'd;
Even Satan glowr'd, and fidg'd fu' fain,
And hotch'd and blew wi' might and main;
Till first ae caper, syne anither,
Tam tint his reason a' thegither,
And roars out, " Weel done, Cutty-Sark!"
And in an instant a' was dark:
And scarcely had he Maggie rallied,
When out the hellish legion sallied.

As bees bizz out wi' angry fyke,
When plundering herds assail their byke,
As open pussie's mortal foes,
When, pop! she starts before their nose;
As eager runs the market-crowd,
When " Catch the thief!" resounds aloud;
So Maggie runs, the witches follow,
Wi' monie an eldritch screech and hollo.

Ah, Tam! ah, Tam! thou'll get thy fairin'!
In hell they'll roast thee like a herrin'!
In vain thy Kate awaits thy comin'!
Kate soon will be a wofu' woman!
Now, do thy speedy utmost, Meg,
And win the keystane of the brig;
There at them thou thy tail may toss,
A running stream they dare na cross!
But ere the keystane she could make,
The fient a tail she had to shake!
For Nannie, far before the rest,
Hard upon noble Maggie prest,
And flew at Tam wi' furious ettle;
But little wist she Maggie's mettle! —

Ae spring brought off her master hale,
But left behind her ain gray tail:
The carlin claught her by the rump,
And left poor Maggie scarce a stump.

Now, wha this tale o' truth shall read,
Ilk man and mother's son, take heed:
Whane'er to drink you are inclin'd,
Or cutty-sarks run in your mind,
Think! ye may buy the joys o'er dear:
Remember Tam O'Shanter's mare.

Robert Burns

THE LATEST DECALOGUE

Thou shalt have one God only; who
Would be at the expense of two?
No graven images may be
Worshipped, except the currency:
Swear not at all; for, for thy curse
Thine enemy is none the worse:
At church on Sunday to attend
Will serve to keep the world thy friend:
Honor thy parents; that is, all
From whom advancement may befall;
Thou shalt not kill; but need'st not strive
Officiously to keep alive:
Do not adultery commit;
Advantage rarely comes of it:
Thou shalt not steal; an empty feat,
When it's so lucrative to cheat:
Bear not false witness; let the lie
Have time on its own wings to fly:
Thou shalt not covet, but tradition
Approves all forms of competition.

Arthur Hugh Clough

ATHEISM

"There is no God," the wicked saith,
   "And truly it's a blessing,
For what He might have done with us
   It's better only guessing."

" The carlin claught her by the rump."

" There is no God," a youngster thinks,
  " Or really, if there may be,
He surely didn't mean a man
  Always to be a baby."

" There is no God, or if there is,"
    The tradesman thinks, " 'twere funny
If He should take it ill in me
  To make a little money."

" Whether there be," the rich man says,
  " It matters very little,
For I and mine, thank somebody,
  Are not in want of victual."

Some others, also, to themselves,
  Who scarce so much as doubt it,
Think there is none, when they are well,
  And do not think about it.

But country folks who live beneath
  The shadow of the steeple;
The parson and the parson's wife,
  And mostly married people;

Youths green and happy in first love,
  So thankful for illusion;
And men caught out in what the world
  Calls guilt, in first confusion;

And almost every one when age,
  Disease, or sorrows strike him,
Inclines to think there is a God,
  Or something very like Him.
                    Arthur Hugh Clough

MISS FLORA McFLIMSEY [1]

Miss Flora McFlimsey, of Madison Square,
Has made three separate journeys to Paris;
And her father assures me, each time she was there,
That she and her friend Mrs. Harris

1 From " Nothing to Wear."

(Not the lady whose name is so famous in history,
But plain Mrs. H., without romance or mystery)
Spent six consecutive weeks without stopping,
In one continuous round of shopping; —
Shopping alone, and shopping together,
At all hours of the day, and in all sorts of weather:
For all manner of things that a woman can put
On the crown of her head or the sole of her foot,
Or wrap round her shoulders, or fit round her waist,
Or that can be sewed on, or pinned on, or laced,
Or tied on with a string, or stitched on with a bow,
In front or behind, above or below;
For bonnets, mantillas, capes, collars, and shawls;
Dresses for breakfasts, and dinners, and balls;
Dresses to sit in, and stand in, and walk in,
Dresses to dance in, and flirt in, and talk in;
Dresses in which to do nothing at all;
Dresses for winter, spring, summer, and fall, —
All of them different in color and pattern,
Silk, muslin, and lace, crape, velvet, and satin,
Brocade, and broadcloth, and other material
Quite as expensive and much more ethereal:
In short, for all things that could ever be thought of,
Or milliner, modiste, or tradesman be bought of,
From ten-thousand-francs robes to twenty-sous frills;
  In all quarters of Paris, and to every store:
  While McFlimsey in vain stormed, scolded, and swore.
They footed the streets, and he footed the bills.

The last trip, their goods shipped by the steamer *Argo*
Formed, McFlimsey declares, the bulk of her cargo,
Not to mention a quantity kept from the rest,
Sufficient to fill the largest-sized chest,
Which did not appear on the ship's manifest,
But for which the ladies themselves manifested
Such particular interest that they invested
Their own proper persons in layers and rows
Of muslins, embroideries, worked underclothes,
Gloves, handkerchiefs, scarfs, and such trifles as those;
Then, wrapped in great shawls, like Circassian beauties,
Gave *good-by* to the ship, and *go-by* to the duties.
Her relations at home all marvelled, no doubt,
Miss Flora had grown so enormously stout

For an actual belle and a possible bride;
But the miracle ceased when she turned inside out,
    And the truth came to light, and the dry-goods beside,
Which, in spite of collector and custom-house sentry,
Had entered the port without any entry.
And yet, though scarce three months have passed since the
    day
This merchandise went, on twelve carts, up Broadway,
This same Miss McFlimsey, of Madison Square,
The last time we met, was in utter despair,
Because she had nothing whatever to wear!

NOTHING TO WEAR! Now, as this is a true ditty,
    I do not assert — this you know is between us —
That she's in a state of absolute nudity,
    Like Powers's Greek Slave, or the Medici Venus;
But I do mean to say I have heard her declare,
    When at the same moment she had on a dress
    Which cost five hundred dollars, and not a cent less,
    And jewelry worth ten times more, I should guess,
That she had not a thing in the wide world to wear!
I should mention just here, that out of Miss Flora's
Two hundred and fifty or sixty adorers,
I had just been selected as he who should throw all
The rest in the shade, by the gracious bestowal
On myself, after twenty or thirty rejections,
Of those fossil remains which she called her "affections,"
And that rather decayed but well-known work of art,
Which Miss Flora persisted in styling "her heart."
So we were engaged. Our troth had been plighted
    Not by moonbeam or starbeam, by fountain or grove;
But in a front parlor, most brilliantly lighted,
    Beneath the gas-fixtures we whispered our love —
Without any romance, or raptures, or sighs,
Without any tears in Miss Flora's blue eyes,
Or blushes, or transports, or such silly actions;
It was one of the quietest business transactions,
With a very small sprinkling of sentiment, if any,
And a very large diamond imported by Tiffany.
On her virginal lips while I printed a kiss,
She exclaimed, as a sort of parenthesis,
And by way of putting me quite at my ease,
"You know, I'm to polka as much as I please,
And flirt when I like, — now stop, — don't you speak, —

And you must not come here more than twice in the week,
Or talk to me either at party or ball;
But always be ready to come when I call:
So don't prose to me about duty and stuff, —
If we don't break this off, there will be time enough
For that sort of thing; but the bargain must be,
That as long as I choose I am perfectly free:
For this is a sort of engagement, you see,
Which is binding on you, but not binding on me."

Well, having thus wooed Miss McFlimsey, and gained her,
With the silks, crinolines, and hoops that contained her,
I had, as I thought, a contingent remainder
At least in the property, and the best right
To appear as its escort by day and by night;
And it being the week of the Stuckups' grand ball, —
    Their cards had been out for a fortnight or so,
    And set all the Avenue on the tiptoe, —
I considered it only my duty to call
    And see if Miss Flora intended to go.
I found her — as ladies are apt to be found
When the time intervening between the first sound
Of the bell and the visitor's entry is shorter
Than usual — I found — I won't say I caught — her
Intent on the pier-glass, undoubtedly meaning
To see if perhaps it didn't need cleaning.
She turned as I entered — "Why, Harry, you sinner,
I thought that you went to the Flashers' to dinner!"
"So I did," I replied; "but the dinner is swallowed,
    And digested, I trust; for 'tis now nine or more:
So being relieved from that duty, I followed
    Inclination, which led me, you see, to your door.
And now will your Ladyship so condescend
As just to inform me if you intend
Your beauty and graces and presence to lend
(All of which, when I own, I hope no one will borrow)
To the Stuckups, whose party, you know, is to-morrow?"
The fair Flora looked up with a pitiful air,
And answered quite promptly, "Why, Harry, *mon cher*,
I should like above all things to go with you there;
But really and truly — I've nothing to wear."

"Nothing to wear? Go just as you are:
Wear the dress you have on, and you'll be by far,

I engage, the most bright and particular star
  On the Stuckup horizon — " I stopped, for her eye,
Notwithstanding this delicate onset of flattery,
Opened on me at once a most terrible battery
  Of scorn and amazement. She made no reply,
But gave a slight turn to the end of her nose
  (That pure Grecian feature), as much as to say,
" How absurd that any sane man should suppose
That a lady would go to a ball in the clothes,
  No matter how fine, that she wears every day ! "
So I ventured again — " Wear your crimson brocade."
(Second turn-up of nose) — " That's too dark by a
  shade." —
" Your blue silk — " " That's too heavy." — " Your pink
  — " " That's too light." —
" Wear tulle over satin." " I can't endure white." —
" Your rose-colored, then, the best of the batch — "
" I haven't a thread of point lace to match." —
" Your brown moire-antique — " " Yes, and look like a
  Quaker." —
" The pearl-colored — " " I would, but that plaguy dress-
  maker
Has had it a week." — ". Then that exquisite lilac,
In which you would melt the heart of a Shylock."
(Here the nose took again the same elevation) —
" I wouldn't wear that for the whole of creation." —
  " Why not ? It's my fancy, there's nothing could strike it
As more *comme il faut*" — " Yes, but, dear me, that lean
  Sophronia Stuckup has got one just like it,
And I won't appear dressed like a chit of sixteen." —
" Then that splendid purple, that sweet mazarine,
That superb *point d'aiguille,* that imperial green,
That zephyr-like tarlatan, that rich grenadine — "
" Not one of all which is fit to be seen,"
Said the lady, becoming excited and flushed.
" Then wear," I exclaimed, in a tone which quite crushed
Opposition, " that gorgeous toilette which you sported
  In Paris last spring, at the grand presentation,
  When you quite turned the head of the head of the
    nation ;
And by all the grand court were so very much courted."
The end of the nose was portentously tipped up,
  And both the bright eyes shot forth indignation,
  As she burst upon me with the fierce exclamation,

"I have worn it three times at the least calculation,
And that and most of my dresses are ripped up!"
Here I *ripped out* something, perhaps rather rash —
  Quite innocent, though; but to use an expression
More striking than classic, it "settled my hash,"
  And proved very soon the last act of our session.
"Fiddlesticks, is it, sir? I wonder the ceiling
Doesn't fall down and crush you! — oh, you men have no
    feeling.
You selfish, unnatural, illiberal creatures,
Who set yourselves up as patterns and preachers,
Your silly pretence — why, what a mere guess it is!
Pray, what do you know of a woman's necessities?
I have told you and shown you I've nothing to wear,
And it's perfectly plain you not only don't care,
But you do not believe me" (here the nose went still
    higher):
"I suppose if you dared you would call me a liar.
Our engagement is ended, sir — yes, on the spot;
You're a brute, and a monster, and — I don't know what."
I mildly suggested the words Hottentot,
Pickpocket, and cannibal, Tartar, and thief,
As gentle expletives which might give relief:
But this only proved as a spark to the powder,
And the storm I had raised came faster and louder;
It blew, and it rained, thundered, lightened, and hailed
Interjections, verbs, pronouns, till language quite failed
To express the abusive, and then its arrears
Were brought up all at once by a torrent of tears;
And my last faint, despairing attempt at an obs-
Ervation was lost in a tempest of sobs.

Well, I felt for the lady, and felt for my hat too,
Improvised on the crown of the latter a tattoo,
In lieu of expressing the feelings which lay
Quite too deep for words, as Wordsworth would say:
Then, without going through the form of a bow,
Found myself in the entry, — I hardly knew how, —
On doorstep and sidewalk, past lamp-post and square,
At home and up-stairs, in my own easy-chair;
  Poked my feet into slippers, my fire into blaze,
And said to myself, as I lit my cigar, —
Supposing a man had the wealth of the Czar
  Of the Russias to boot, for the rest of his days,

On the whole do you think he would have much to spare
If he married a woman with nothing to wear?
William Allen Butler

THE POSITIVISTS

Life and the Universe show spontaneity:
Down with ridiculous notions of Deity!
    Churches and creeds are all lost in the mists;
    Truth must be sought with the Positivists.

Wise are their teachers beyond all comparison,
Comte, Huxley, Tyndall, Mill, Morley, and Harrison;
    Who will adventure to enter the lists
    With such a squadron of Positivists?

Social arrangements are awful miscarriages;
Cause of all crime is our system of marriages.
    Poets with sonnets, and lovers with trysts,
    Kindle the ire of the Positivists.

Husbands and wives should be all one community,
Exquisite freedom with absolute unity.
    Wedding-rings worse are than manacled wrists —
    Such is the creed of the Positivists.

There was an ape in the days that were earlier;
Centuries passed, and his hair became curlier;
    Centuries more gave a thumb to his wrist —
    Then he was Man, and a Positivist.

If you are pious (mild form of insanity)
Bow down and worship the mass of humanity.
    Other religions are buried in mists;
    We're our own Gods, say the Positivists.
Mortimer Collins

THE BOHEMIANS OF BOSTON

The " Orchids " were as tough a crowd
As Boston anywhere allowed;
It was a club of wicked men —
The oldest, twelve, the youngest, ten;
They drank their soda colored green,
They talked of " Art," and " Philistine,"
They wore buff " wescoats," and their hair
It used to make the waiters stare!
They were so shockingly behaved
And Boston thought them *so* depraved,
Policemen, stationed at the door,
Would raid them every hour or more!
They used to smoke (!) and laugh out loud (!)
They were a very devilish crowd!
They formed a Cult, far subtler, brainier,
Than ordinary Anglomania,
For all as Jacobites were reckoned,
And gaily toasted Charles the Second!
(What would the Bonnie Charlie say,
If he could see that crowd to-day?)
Fitz-Willieboy McFlubadub
Was Regent of the Orchids' Club;
A wild Bohemian was he,
And spent his money fast and free.
He thought no more of spending dimes
On some debauch of pickled limes,
Than you would think of spending nickels
To buy a pint of German pickles!
The Boston maiden passed him by
With sidelong glances of her eye,
She dared not speak (he *was* so wild),
Yet worshipped this Lotharian child.
Fitz-Willieboy was so *blasé*,
He burned a *Transcript* up, one day!
The Orchids fashioned all their style
On Flubadub's infernal guile.
That awful Boston oath was his, —
He used to jaculate, " Gee-Whiz! "
He showed them that immoral haunt,

The dirty Chinese Restaurant,
And there they'd find him, even when
It got to be as late as ten!
He ate chopped *suey* (with a fork),
You should have heard the villain talk
Of one *reporter* that he knew (!)
An artist, and an actor, too!!!
The Orchids went from bad to worse,
Made epigrams — attempted verse!
Boston was horrified and shocked
To hear the way those Orchids mocked;
For they made fun of Boston ways,
And called good men Provincial Jays!
The end must come to such a story,
Gone is the wicked Orchids' glory,
The room was raided by police,
One night, for breaches of the Peace
(There had been laughter, long and loud,
In Boston this is not allowed),
And there, the sergeant of the squad
Found awful evidence — my God! —
Fitz-Willieboy McFlubadub,
The Regent of the Orchids' Club,
Had written on the window-sill,
This shocking outrage — " Beacon H—ll! "

Gelett Burgess
(*In " The Burgess Nonsense Book "*)

TO JULIA IN SHOOTING TOGS

AND A HERRICKOSE VEIN

Whenas to shoot my Julia goes,
Then, then (methinks), how bravely shows
That rare arrangement of her clothes!

So shod as when the Huntress Maid
With thumping buskin bruised the glade,
She moveth, making earth afraid.

Against the sting of random chaff
Her leathern gaiters circle half
The arduous crescent of her calf.

Unto th' occasion timely fit,
My love's attire doth show her wit,
And of her legs a little bit.

Sorely it sticketh in my throat,
She having nowhere to bestow't,
To name the absent petticoat.

In lieu whereof a wanton pair
Of knickerbockers she doth wear,
Full windy and with space to spare.

Enlargèd by the bellying breeze,
Lord! how they playfully do ease
The urgent knocking of her knees!

Lengthways curtailèd to her taste
A tunic circumvents her waist,
And soothly it is passing chaste.

Upon her head she hath a gear
Even such as wights of ruddy cheer
Do use in stalking of the deer.

Haply her truant tresses mock
Some coronal of shapelier block,
To wit, the bounding billy-cock.

Withal she hath a loaded gun,
Whereat the pheasants, as they run,
Do make a fair diversiòn.

For very awe, if so she shoots,
My hair upriseth from the roots,
And lo! I tremble in my boots!

Owen Seaman

A PARENTAL ODE TO MY SON, AGED THREE
YEARS AND FIVE MONTHS

Thou happy, happy elf!
(But stop, — first let me kiss away that tear) —
Thou tiny image of myself!
(My love, he's poking peas into his ear!)
Thou merry, laughing sprite!
With spirits feather-light,
Untouched by sorrow, and unsoiled by sin —
(Good Heavens! the child is swallowing a pin!)

Thou little tricksy Puck!
With antic toys so funnily bestuck,
Light as the singing bird that wings the air —
(The door! the door! he'll tumble down the stair!)
Thou darling of thy sire!
(Why, Jane, he'll set his pinafore afire!)
Thou imp of mirth and joy!
In love's dear chain, so strong and bright a link,
Thou idol of thy parents — (Drat the boy!
There goes my ink!)

Thou cherub — but of earth;
Fit playfellow for Fays, by moonlight pale,
In harmless sport and mirth,
(That dog will bite him if he pulls its tail!)
Thou human humming-bee, extracting honey
From every blossom in the world that blows,
Singing in youth's elysium ever sunny,
(Another tumble! — that's his precious nose!)

Thy father's pride and hope!
(He'll break the mirror with that skipping-rope!)
With pure heart newly stamped from Nature's mint —
(Where *did* he learn that squint?)
Thou young domestic dove!
(He'll have that jug off, with another shove!)
Dear nursling of the Hymeneal nest!
(Are those torn clothes his best?)
Little epitome of man!

(He'll climb upon the table, that's his plan!)
Touched with the beautous tints of dawning life
    (He's got a knife!)

    Thou enviable being!
No storms, no clouds, in thy blue sky foreseeing,
    Play on, play on,
    My elfin John!
Toss the light ball — bestride the stick —
(I knew so many cakes would make him sick!)
With fancies, buoyant as the thistle-down,
Prompting the face grotesque, and antic brisk,
    With many a lamb-like frisk,
(He's got the scissors, snipping at your gown!)

    Thou pretty opening rose!
(Go to your mother, child, and wipe your nose!)
Balmy and breathing music like the South,
(He really brings my heart into my mouth!)
Fresh as the morn, and brilliant as its star, —
(I wish that window had an iron bar!)
Bold as the hawk, yet gentle as the dove, —
    (I'll tell you what, my love,
I cannot write unless he's sent above!)

                    Thomas Hood

THE AMERICAN TRAVELLER

To Lake Aghmoogenegamook
    All in the State of Maine,
A man from Wittequergaugaum came
    One evening in the rain.

"I am a traveller," said he,
    "Just started on a tour,
And go to Nomjamskillicook
    To-morrow morn at four."

He took a tavern-bed that night,
    And, with the morrow's sun,
By way of Sekledobskus went,
    With carpet-bag and gun.

A week passed on, and next we find
  Our native tourist come
To that sequestered village called
  Genasagarnagum.

From thence he went to Absequoit,
  And there — quite tired of Maine —
He sought the mountains of Vermont,
  Upon a railroad train.

Dog Hollow, in the Green Mount State,
  Was his first stopping-place ;
And then Skunk's Misery displayed
  Its sweetness and its grace.

By easy stages then he went
  To visit Devil's Den ;
And Scrabble Hollow, by the way,
  Did come within his ken.

Then *via* Nine Holes and Goose Green
  He travelled through the State ;
And to Virginia, finally,
  Was guided by his fate.

Within the Old Dominion's bounds,
  He wandered up and down ;
To-day at Buzzard's Roost ensconced,
  To-morrow, at Hell Town.

At Pole Cat, too, he spent a week,
  Till friends from Bull Ring came,
And made him spend a day with them
  In hunting forest-game.

Then, with his carpet-bag in hand,
  To Dog Town next he went ;
Though stopping at Free Negro Town,
  Where half a day he spent.

From thence, into Negationburg
  His route of travel lay;
Which having gained, he left the State,
  And took a southward way.

North Carolina's friendly soil
  He trod at fall of night,
And, on a bed of softest down,
  He slept at Hell's Delight.

Morn found him on the road again,
  To Lousy Level bound;
At Bull's Tail, and Lick Lizard, too,
  Good provender he found.

The country all about Pinch Gut
  So beautiful did seem
That the beholder thought it like
  A picture in a dream.

But the plantations near Burnt Coat
  Were even finer still,
And made the wondering tourist feel
  A soft, delicious thrill.

At Tear Shirt, too, the scenery
  Most charming did appear,
With Snatch It in the distance far,
  And Purgatory near.

But, spite of all these pleasant scenes,
  The tourist stoutly swore
That home is brightest, after all,
  And travel is a bore.

So back he went to Maine, straightway;
  A little wife he took;
And now is making nutmegs at
  Moosehicmagunticook.

                            Robert Henry Newell

SONG

OF ONE ELEVEN YEARS IN PRISON

I.

Whene'er with haggard eyes I view
This dungeon that I'm rotting in,
I think of those companions true
Who studied with me at the U
    niversity of Gottingen,
    niversity of Gottingen.

> [Weeps, and pulls out a blue kerchief, with which he wipes his
> eyes; gazing tenderly at it, he proceeds —

II.

Sweet kerchief, check'd with heavenly blue,
Which once my love sat knotting in! —
Alas! Matilda *then* was true!
At least I thought so at the U
    niversity of Gottingen,
    niversity of Gottingen.

> [At the repetition of this line he clanks his chains in cadence.

III.

Barbs! Barbs! alas! how swift you flew,
Her neat post-wagon trotting in!
Ye bore Matilda from my view;
Forlorn I languish'd at the U
    niversity of Gottingen,
    niversity of Gottingen.

IV.

This faded form! this pallid hue!
This blood my veins is clotting in,
My years are many — they were few
When first I entered at the U
    niversity of Gottingen,
    niversity of Gottingen.

v.

There first for thee my passion grew,
  Sweet, sweet Matilda Pottengen!
Thou wast the daughter of my tu
  tor, law professor at the U
          niversity of Gottingen,
          niversity of Gottingen.

vi.

Sun, moon and thou, vain world, adieu,
  That kings and priests are plotting in;
Here doom'd to starve on water gru
  el, never shall I see the U
          niversity of Gottingen,
          niversity of Gottingen.

[During the last stanza he dashes his head repeatedly against the walls of his
prison; and, finally, so hard as to produce a visible contusion; he then throws
himself on the floor in an agony. The curtain drops; the music still continuing
to play till it is wholly fallen.

George Canning

MARY THE COOK-MAID'S LETTER TO DOCTOR SHERIDAN

Well, if ever I saw such another man since my mother
  bound my head!
You a gentleman! marry come up! I wonder where you
  were bred.
I'm sure such words do not become a man of your cloth;
I would not give such language to a dog, faith and troth.
Yes, you call'd my master a knave; fie, Mr. Sheridan! it's
  a shame!
For a parson, who should know better things, to come out
  with such a name.
Knave in your teeth, Mr. Sheridan! 'tis both a shame and
  a sin;
And the Dean, my master, is an honester man than you and
  all your kin:
He has more goodness in his little finger, than you have in
  your whole body:

My master is a parsonable man, and not a spindle-shank'd
 hoddy-doddy.
And now, whereby I find you would fain make an excuse,
Because my master one day, in anger, call'd you a goose;
Which, and I am sure I have been his servant four years
 since October,
And he never call'd me worse than sweetheart, drunk or
 sober:
Not that I know his reverence was ever concern'd to my
 knowledge,
Though you and your come-rogues keep him out so late
 in your college.
You say you will eat grass on his grave: a Christian eat
 grass!
Whereby you now confess yourself to be a goose or an
 ass:
But that's as much as to say, that my master should die
 before ye;
Well, well, that's as God pleases; and I don't believe that's
 a true story:
And so say I told you so, and you may go tell my master;
 what care I?

And I don't care who knows it; 'tis all one to Mary;
Every one knows that I love to tell truth and shame the
 Devil;
I am but a poor servant; but I think gentlefolks should
 be civil.
Besides, you found fault with our victuals one day that
 you was here:
I remember it was on a Tuesday of all days in the year.
And Saunders the man says you are always jesting and
 mocking:
"Mary," said he (one day as I was mending my master's
 stocking),
"My master is so fond of that minister that keeps the
 school,
I thought my master a wise man, but that man makes him
 a fool."
"Saunders," said I, "I would rather than a quart of ale
He would come into our kitchen, and I would pin a dish-
 clout to his tail."
And now I must go and get Saunders to direct this letter;

For I write but a sad scrawl; but my sister Marget she
    writes better.
Well, but I must run and make the bed, before my master
    comes from prayers;
And see now, it strikes ten, and I hear him coming up-
    stairs;
Whereof I could say more to your verses, if I could write
    written hand:
And so I remain in a civil way, your servant to command,
                                                    MARY.
                                        Jonathan Swift

THE BELLE OF THE BALL

Years — years ago, — ere yet my dreams
    Had been of being wise and witty, —
Ere I had done with writing themes,
    Or yawn'd o'er this infernal Chitty; —
Years, years ago, while all my joy
    Was in my fowling-piece and filly:
In short, while I was yet a boy,
    I fell in love with Laura Lily.

I saw her at the county ball;
    There, when the sounds of flute and fiddle
Gave signal sweet in that old hall
    Of hands across and down the middle,
Hers was the subtlest spell by far
    Of all that set young hearts romancing:
She was our queen, our rose, our star;
    And when she danced — O Heaven, her dancing!

Dark was her hair, her hand was white;
    Her voice was exquisitely tender,
Her eyes were full of liquid light;
    I never saw a waist so slender;
Her every look, her every smile,
    Shot right and left a score of arrows;
I thought 'twas Venus from her isle,
    And wonder'd where she'd left her sparrows.

She talk'd, — of politics or prayers;
  Of Southey's prose, or Wordsworth's sonnets;
Of daggers or of dancing bears,
  Of battles, or the last new bonnets;
By candle-light, at twelve o'clock,
  To me it matter'd not a tittle,
If those bright lips had quoted Locke,
  I might have thought they murmur'd Little.

Through sunny May, through sultry June,
  I loved her with a love eternal;
I spoke her praises to the moon,
  I wrote them for the *Sunday Journal.*
My mother laugh'd; I soon found out
  That ancient ladies have no feeling;
My father frown'd; but how should gout
  See any happiness in kneeling?

She was the daughter of a Dean,
  Rich, fat, and rather apoplectic;
She had one brother, just thirteen,
  Whose color was extremely hectic;
Her grandmother for many a year
  Had fed the parish with her bounty;
Her second cousin was a peer,
  And lord lieutenant of the county.

But titles and the three per cents,
  And mortgages, and great relations,
And India bonds, and tithes and rents,
  Oh! what are they to love's sensations?
Black eyes, fair forehead, clustering locks,
  Such wealth, such honors, Cupid chooses;
He cares as little for the stocks,
  As Baron Rothschild for the Muses.

She sketch'd; the vale, the wood, the beach,
  Grew lovelier from her pencil's shading;
She botanized; I envied each
  Young blossom in her boudoir fading;
She warbled Handel; it was grand —
  She made the Catalani jealous;

She touch'd the organ; I could stand
  For hours and hours to blow the bellows.

She kept an album, too, at home,
  Well fill'd with all an album's glories;
Paintings of butterflies, and Rome,
  Patterns for trimming, Persian stories;
Soft songs to Julia's cockatoo,
  Fierce odes to Famine and to Slaughter;
And autographs of Prince Leboo,
  And recipes for elder water.

And she was flatter'd, worshipp'd, bored;
  Her steps were watch'd, her dress was noted;
Her poodle dog was quite adored,
  Her sayings were extremely quoted.
She laugh'd, and every heart was glad,
  As if the taxes were abolish'd;
She frown'd, and every look was sad,
  As if the Opera were demolished.

She smil'd on many just for fun —
  I knew that there was nothing in it;
I was the first — the only one
  Her heart had thought of for a minute;
I knew it, for she told me so,
  In phrase which was divinely moulded;
She wrote a charming hand, — and oh!
  How sweetly all her notes were folded!

Our love was like most other loves —
  A little glow, a little shiver;
A rosebud and a pair of gloves,
  And " Fly Not Yet," upon the river;
Some jealousy of some one's heir,
  Some hopes of dying broken-hearted,
A miniature, a lock of hair,
  The usual vows — and then we parted.

We parted; — months and years roll'd by;
  We met again four summers after;
Our parting was all sob and sigh —
  Our meeting was all mirth and laughter;

For in my heart's most secret cell,
  There had been many other lodgers;
And she was not the ballroom belle,
  But only — Mrs. Something Rogers.
               Winthrop Mackworth Praed

THE STAMMERING WIFE

When deeply in love with Miss Emily Pryne,
I vowed, if the maiden would only be mine,
  I would always endeavor to please her.
She blushed her consent, though the stuttering lass
Said never a word except " You're an ass —
  An ass — an ass-iduous teaser!"

But when we were married, I found to my ruth,
The stammering lady had spoken the truth;
  For often, in obvious dudgeon,
She'd say if I ventured to give her a jog
In the way of reproof — "You're a dog — you're
    a dog —
  A dog — a dog-matic curmudgeon!"

And once when I said, "We can hardly afford
This extravagant style, with our moderate hoard,"
  And hinted we ought to be wiser,
She looked, I assure you, exceedingly blue,
And fretfully cried, "You're a Jew — you're a
    Jew —
  A very ju-dicious adviser!"

Again, when it happened that, wishing to shirk
Some rather unpleasant and arduous work,
  I begged her to go to a neighbor,
She wanted to know why I made such a fuss,
And saucily said, "You're a cuss — cuss — cuss —
  You were always ac-cus-tomed to labor!"

Out of temper at last with the insolent dame,
And feeling that madame was greatly to blame
  To scold me instead of caressing,

I mimicked her speech — like a churl that I am —
And angrily said, "You're a dam — dam — dam —
A dam-age instead of a blessing!"

John Godfrey Saxe

HOLY WILLIE'S PRAYER

O Thou wha in the heavens dost dwell,
Wha, as it pleases best Thysel,
Sends ane to Heaven, an' ten to Hell,
   A' for Thy glory,
And no for onie guid or ill
    They've done before Thee!

I bless and praise Thy matchless might,
When thousands Thou hast left in night,
That I am here, before Thy sight,
    For gifts an' grace,
A burnin' an' a shinin' light
    To a' this place.

What was I, or my generation,
That I should get sic exaltation!
I, wha deserv'd most just damnation,
    For broken laws
Sax thousand years ere my creation,
    Thro' Adam's cause.

When frae my mither's womb I fell,
Thou might hae plung'd me deep in Hell,
To gnash my gooms, to weep and wail
    In burnin' lakes,
Whare damnèd devils roar and yell,
    Chain'd to their stakes.

Yet I am here, a chosen sample,
To show Thy grace is great and ample;
I'm here a pillar o' Thy temple,
    Strong as a rock,
A guide, a buckler, an example
    To a' Thy flock!

But yet, O Lord! confess I must,
At times I'm fash'd wi' fleshly lust;
An' sometimes, too, in warldly trust,
   Vile self gets in;
But Thou remembers we are dust,
   Defil'd wi' sin.

May be Thou lets this fleshly thorn
Beset Thy servant e'en and morn,
Lest he owre proud and high should turn
   That he's sae gifted:
If sae, Thy han' maun e'en be borne
   Until Thou lift it.

Lord, bless Thy chosen in this place,
For here Thou has a chosen race:
But God confound their stubborn face,
   An' blast their name,
Wha bring Thy elders to disgrace
   An' open shame!

Lord, mind Gawn Hamilton's deserts,
He drinks, an' swears, an' plays at cartes,
Yet has sae monie takin' arts,
   Wi' great and sma',
Frae God's ain priest the people's hearts
   He steals awa.

An' when we chasten'd him therefore,
Thou kens how he bred sic a splore,
As set the warld in a roar
   O' laughin' at us; —
Curse Thou his basket and his store,
   Kail an' potatoes!

Lord, hear my earnest cry and pray'r
Against the Presbyt'ry of Ayr!
Thy strong right hand, Lord, mak it bare
   Upo' their heads!
Lord, visit them, an' dinna spare,
   For their misdeeds!

O Lord, my God! that glib-tongu'd Aiken,
My vera heart and saul are quakin'
To think how we stood sweatin', shakin',
      An' pish'd wi' dread,
While he wi' hingin' lip an' snakin',
      Held up his head.

Lord, in Thy day o' vengeance try him!
Lord, visit them wha did employ him,
And pass not in Thy mercy by them,
      Nor hear their pray'r;
But for Thy people's sake destroy them,
      An' dinna spare!

But, Lord, remember me and mine,
Wi' mercies temp'ral and divine,
That I for grace and gear may shine,
      Excell'd by nane,
An' a' the glory shall be Thine,
      Amen, Amen!

Robert Burns

WHAT MR. ROBINSON THINKS

Guvener B. is a sensible man;
  He stays to his home an' looks arter his folks;
He draws his furrer ez straight ez he can,
  An' into nobody's tater-patch pokes;
      But John P.
      Robinson he
Sez he wun't vote fer Guvener B.

My! ain't it terrible? Wut shall we du?
  We can't never choose him o' course, — thet's flat;
Guess we shall hev to come round (don't you?)
  An' go in fer thunder an' guns, an' all that;
      Fer John P.
      Robinson he
Sez he wun't vote fer Guvener B.

Gineral C. is a dreffle smart man:
  He's ben on all sides thet give places or pelf;
But consistency still wuz a part of his plan, —
  He's ben true to *one* party, — an' thet is himself; —
      So John P.
        Robinson he
Sez he shall vote fer Gineral C.

Gineral C. he goes in fer the war;
  He don't vally principle more'n an old cud;
Wut did God make us raytional creeturs fer,
  But glory an' gunpowder, plunder an' blood?
      So John P.
        Robinson he
Sez he shall vote fer Gineral C.

We were gittin' on nicely up here to our village,
  With good old idees o' wut's right an' wut ain't,
We kind o' thought Christ went agin war an' pillage,
  An' thet eppyletts worn't the best mark of a saint;
      But John P.
        Robinson he
Sez this kind o' thing's an exploded idee.

The side of our country must ollers be took,
  An' President Polk, you know, *he* is our country.
An' the angel thet writes all our sins in a book
  Puts the *debit* to him, an' to us the *per contry;*
      An' John P.
        Robinson he
Sez this is his view o' the thing to a T.

Parson Wilbur he calls all these argimunts lies;
  Sez they're nothin' on airth but jest *fee, faw, fum:*
An' thet all this big talk of our destinies
  Is half on it ign'ance, an' t'other half rum;
      But John P.
        Robinson he
Sez it ain't no sech thing; an', of course, so must we.

Parson Wilbur sez *he* never heerd in his life
  Thet th' Apostles rigged out in their swaller-tail coats,

An' marched round in front of a drum an' a fife,
  To git some on 'em office, and some on 'em votes;
      But John P.
      Robinson he
  Sez they didn't know everythin' down in Judee.

Wal, it's a marcy we've gut folks to tell us
  The rights an' the wrongs o' these matters, I vow, —
God sends country lawyers, an' other wise fellers,
  To start the world's team wen it gits in a slough;
      Fer John P.
      Robinson he
  Sez the world'll go right, ef he hollers out Gee!
                                James Russell Lowell

THE DIVERTING HISTORY OF JOHN GILPIN

SHOWING HOW HE WENT FARTHER THAN HE INTENDED
AND CAME SAFE HOME AGAIN

John Gilpin was a citizen of credit and renown;
A train-band captain eke was he, of famous London town.

John Gilpin's spouse said to her dear — "Though wedded
  we have been
These twice ten tedious years, yet we no holiday have seen.

"To-morrow is our wedding-day, and we will then repair
Unto the Bell at Edmonton all in a chaise and pair.

"My sister, and my sister's child, myself, and children
  three,
Will fill the chaise; so you must ride on horseback after
  we."

He soon replied, "I do admire of womankind but one,
And you are she, my dearest dear; therefore it shall be
  done.

"I am a linendraper bold, as all the world doth know;
And my good friend, the calender, will lend his horse to
  go."

Quoth Mrs. Gilpin, " That's well said; and, for that wine
 is dear,
We will be furnished with our own, which is both bright
 and clear."

John Gilpin kissed his loving wife; o'erjoyed was he to
 find
That, though on pleasure she was bent, she had a frugal
 mind.

The morning came, the chaise was brought, but yet was not
 allowed
To drive up to the door, lest all should say that she was
 proud.

So three doors off the chaise was stayed, where they did
 all get in —
Six precious souls, and all agog to dash through thick and
 thin.

Smack went the whip, round went the wheels — were never
 folks so glad;
The stones did rattle underneath, as if Cheapside were mad.

John Gilpin at his horse's side seized fast the flowing
 mane,
And up he got, in haste to ride — but soon came down
 again:

For saddletree scarce reached had he, his journey to begin,
When, turning round his head, he saw three customers
 come in.

So down he came: for loss of time, although it grieved
 him sore,
Yet loss of pence, full well he knew, would trouble him
 much more.

'Twas long before the customers were suited to their mind;
When Betty, screaming, came down-stairs — " The wine is
 left behind!"

"Good lack!" quoth he — "yet bring it me, my leathern
    belt likewise,
In which I wear my trusty sword when I do exercise."

Now Mistress Gilpin (careful soul!) had two stone bottles
    found,
To hold the liquor that she loved, and keep it safe and
    sound.

Each bottle had a curling ear, through which the belt he
    drew,
And hung a bottle on each side to make his balance true.

Then over all, that he might be equipped from top to toe,
His long red cloak, well brushed and neat, he manfully did
    throw.

Now see him mounted once again upon his nimble steed,
Full slowly pacing o'er the stones, with caution and good
    heed.

But finding soon a smoother road beneath his well-shod
    feet,
The snorting beast began to trot, which galled him in his
    seat.

So, "Fair and softly," John he cried, but John he cried in
    vain;
That trot became a gallop soon, in spite of curb and rein.

So stooping down, as needs he must who cannot sit up-
    right,
He grasped the mane with both his hands, and eke with all
    his might.

His horse, who never in that sort had handled been before,
What thing upon his back had got did wonder more and
    more.

Away went Gilpin, neck or nought; away went hat and
    wig;
He little dreamt, when he set out, of running such a rig.

The wind did blow — the cloak did fly, like streamer long
 and gay;
Till, loop and button failing both, at last it flew away.

Then might all people well discern the bottles he had
 slung —
A bottle swinging at each side, as hath been said or sung.

The dogs did bark, the children screamed, up flew the windows all;
And every soul cried out, " Well done ! " as loud as he
 could bawl.

Away went Gilpin — who but he? His fame soon spread
 around —
" He carries weight ! he rides a race ! 'Tis for a thousand
 pound ! "

And still as fast as he drew near, 'twas wonderful to view
How in a trice the turnpike men their gates wide open
 threw.

And now, as he went bowing down his reeking head full
 low,
The bottles twain behind his back were shattered at a blow.

Down ran the wine into the road, most piteous to be seen,
Which made his horse's flanks to smoke as they had basted
 been.

But still he seemed to carry weight, with leathern girdle
 braced;
For all might see the bottle necks still dangling at his
 waist.

Thus all through merry Islington these gambols did he
 play,
Until he came unto the Wash of Edmonton so gay;

And there he threw the wash about on both sides of the
 way,
Just like unto a trundling mop, or a wild goose at play.

At Edmonton his loving wife from the balcony spied
Her tender husband, wondering much to see how he did
    ride.

"Stop, stop, John Gilpin! here's the house," they all at
    once did cry;
"The dinner waits, and we are tired." Said Gilpin —
    "So am I!"

But yet his horse was not a whit inclined to tarry there;
For why? — his owner had a house full ten miles off, at
    Ware.

So like an arrow swift he flew, shot by an archer strong:
So did he fly — which brings me to the middle of my song.

Away went Gilpin out of breath, and sore against his will,
Till at his friend the calender's his horse at last stood still.

The calender, amazed to see his neighbor in such trim,
Laid down his pipe, flew to the gate, and thus accosted
    him:

"What news? what news? your tidings tell; tell me you
    must and shall —
Say why bareheaded you are come, or why you come at
    all?"

Now Gilpin had a pleasant wit, and loved a timely joke;
And thus unto the calender in merry guise he spoke:

"I came because your horse would come; and, if I well
    forebode,
My hat and wig will soon be here, they are upon the road."

The calender, right glad to find his friend in merry pin,
Returned him not a single word, but to the house went in;

Whence straight he came with hat and wig: a wig that
    flowed behind,
A hat not much the worse for wear — each comely in its
    kind.

*" ' Stop, stop, John Gilpin! here's the house,' they
all at once did cry."*

He held them up, and in his turn thus showed his ready
wit —
"My head is twice as big as yours, they therefore needs
must fit.

"But let me scrape the dirt away that hangs upon your
face,
And stop and eat, for well you may be in a hungry case."

Said John, "It is my wedding-day, and all the world would
stare,
If wife should dine at Edmonton, and I should dine at
Ware."

So, turning to his horse, he said, "I am in haste to dine;
'Twas for your pleasure you came here — you shall go back
for mine."

Ah, luckless speech, and bootless boast, for which he paid
full dear!
For, while he spake, a braying ass did sing most loud and
clear;

Whereat his horse did snort, as he had heard a lion roar,
And galloped off with all his might, as he had done before.

Away went Gilpin, and away went Gilpin's hat and wig:
He lost them sooner than at first, for why? — they were too
big.

Now Mistress Gilpin, when she saw her husband posting
down
Into the country far away, she pulled out half a crown;

And thus unto the youth she said, that drove them to the
Bell,
"This shall be yours when you bring back my husband safe
and well."

The youth did ride, and soon did meet John coming back
amain —
Whom in a trice he tried to stop, by catching at his **rein;**

But not performing what he meant, and gladly would have
    done,
The frighted steed he frighted more, and made him faster
    run.

Away went Gilpin, and away went post-boy at his heels,
The post-boy's horse right glad to miss the lumbering of
    the wheels.

Six gentlemen upon the road, thus seeing Gilpin fly,
With post-boy scampering in the rear, they raised the hue
    and cry:

"Stop thief! stop thief! — a highwayman!" Not one of
    them was mute;
And all and each that passed that way did join in the pur-
    suit.

And now the turnpike gates again flew open in short space;
The tollmen thinking, as before, that Gilpin rode a race.

And so he did, and won it, too, for he got first to town;
Nor stopped till where he had got up he did again get
    down.

Now let us sing, long live the king! and Gilpin, long live
    he;
And when he next doth ride abroad, may I be there to see!
                             William Cowper

CANDOR [1]

OCTOBER — A WOOD

"I know what you're going to say," she said,
    And she stood up looking uncommonly tall;
    "You are going to speak of the hectic Fall,
And say you're sorry the summer's dead.
    And no other summer was like it, you know,
    And can I imagine what made it so?
Now aren't you, honestly?" "Yes," I said.

[1] From the "Poems of H. C. Bunner," Copyright 1899 by Charles Scribner's
Sons.

"I know what you're going to say," she said;
   "You are going to ask if I forget
   That day in June when the woods were wet,
And you carried me" — here she dropped her head —
   "Over the creek; you are going to say,
   Do I remember that horrid day.
Now aren't you, honestly?" "Yes," I said.

"I know what you're going to say," she said;
   "You are going to say that since that time
   You have rather tended to run to rhyme,
And" — her clear glance fell and her cheek grew red —
   "And have I noticed your tone was queer? —
   Why, everybody has seen it here! —
Now aren't you, honestly?" "Yes," I said.

"I know what you're going to say," I said;
   "You're going to say you've been much annoyed,
   And I'm short of tact — you will say devoid —
And I'm clumsy and awkward, and call me Ted,
   And I bear abuse like a dear old lamb,
   And you'll have me, anyway, just as I am,
Now aren't you, honestly?" "Ye-es," she said.
                     Henry Cuyler Bunner

THE IRISHMAN AND THE LADY

There was a lady liv'd at Leith,
   A lady very stylish, man;
And yet, in spite of all her teeth,
   She fell in love with an Irishman —
     A nasty, ugly Irishman,
     A wild, tremendous Irishman,
A tearing, swearing, thumping, bumping, ranting, roaring
  Irishman.

     His face was no ways beautiful,
       For with small-pox 'twas scarr'd across;
     And the shoulders of the ugly dog
       Were almost double a yard across.

Oh, the lump of an Irishman,
The whiskey-devouring Irishman,
The great he-rogue with his wonderful brogue — the fighting, rioting Irishman!

One of his eyes was bottle-green,
And the other eye was out, my dear;
And the calves of his wicked-looking legs
Were more than two feet about, my dear.
Oh, the great big Irishman,
The rattling, battling Irishman —
The stamping, ramping, swaggering, staggering, leathering
swash of an Irishman!

He took so much of Lundy-foot
That he used to snort and snuffle — O!
And in shape and size the fellow's neck
Was as bad as the neck of a buffalo.
Oh, the horrible Irishman,
The thundering, blundering Irishman —
The slashing, dashing, smashing, lashing, thrashing, hashing Irishman!

His name was a terrible name, indeed,
Being Timothy Thady Mulligan;
And whenever he emptied his tumbler of punch
He'd not rest till he fill'd it full again.
The boosing, bruising Irishman,
The 'toxicated Irishman —
The whiskey, frisky, rummy, gummy, brandy, no dandy
Irishman!

This was the lad the lady lov'd,
Like all the girls of quality;
And he broke the skulls of the men of Leith,
Just by the way of jollity.
Oh, the leathering Irishman,
The barbarous, savage Irishman —
The hearts of the maids, and the gentlemen's heads, were
bothered, I'm sure, by this Irishman!

William Maginn

ST. PATRICK OF IRELAND, MY DEAR!

A fig for St. Denis of France —
  He's a trumpery fellow to brag on;
A fig for St. George and his lance,
  Which spitted a heathenish dragon;
And the saints of the Welshman or Scot
  Are a couple of pitiful pipers,
Both of whom may just travel to pot,
  Compared with that patron of swipers —
    St. Patrick of Ireland, my dear!

He came to the Emerald Isle
  On a lump of a paving-stone mounted;
The steamboat he beat by a mile,
  Which mighty good sailing was counted.
Says he, " The salt water, I think,
  Has made me most bloodily thirsty;
So bring me a flagon of drink
  To keep down the mulligrubs, burst ye!
    Of drink that is fit for a saint! "

He preached, then, with wonderful force,
  The ignorant natives a-teaching;
With a pint he washed down his discourse,
  " For," says he, " I detest your dry preaching."
The people, with wonderment struck
  At a pastor so pious and civil,
Exclaimed — " We're for you, my old buck!
  And we pitch our blind gods to the devil,
    Who dwells in hot water below! "

This ended, our worshipful spoon
  Went to visit an elegant fellow,
Whose practice, each cool afternoon,
  Was to get most delightfully mellow.
That day with a black-jack of beer,
  It chanced he was treating a party;
Says the saint — " This good day, do you hear,
  I drank nothing to speak of, my hearty!
    So give me a pull at the pot! "

The pewter he lifted in sport
  (Believe me, I tell you no fable);
A gallon he drank from the quart,
  And then placed it full on the table.
"A miracle!" every one said —
  And they all took a haul at the stingo;
They were capital hands at the trade,
  And drank till they fell; yet, by jingo,
    The pot still frothed over the brim.

Next day, quoth his host, "'Tis a fast,
  And I've nought in my larder but mutton;
And on Fridays who'd make such repast,
  Except an unchristian-like glutton?"
Says Pat, "Cease your nonsense, I beg —
  What you tell me is nothing but gammon;
Take my compliments down to the leg,
  And bid it come hither a salmon!"
    And the leg most politely complied.

You've heard, I suppose, long ago,
  How the snakes, in a manner most antic,
He marched to the county Mayo,
  And trundled them into th' Atlantic.
Hence, not to use water for drink,
  The people of Ireland determine —
With mighty good reason, I think,
  Since St. Patrick has filled it with vermin
    And vipers, and other such stuff!

Oh, he was an elegant blade
  As you'd meet from Fairhead to Kilcrumper;
And though under the sod he is laid,
  Yet here goes his health in a bumper!
I wish he was here, that my glass
  He might by art magic replenish;
But since he is not — why, alas!
  My ditty must come to a finish, —
    Because all the liquor is out!

William Maginn

" The snakes, in a manner most antic."

HE CAME TO PAY

The editor sat with his head in his hands
And his elbows at rest on his knees;
He was tired of the ever-increasing demands
On his time, and he panted for ease.
The clamor for copy was scorned with a sneer,
And he sighed in the lowest of tones:
"Won't somebody come with a dollar to cheer
The heart of Emanuel Jones?"

Just then on the stairway a footstep was heard
And a rap-a-tap loud at the door,
And the flickering hope that had been long deferred
Blazed up like a beacon once more;
And there entered a man with a cynical smile
That was fringed with a stubble of red,
Who remarked, as he tilted a sorry old tile
To the back of an average head:

"I have come here to pay" — Here the editor cried:
"You're as welcome as flowers in spring!
Sit down in this easy armchair by my side,
And excuse me awhile till I bring
A lemonade dashed with a little old wine
And a dozen cigars of the best . . .
Ah! Here we are! This, I assure you, is fine;
Help yourself, most desirable guest."

The visitor drank with a relish, and smoked
Till his face wore a satisfied glow,
And the editor, beaming with merriment, joked
In a joyous, spontaneous flow;
And then, when the stock of refreshments was gone,
His guest took occasion to say,
In accents distorted somewhat by a yawn,
"My errand up here is to pay — "

But the generous scribe, with a wave of his hand,
Put a stop to the speech of his guest,

And brought in a melon, the finest the land
  Ever bore on its generous breast;
And the visitor, wearing a singular grin,
  Seized the heaviest half of the fruit,
And the juice, as it ran in a stream from his chin,
  Washed the mud of the pike from his boot.

Then, mopping his face on a favorite sheet
  Which the scribe had laid carefully by,
The visitor lazily rose to his feet
  With the dreariest kind of a sigh,
And he said, as the editor sought his address,
  In his books to discover his due:
" I came here to pay — my respects to the press,
  And to borrow a dollar of you! "

                    Andrew V. Kelley ("*Parmenas Mix*")

THE BUMBOAT WOMAN'S STORY

I'm old, my dears, and shrivelled with age, and work and
    grief,
My eyes are gone, and my teeth have been drawn by Time,
    the Thief!
For terrible sights I've seen, and dangers great I've run —
I'm nearly seventy now, and my work is almost done.

Ah! I've been young in my time, and I've played the deuce
    with men!
I'm speaking of ten years past — I was barely sixty then:
My cheeks were mellow and soft, and my eyes were large
    and sweet,
Poll Pineapple's eyes were the standing toast of the Royal
    Fleet.

A bumboat woman was I, and I faithfully served the ships
With apples and cakes, and fowls and beer, and halfpenny
    dips,
Ard beef for the generous mess, where the officers dine at
    nights,
And fine fresh peppermint drops for the rollicking midship-
    mites.

Of all the kind commanders who anchored in Portsmouth
   Bay,
By far the sweetest of all was kind Lieutenant Belaye.
Lieutenant Belaye commanded the gunboat, *Hot Cross Bun*,
She was seven and thirty feet in length, and she carried a
   gun.

With the laudable view of enhancing his country's naval
   pride,
When people inquired her size, Lieutenant Belaye replied,
"Oh, my ship, my ship is the first of the Hundred and
   Seventy-ones!"
Which meant her tonnage, but people imagined it meant her
   guns.

Whenever I went on board he would beckon me down
   below,
"Come down, Little Buttercup, come" (for he loved to
   call me so),
And he'd tell of the fights at sea in which he'd taken a
   part,
And so Lieutenant Belaye won poor Poll Pineapple's heart!

But at length his orders came, and he said one day, said he,
"I'm ordered to sail with the *Hot Cross Bun* to the German
   Sea."
And the Portsmouth maidens wept when they learnt the
   evil day,
For every Portsmouth maid loved good Lieutenant Belaye.

And I went to a back back street, with plenty of cheap
   cheap shops,
And I bought an oilskin hat, and a second-hand suit of
   slops,
And I went to Lieutenant Belaye (and he never suspected
   me!)
And I entered myself as a chap as wanted to go to sea.

We sailed that afternoon at the mystic hour of one, —
Remarkably nice young men were the crew of the *Hot
   Cross Bun*.

I'm sorry to say that I've heard that sailors sometimes
    swear,
But I never yet heard a *Bun* say anything wrong, I declare.

When Jack Tars meet, they meet with a " Messmate, ho!
    What cheer? "
But here, on the *Hot Cross Bun,* it was " How do you do,
    my dear? "
When Jack Tars growl, I believe they growl with a big
    big D—,
But the strongest oath of the *Hot Cross Bun* was a mild
    " Dear me! "

Yet, though they were all well-bred, you could scarcely call
    them slick:
Whenever a sea was on, they were all extremely sick;
And whenever the weather was calm, and the wind was light
    and fair,
They spent more time than a sailor should on his back
    back hair.

They certainly shivered and shook when ordered aloft to
    run,
And they screamed when Lieutenant Belaye discharged his
    only gun,
And as he was proud of his gun — such pride is hardly
    wrong —
The Lieutenant was blazing away at intervals all day long.

They all agreed very well, though at times you heard it
    said
That Bill had a way of his own of making his lips look
    red —
That Joe looked quite his age — or somebody might de-
    clare
That Barnacle's long pig-tail was never his own own hair.

Belaye would admit that his men were of no great use to
    him,
" But then," he would say, " there is little to do on a gun-
    boat trim.
I can hand, and reef, and steer, and fire my big gun, too —
And it is such a treat to sail with a gentle well-bred crew."

I saw him every day! How the happy moments sped!
Reef topsails! Make all taut! There's dirty weather ahead!
(I do not mean that tempest threatened the *Hot Cross
    Bun;*
In *that* case, I don't know whatever we *should* have done!)

After a fortnight's cruise, we put into port one day,
And off on leave for a week went kind Lieutenant Belaye,
And after a long long week had passed (and it seemed like
    a life),
Lieutenant Belaye returned to his ship with a fair young
    wife!

He up and he says, says he, " O crew of the *Hot Cross Bun,*
Here is the wife of my heart, for the Church has made us
    one ! "
And as he uttered the word, the crew went out of their
    wits,
And all fell down in so many separate fainting fits.

And then their hair came down, or off, as the case might
    be,
And lo! the rest of the crew were simple girls, like me,
Who all had fled from their homes in a sailor's blue array,
To follow the shifting fate of kind Lieutenant Belaye.

.   .   .   .

It's strange to think that *I* should ever have loved young
    men,
But I'm speaking of ten years past — I was barely sixty
    then,
And now my cheeks are furrowed with grief and age, I
    trow!
And poor Poll Pineapple's eyes have lost their lustre now!
                                    William S. Gilbert

THE WIFE

Her washing ended with the day,
    Yet lived she at its close,
And passed the long, long night away
    In darning ragged hose.

But when the sun in all its state
   Illumed the Eastern skies,
She passed about the kitchen grate
   And went to making pies.

Phœbe Cary

BEHAVE YOURSEL' BEFORE FOLK

  Behave yoursel' before folk,
  Behave yoursel' before folk;
And dinna be sae rude to me,
  As kiss me sae before folk.

It wadna gie me meikle pain,
Gin we were seen and heard by nane,
To tak' a kiss, or grant you ane;
  But guidsake! no before folk.
    Behave yoursel' before folk,
    Behave yoursel' before folk;
  Whate'er ye do, when out o' view,
    Be cautious aye before folk.

Consider, lad, how folk will crack,
And what a great affair they'll mak'
O' naething but a simple smack,
  That's gi'en or ta'en before folk.
    Behave yoursel' before folk,
    Behave yoursel' before folk;
  Nor gie the tongue o' auld or young
    Occasion to come o'er folk.

It's no through hatred o' a kiss,
That I sae plainly tell you this;
But, losh! I tak' it sair amiss
  To be sae teased before folk.
    Behave yoursel' before folk,
    Behave yoursel' before folk;
  When we're our lane ye may tak' ane,
    But fient a ane before folk.

I'm sure wi' you I've been as free
As ony modest lass should be;
But yet it doesna do to see
  Sic freedom used before folk.
    Behave yoursel' before folk,
    Behave yoursel' before folk;
  I'll ne'er submit again to it —
    So mind you that — before folk.

Ye tell me that my face is fair;
It may be sae — I dinna care —
But ne'er again gar't blush sae sair
  As ye hae done before folk.
    Behave yoursel' before folk,
    Behave yoursel' before folk;
  Nor heat my cheeks wi' your mad freaks,
    But aye be douce before folk.

Ye tell me that my lips are sweet,
Sic tales, I doubt, are a' deceit;
At ony rate, it's hardly meet
  To pree their sweets before folk.
    Behave yoursel' before folk,
    Behave yoursel' before folk;
  Gin that's the case, there's time, and place,
    But surely no before folk.

But, gin you really do insist
That I should suffer to be kiss'd,
Gae, get a license frae the priest,
  And mak' me yours before folk.
    Behave yoursel' before folk,
    Behave yoursel' before folk;
  And when we're ane, baith flesh and bane,
    Ye may tak' ten — before folk.
                            Alexander Rodger

GENTLE ALICE BROWN

It was a robber's daughter, and her name was Alice Brown,
Her father was the terror of a small Italian town;
Her mother was a foolish, weak, but amiable old thing;
But it isn't of her parents that I'm going for to sing.

As Alice was a-sitting at her window-sill one day,
A beautiful young gentleman he chanced to pass that way;
She cast her eyes upon him, and he looked so good and true,
That she thought, " I could be happy with a gentleman like
    you! "

And every morning passed her house that cream of gentle-
    men,
She knew she might expect him at a quarter unto ten;
A sorter in the Custom-house, it was his daily road
(The Custom-house was fifteen minutes' walk from her
    abode).

For Alice was a pious girl, who knew it wasn't wise
To look at strange young sorters with expressive purple
    eyes;
So she sought the village priest to whom her family con-
    fessed,
The priest by whom their little sins were carefully assessed.

" Oh, holy father," Alice said, " 'twould grieve you, would it
    not,
To discover that I was a most disreputable lot?
Of all unhappy sinners I'm the most unhappy one! "
The padre said, " Whatever have you been and gone and
    done? "

" I have helped mamma to steal a little kiddy from its dad,
I've assisted dear papa in cutting up a little lad,
I've planned a little burglary and forged a little cheque,
And slain a little baby for the coral on its neck! "

The worthy pastor heaved a sigh, and dropped a silent tear,
And said, "You mustn't judge yourself too heavily, my
    dear:
It's wrong to murder babies, little corals for to fleece;
But sins like these one expiates at half-a-crown apiece.

"Girls will be girls — you're very young, and flighty in
    your mind;
Old heads upon young shoulders we must not expect to
    find:
We mustn't be too hard upon these little girlish tricks.
Let's see — five crimes at half-a-crown — exactly twelve-
    and-six."

"Oh, father," little Alice cried, "your kindness makes me
    weep,
You do these little things for me so singularly cheap —
Your thoughtful liberality I never can forget;
But, oh! There is another crime I haven't mentioned yet!

"A pleasant-looking gentleman, with pretty purple eyes,
I've noticed at my window, as I've sat a-catching flies;
He passes by it every day as certain as can be —
I blush to say I've winked at him, and he has winked at
    me!"

"For shame!" said Father Paul, "my erring daughter!
    On my word
This is the most distressing news that I have ever heard.
Why, naughty girl, your excellent papa has pledged your
    hand
To a promising young robber, the lieutenant of his band!

"This dreadful piece of news will pain your worthy parents
    so!
They are the most remunerative customers I know;
For many many years they've kept starvation from my
    doors:
I never knew so criminal a family as yours!

"The common country folk in this insipid neighborhood
Have nothing to confess, they're so ridiculously good;

And if you marry any one respectable at all,
Why, you'll reform, and what will then become of Father
      Paul? "

The worthy priest, he up and drew his cowl upon his
      crown,
And started off in haste to tell the news to Robber Brown —
To tell him how his daughter, who was now for marriage
      fit,
Had winked upon a sorter, who reciprocated it.

Good Robber Brown, he muffled up his anger pretty well:
He said, "I have a notion, and that notion I will tell;
I will nab this gay young sorter, terrify him into fits,
And get my gentle wife to chop him into little bits.

"I've studied human nature, and I know a thing or two;
Though a girl may fondly love a living gent, as many do,
A feeling of disgust upon her senses there will fall
When she looks upon his body chopped particularly small."

He traced that gallant sorter to a still suburban square;
He watched his opportunity, and seized him unaware;
He took a life-preserver and he hit him on the head,
And Mrs. Brown dissected him before she went to bed.

And pretty little Alice grew more settled in her mind,
She never more was guilty of a weakness of the kind,
Until at length good Robber Brown bestowed her pretty
      hand
On the promising young robber, the lieutenant of his band.
                            William S. Gilbert

THE POSTER-GIRL

The blessed Poster-girl leaned out
    From a pinky-purple heaven;
One eye was red and one was green;
    Her bang was cut uneven;
She had three fingers on her hand,
    And the hairs on her head were seven.

Her robe, ungirt from clasp to hem,
  No sunflowers did adorn;
But a heavy Turkish portière
  Was very neatly worn;
And the hat that lay along her back
  Was yellow like canned corn.

It was a kind of wobbly wave
  That she was standing on,
And high aloft she flung a scarf
  That must have weighed a ton;
And she was rather tall — at least
  She reached up to the sun.

She curved and writhed, and then she said,
  Less green of speech than blue:
"Perhaps I *am* absurd — perhaps
  I *don't* appeal to you;
But my artistic worth depends
  Upon the point of view."

I saw her smile, although her eyes
  Were only smudgy smears;
And then she swished her swirling arms,
  And wagged her gorgeous ears,
She sobbed a blue-and-green-checked sob,
  And wept some purple tears.

                    Carolyn Wells

THE ARAB

On, on, my brown Arab, away, away!
Thou hast trotted o'er many a mile to-day,
And I trow right meagre hath been thy fare
Since they roused thee at dawn from thy straw-piled lair,
To tread with those echoless unshod feet
Yon weltering flats in the noontide heat,
Where no palm-tree proffers a kindly shade
And the eye never rests on a cool grass blade;
And lank is thy flank, and thy frequent cough
Oh! it goes to my heart — but away, friend, off!

And yet, ah! what sculptor who saw thee stand,
As thou standest now, on thy Native Strand,
With the wild wind ruffling thine uncomb'd hair,
And thy nostrils upturn'd to the od'rous air,
Would not woo thee to pause till his skill might trace
At leisure the lines of that eager face;
The collarless neck and the coal-black paws
And the bit grasp'd tight in the massive jaws;
The delicate curve of the legs, that seem
Too slight for their burden — and, oh, the gleam
Of that eye, so sombre and yet so gay!
Still away, my lithe Arab, once more away!

Nay, tempt me not, Arab, again to stay;
Since I crave neither Echo nor Fun to-day.
For thy *hand* is not Echoless — there they are —
Fun, Glowworm, and Echo, and Evening Star:
And thou hintest withal that thou fain would'st shine,
As I con them, these bulgy old boots of mine.
But I shrink from thee, Arab! Thou eatest eel-pie,
Thou evermore hast at least one black eye;
There is brass on thy brow, and thy swarthy hues
Are due not to nature but handling shoes;
And the bit in thy mouth, I regret to see,
Is a bit of tobacco-pipe — Flee, child, flee!

Charles Stuart Calverley

THE PRAYER OF CYRUS BROWN

" The proper way for a man to pray,"
    Said Deacon Lemuel Keyes,
" And the only proper attitude
    Is down upon his knees."

" No, I should say the way to pray,"
    Said Rev. Doctor Wise,
" Is standing straight with outstretched arms
    And rapt and upturned eyes."

" Oh, no; no, no," said Elder Slow,
    " Such posture is too proud:

A man should pray with eyes fast closed
And head contritely bowed."

"It seems to me his hands should be
   Austerely clasped in front,
With both thumbs pointing toward the ground,"
   Said Rev. Doctor Blunt.

"Las' year I fell in Hodgkin's well
   Head first," said Cyrus Brown,
"With both my heels a-stickin' up,
   My head a-pinting down;

"An' I made a prayer right then an' there —
   Best prayer I ever said,
The prayingest prayer I ever prayed,
   A-standing on my head."

                          Sam Walter Foss

PADDY O'RAFTHER

Paddy, in want of a dinner one day,
Credit all gone, and no money to pay,
Stole from a priest a fat pullet, they say,
   And went to confession just afther;
"Your riv'rince," says Paddy, "I stole this fat hen."
"What, what!" says the priest, "at your ould thricks
   again?
Faith, you'd rather be staalin' than sayin' *amen,*
             Paddy O'Rafther!"

"Sure, you wouldn't be angry," says Pat, "if you knew
That the best of intintions I had in my view —
For I stole it to make it a present to you,
   And you can absolve me afther."
"Do you think," says the priest, "I'd partake of your theft?
Of your seven small senses you must be bereft —
You're the biggest blackguard that I know, right and left,
             Paddy O'Rafther."

" Then what shall I do with the pullet," says Pat,
" If your riv'rince won't take it? By this and by that
I don't know no more than a dog or a cat
   What your riv'rince would have me be afther."
"Why, then," says his rev'rence, " you sin-blinded owl,
Give back to the man that you stole from his fowl:
For if you do not, 'twill be worse for your sowl,
            Paddy O'Rafther."

Says Paddy, " I ask'd him to take it — 'tis thrue
As this minit I'm talkin', your riv'rince, to you;
But he wouldn't resaive it — so what can I do? "
   Says Paddy, nigh choken with laughter.
" By my throth," says the priest, " but the case is absthruse;
If he won't take his hen, why the man is a goose:
'Tis not the first time my advice was no use,
            Paddy O'Rafther.

"But, for sake of your sowl, I would sthrongly advise
To some one in want you would give your supplies —
Some widow, or orphan, with tears in their eyes;
   And *then* you may come to *me* afther."
So Paddy went off to the brisk Widow Hoy,
And the pullet between them was eaten with joy,
And, says she, " 'Pon my word you're the cleverest boy,
            Paddy O'Rafther! "

Then Paddy went back to the priest the next day,
And told him the fowl he had given away
To a poor lonely widow, in want and dismay,
   The loss of her spouse weeping afther.
"Well, now," says the priest, " I'll absolve you, my lad,
For repentantly making the best of the bad,
In feeding the hungry and cheering the sad,
            Paddy O'Rafther! "
                Samuel Lover

SOME HALLUCINATIONS

He thought he saw an Elephant,
    That practised on a fife:
He looked again, and found it was
    A letter from his wife.
" At length I realize," he said,
    " The bitterness of Life!"

He thought he saw a Buffalo
    Upon the chimneypiece:
He looked again, and found it was
    His Sister's Husband's Niece.
" Unless you leave this house," he said,
    " I'll send for the Police!"

He thought he saw a Rattlesnake
    That questioned him in Greek:
He looked again, and found it was
    The Middle of Next Week.
" The one thing I regret," he said,
    " Is that it cannot speak!"

He thought he saw a Banker's Clerk
    Descending from the 'bus:
He looked again, and found it was
    A Hippopotamus.
" If this should stay to dine," he said,
    " There won't be much for us!"

                                Lewis Carroll

THE CHIMPANZOR AND THE CHIMPANZEE

One Balaam Vermicelli Lepidoptera FitzApe
(Zoological Professor in a College at the Cape),
As a competent authority is quoted even now,
As the Royal Zoological Society allow.

Without ever introducing any element of chance,
He could tell an armadillo from a spider at a glance;
A beetle from a buffalo, a lobster from a leech,
And he knew the scientific terminology for each.

And he hesitated rarely to pronounce upon the spot
Whether any given object was an animal or not;
He was clever at comparative anatomy — he knew
The aurora borealis from the common cockatoo.

He studied perseveringly, and had,.so people said,
For a work on entomology material in his head;
But he left it there to germinate, and hopefully began
To investigate the question of the origin of man.

Humanity descended, as he confidently showed,
From the ape, the sloth, the otter, the chameleon, and the
    toad;
And the latter from a tadpole, which was only head and
    tail,
And whose parents were respectively a minnow and a snail.

Those who noted his appearance were contented to agree
That such, for anything they knew, was his ancestral tree;
His claim to such progenitors they scrupled to condemn,
But the Adam and the Eve descent was good enough for
    them.

He said, " The use of weapons is depriving man of nails;
For the element of artificiality prevails.
The nails of men — no longer claws — grow softer every
    day :
And even those of women have a tendency that way.

" Abnormally hirsute myself, I think it only fair
To publish the humiliating theory that hair
Is a remnant of the monkey — as the ' mannikin ' is called;
And men of real intellect are generally bald."

He started for the central parts of Africa, and he
Found the hairier inhabitants the further from the sea,
Till finally he came upon a most undoubted ape,
Which resembled him remarkably in feature and in shape.

It possessed the human instincts in a marvellous degree;
It could readily distinguish between alcohol and tea,
And developed such a fancy for the former of the two,
That it followed him to Cape Town, where he put it in the
    Zoo.

He delivered then a lecture to the *savants* of the place,
And they said it served to illustrate his theory of race.
He dressed it up in clothes of his, which seemed to make it
    proud,
And it smoked, and drank, and chattered, and attracted
    quite a crowd.

The two were seldom separate — the Doctor and his prize —
And the latter soon was looking preternaturally wise;
For the sake of wearing glasses, it had feigned its sight
    was dim;
For in everything conceivable it imitated him.

" Observe this cultured creature," said FitzApe, " and, if
    you can,
Discriminate at sight between the monkey and the man."
But as they looked from it to him, and then from him to it,
They declared themselves unable to discriminate a bit.

" I now shall bring it home," he said, " to stay with me a
    week;
And, before that time is over, I'll have taught it how to
    speak.
I've had a cage constructed in my study, though indeed
For such coercive measures there's no longer any need."

The Professor and his *protégé* were sitting, after tea,
Enjoying some Havannahs, and liqueurs of *eau de vie*,
When the animal was seized with such ungovernable rage
That the man suspected violence, and got into the cage.

But, further disconcerting the distinguished refugee,
The monkey calmly locked the cage and pocketed the key;
It took the flask of brandy and a bundle of cigars,
And scornfully regarded the Professor through the bars.

It seized its patron's hat and cane, umbrellas, overcoats,
A purse or two of sovereigns, a roll or so of notes;

Then — consulting the barometer — a mackintosh or two,
And, bowing to him more or less respectfully, withdrew.

His friends next morning found him in a pitiable plight;
He said, " Pray let me out of this, I've been locked up all
　　night.
That most inhuman monkey has incarcerated me:
Run after him, and force him to deliver up the key."

Then one of them remarked: "I heard our good Professor
　　tell
That a monkey might articulate, and this one does it well."
Another said, " FitzApe has gone to travel north again,
I met him muffled up last night, and making for the train."

In vain the Doctor pleaded; it was all of no avail.
He said, " The real monkey had a little bit of tail."
But " No," they said, " your friend has gone to bring you
　　home a mate,
And, pending his arrival, you will only have to wait."

MORAL

In starting a menagerie, you safely may assume
That a cage is less commodious than an ordinary room.
So, harbor no phenomenon too like yourself in shape,
Like Balaam Vermicelli Lepidoptera FitzApe.

Edwin Hamilton

A RHYME FOR PRISCILLA

Dear Priscilla, quaint and very
　　Like a modern Puritan,
Is a modest, literary,
　　Merry young American:
Horace she has read, and Bion
　　Is her favorite in Greek;
Shakespeare is a mighty lion
　　In whose den she dares but peek;
Him she leaves to some sage Daniel,
　　Since of lions she's afraid, —

She prefers a playful spaniel,
  Such as Herrick or as Praed;
And it's not a bit satiric
  To confess her fancy goes
From the epic to a lyric
  On a rose.

Wise Priscilla, dilettante,
  With a sentimental mind,
Doesn't deign to dip in Dante,
  And to Milton isn't kind;
L'Allegro, Il Penseroso
  Have some merits she will grant,
All the rest is only so-so, —
  Enter Paradise she can't!
She might make a charming angel
  (And she will if she is good),
But it's doubtful if the change'll
  Make the Epic understood:
Honey-suckling, like a bee she
  Goes and pillages his sweets,
And it's plain enough to see she
  Worships Keats.

Gay Priscilla, — just the person
  For the Locker whom she loves;
What a captivating verse on
  Her neat-fitting gowns or gloves
He could write in catching measure,
  Setting all the heart astir!
And to Aldrich what a pleasure
  It would be to sing of her, —
He, whose perfect songs have won her
  Lips to quote them day by day.
She repeats the rhymes of Bunner
  In a fascinating way,
And you'll often find her lost in —
  She has reveries at times —
Some delightful one of Austin
  Dobson's rhymes.

O Priscilla, sweet Priscilla,
  Writing of you makes me think,

As I burn my brown Manila
  And immortalize my ink,
How well satisfied these poets
  Ought to be with what they do
When, especially, they know it's
  Read by such a girl as you:
I who sing of you would marry
  Just the kind of girl you are, —
One who doesn't care to carry
  Her poetic taste too far, —
One whose fancy is a bright one,
  Who is fond of poems fine,
And appreciates a light one
  Such as mine.

                              Frank Dempster Sherman

MRS. JONES'S PIRATE

A sanguinary pirate sailed upon the Spanish Main
In a rakish-looking schooner which was called the *Mary
    Jane.*
She carried lots of howitzers, and deadly rifled guns,
With shot and shell and powder and percussion caps in
    tons.

The pirate was a homely man, and short and grum and fat;
He wore a wild and awful scowl beneath his slouching hat.
Swords, pistols, and stilettos were arranged around his
    thighs,
And demoniacal glaring was quite common with his eyes.

His heavy black moustaches curled away beneath his nose,
And dropped in elegant festoons about his very toes.
He hardly ever spoke at all; but when such was the case,
His voice, 'twas easy to perceive, was quite a heavy bass.

He was not a serious pirate; and despite his anxious cares,
He rarely went to Sunday-school, and seldom said his
    prayers.
He worshipped lovely woman, and his hope in life was this:
To calm his wild tumultuous soul with pure domestic bliss.

When conversing with his shipmates, he very often swore
That he longed to give up piracy and settle down on shore.
He tired of blood and plunder; of the joys that they could
bring;
He sighed to win the love of some affectionate young thing.

One morning as the *Mary Jane* went bounding o'er the sea
The pirate saw a merchant bark far off upon his lee.
He ordered a pursuit, and spread all sail that he could
spare,
And then went down, in hopeful mood, to shave and curl
his hair.

He blacked his boots and pared his nails and tied a fresh
cravat;
He cleansed his teeth, pulled down his cuffs, and polished
up his hat;
He dimmed with flour the radiance of his fiery red nose,
For, hanging with that vessel's wash, *he saw some ladies'
hose.*

Once more on deck, the stranger's hull he riddled with a
ball,
And yelled, "I say, what bark is that?" In answer to his
call
The skipper on the other boat replied in thunder tones:
"This here's the bark *Matilda,* and her captain's name is
Jones."

The pirate told his bold corsairs to man the jolly-boats,
To board the bark and seize the crew, and slit their tarry
throats,
And then to give his compliments to Captain Jones, and
say
He wished that he and Mrs. Jones would come and spend
the day.

They reached the bark, they killed the crew, they threw
them in the sea,
And then they sought the captain, who was mad as he
could be,
Because his wife — who saw the whole sad tragedy, it
seems —
Made all the ship vociferous with her outrageous screams.

But when the pirate's message came, she dried her streaming
  tears,
And said, although she'd like to come, she had unpleasant
  fears,
That, his social status being very evidently low,
She might meet some common people whom she wouldn't
  care to know.

Her husband's aged father, she admitted, dealt in bones,
But the family descended from the famous Duke de Jones;
And such blue-blooded people, that the rabble might be
  checked,
Had to make their social circle excessively select.

Before she visited his ship she wanted him to say
If the Smythes had recognized him in a social, friendly
  way;
Did the Jonsons ever ask him 'round to their ancestral
  halls?
Was he noticed by the Thomsons? Was he asked to
  Simms's balls?

The pirate wrote that Thomson was his best and oldest
  friend,
That he often stopped at Jonson's when he had a week to
  spend;
As for the Smythes, they worried him with their incessant
  calls;
His very legs were weary with the dance at Simms's balls.

(The scoundrel fibbed most shamelessly. In truth he only
  knew
A lot of Smiths without a y — a most plebeian crew.
His Johnsons used a vulgar h, his Thompsons spelled
  with p,
His Simses had one m, and they were common as could be.)

Then Mrs. Jones mussed up her hair and donned her best
  delaine,
And went with Captain Jones aboard the schooner *Mary
  Jane.*
The pirate won her heart at once by saying, with a smile,
He never saw a woman dressed in such exquisite style.

The pirate's claim to status she was very sure was just
When she noticed how familiarly the Johnsons he dis-
cussed.
Her aristocratic scruples then were quickly laid aside,
And when the pirate sighed at her, reciproc'ly she sighed.

No sooner was the newer love within her bosom born
Than Jones was looked upon by her with hatred and with
scorn.
She said 'twas true his ancestor was famous Duke de Jones,
But she shuddered to remember that his father dealt in
bones.

So then they got at Captain Jones and hacked him with a
sword,
And chopped him into little bits and tossed him overboard.
The chaplain read the service, and the captain of the bark
Before his widow's weeping eyes was gobbled by a shark.

The chaplain turned the prayer-book o'er; the bride took
off her glove;
They swore to honor, to obey, to cherish, and to love.
And, freighted full of happiness, across the ocean's foam
The schooner glided rapidly toward the pirate's home.

And when of ecstasy and joy their hearts could hold no
more,
The pirate dropped his anchor down and rowed his love
ashore.
And as they sauntered up the street he gave his bride a
poke,
And said, "In them there mansions live the friends of
whom I spoke."

She glanced her eye along the plates of brass upon each
door,
And then her anger rose as it had never done before.
She said, "That Johnson has an h! that Thompson has
a p!
The Smith that spells without a y is not the Smith for
me!"

And darkly scowled she then upon that rover of the wave;
"False! false!" she shrieked, and spoke of him as "Monster, traitor, slave!"
And then she wept and tore her hair, and filled the air with groans,
And cursed with bitterness the day she let them chop up Jones.

And when she'd spent on him at last the venom of her tongue,
She seized her pongee parasol and stabbed him in the lung.
A few more energetic jabs were at his heart required,
And then this scand'lous buccaneer rolled over and expired.

Still brandishing her parasol she sought the pirate boat;
She loaded up a gun and jammed her head into its throat;
And fixing fast the trigger, with a string tied to her toe,
She breathed "Mother!" through the touch-hole, and kicked and let her go.

A snap, a fizz, a rumble; some stupendous roaring tones —
And where upon earth's surface was the recent Mrs. Jones?
Go ask the moaning winds, the sky, the mists, the murmuring sea;
Go ask the fish, the coroner, the clams — but don't ask me.

Charles Heber Clark ("Max Adeler")

THE USUAL WAY

There was once a little man, and his rod and line he took,
For he said, "I'll go a-fishing in the neighboring brook."
And it chanced a little maiden was walking out that day,
And they met — in the usual way.

Then he sat him down beside her, and an hour or two went by,
But still upon the grassy brink his rod and line did lie;
"I thought," she shyly whispered, "you'd be fishing all the day!"
And he was — in the usual way.

So he gravely took his rod in hand, and threw the line
    about,
But the fish perceived distinctly that he was not looking
    out;
And he said, "Sweetheart, I love you!" but she said she
    could not stay:
           But she did — in the usual way.

Then the stars came out above them, and she gave a little
    sigh,
As they watched the silver ripples, like the moments, run-
    ning by;
"We must say good-by," she whispered, by the alders old
    and gray,
           And they did — in the usual way.

And day by day beside the stream they wandered to and fro,
And day by day the fishes swam securely down below;
Till this little story ended, as such little stories may,
           Very much — in the usual way.

And now that they are married, do they always bill and
    coo?
Do they never fret and quarrel as other couples do?
Does he cherish her and love her? Does she honor and
    obey?
           Well — they do — in the usual way.
                Frederic E. Weatherley

BALLAD OF THE MERMAID

Der noble Ritter Hugo
  Von Schwillensaufenstein,
Rode out mit shpeer und helmet,
  Und he coom to de panks of de Rhine.

Und oop dere rose a meermaid,
  Vot hadn't got nodings on,
Und she say, "Oh, Ritter Hugo,
  Vhere you goes mit yourself alone?"

Und he says, "I rides in de creenwood
    Mit helmet und mit shpeer,
Till I cooms into ein Gasthaus,
    Und dere I trinks some beer."

Und den outshpoke de maiden
    Vot hadn't got nodings on:
"I ton't dink mooch of beoplesh
    Dat goes mit demselfs alone.

"You'd petter coom down in de wasser,
    Vhere dere's heaps of dings to see,
Und hafe a shplendid tinner
    Und drafel along mit me.

"Dere you sees de fisch a-schwimmin',
    Und you catches dem efery one:"
So sang dis wasser maiden
    Vot hadn't got nodings on.

"Dere ish drunks all full mit money
    In ships dat vent down of old;
Und you helpsh yourself, by dunder!
    To shimmerin' crowns of gold.

"Shoost look at dese shpoons und vatches!
    Shoost see dese diamant rings!
Coom down und fill your bockets,
    Und I'll giss you like efery dings.

"Vot you vantsh mit your schnapps und lager?
    Coom down into der Rhine!
Der ish pottles der Kaiser Charlemagne
    Vonce filled mit gold-red wine!"

Dat fetched him — he shtood all shpell-pound.;
    She pooled his coat-tails down,
She drawed him oonder der wasser,
    De maiden mit nodings on.
                      Charles Godfrey Leland

" I danced last year my first quadrille
With old Sir Geoffrey's daughter."

MY PARTNER

At Cheltenham, where one drinks one's fill,
  Of folly and cold water,
I danced last year my first quadrille
  With old Sir Geoffrey's daughter.
Her cheek with summer's rose might vie,
  When summer's rose is newest;
Her eyes were blue as autumn's sky,
  When autumn's sky is bluest;
And well my heart might deem her one
  Of life's most precious flowers,
For half her thoughts were of its sun,
  And half were of its showers.

I spoke of novels: — " Vivian Grey "
  Was positively charming,
And " Almacks " infinitely gay,
  And " Frankenstein " alarming;
I said " De Vere " was chastely told,
  Thought well of " Herbert Lacy,"
Called Mr. Banim's sketches "bold,"
  And Lady Morgan's " racy; "
I vowed that last new thing of Hook's
  Was vastly entertaining:
And Laura said — " I dote on books,
  Because it's always raining! "

I talked of Music's gorgeous fane;
  I raved about Rossini,
Hoped Renzi would come back again,
  And criticised Pacini;
I wished the chorus-singers dumb,
  The trumpets more pacific,
And eulogized Brocard's *à plomb,*
  And voted Paul " terrific! "
What cared she for Medea's pride,
  Or Desdemona's sorrow?
" Alas! " my beauteous listener sighed,
  " We must have rain to-morrow! "

I told her tales of other lands;
  Of ever-boiling fountains,
Of poisonous lakes and barren sands,
  Vast forests, trackless mountains;
I painted bright Italian skies,
  I lauded Persian roses,
Coined similes for Spanish eyes,
  And jests for Indian noses;
I laughed at Lisbon's love of mass,
  Vienna's dread of treason:
And Laura asked me — where the glass
  Stood, at Madrid, last season.

I broached whate'er had gone its rounds,
  The week before, of scandal;
What made Sir Luke lay down his hounds,
  And Jane take up her Handel;
Why Julia walked upon the heath,
  With the pale moon above her;
Where Flora lost her false front teeth,
  And Anna her falser lover;
How Lord de B. and Mrs. L.
  Had crossed the sea together:
My shuddering partner cried, "*O Ciel!*
  How *could* they, — in such weather?"

Was she a Blue? — I put my trust
  In strata, petals, gases;
A boudoir-pedant? I discussed
  The toga and the fasces:
A Cockney-Muse? I mouthed a deal
  Of folly from "Endymion;"
A saint? I praised the pious zeal
  Of Messrs. Way and Simeon;
A politician? — It was vain
  To quote the morning paper;
The horrid phantoms came again,
  Rain, Hail, and Snow, and Vapor.

Flat flattery was my only chance:
  I acted deep devotion,
Found magic in her every glance,
  Grace in her every motion;

I wasted all a stripling's lore,
  Prayer, passion, folly, feeling;
And wildly looked upon the floor,
  And mildly on the ceiling.
I envied gloves upon her arm
  And shawls upon her shoulder;
And, when my worship was most warm, —
  She — "never found it colder."

I don't object to wealth or land;
  And she will have the giving
Of an extremely pretty hand,
  Some thousands, and a living.
She makes silk purses, broiders stools,
  Sings sweetly, dances finely,
Paints screens, subscribes to Sunday-schools,
  And sits a horse divinely.
But to be linked for life to her! —
  The desperate man who tried it
Might marry a Barometer
  And hang himself beside it!
                 Winthrop Mackworth Praed

WITHOUT AND WITHIN

My coachman, in the moonlight there,
  Looks through the side-light of the door;
I hear him with his brethren swear,
  As I could do, — but only more.

Flattening his nose against the pane,
  He envies me my brilliant lot,
Breathes on his aching fist in vain,
  And dooms me to a place more hot.

He sees me in to supper go,
  A silken wonder by my side,
Bare arms, bare shoulders, and a row
  Of flounces, for the door too wide.

He thinks how happy is my arm,
  'Neath its white-gloved and jewelled load;

And wishes me some dreadful harm,
    Hearing the merry corks explode.

Meanwhile I inly curse the bore
    Of hunting still the same old coon,
And envy him, outside the door,
    The golden quiet of the moon.

The winter wind is not so cold
    As the bright smile he sees me win,
Nor the host's oldest wine so old
    As our poor gabble, sour and thin.

I envy him the rugged prance
    By which his freezing feet he warms,
And drag my lady's chains, and dance,
    The galley-slave of dreary forms.

Oh, could he have my share of din,
    And I his quiet — past a doubt
'Twould still be one man bored within,
    And just another bored without.

                    James Russell Lowell

ON AN OLD MUFF

Time has a magic wand!
What is this meets my hand,
Moth-eaten, mouldy, and
    Cover'd with fluff?
Faded, and stiff, and scant;
Can it be? no, it can't —
Yes, I declare, it's Aunt
    Prudence's Muff!

Years ago, twenty-three,
Old Uncle Doubledee
Gave it to Aunty P.
    Laughing and teasing —
" Pru., of the breezy curls,
Question those solemn churls, —

> *What holds a pretty girl's*
> *Hand without squeezing?"*

Uncle was then a lad
Gay, but, I grieve to add,
Sinful, if smoking bad
   'Baccy's a vice:
Glossy was then this mink
Muff, lined with pretty pink
Satin, which maidens think
" Awfully nice ! "

I seem to see again
Aunt in her hood and train,
Glide, with a sweet disdain,
   Gravely to Meeting:
Psalm-book and kerchief new,
Peep'd from the Muff of Pru.;
Young men, and pious too,
   Giving her greeting.

Sweetly her Sabbath sped
Then; from this muff, it's said,
Tracts she distributed : —
   Converts (till Monday),
Lured by the grace they lack'd,
Follow'd her. One, in fact,
Ask'd for — and got his tract
   Twice of a Sunday!

Love has a potent spell;
Soon this bold *Ne'er-do-well,*
Aunt's too susceptible
   Heart undermining,
Slipt, so the scandal runs,
Notes in the pretty nun's
Muff, triple-corner'd ones,
   Pink as its lining.

Worse follow'd — soon the jade
Fled (to oblige her blade!)
Whilst her friends thought that they'd
   Lock'd her up tightly :

After such shocking games
Aunt is of wedded dames
Gayest, and now her name's
   Mrs. Golightly.

In female conduct flaw
Sadder I never saw,
Faith still I've in the law
   Of compensation.
Once Uncle went astray,
Smoked, joked, and swore away,
Sworn by he's now, by a
   Large congregation.

Changed is the Child of Sin,
Now he's (he once was thin)
Grave, with a double chin, —
   Blest be his fat form!
Changed is the garb he wore,
Preacher was never more
Prized than is Uncle for
   Pulpit or platform.

If all's as best befits
Mortals of slender wits,
Then beg this Muff and its
   Fair owner pardon:
All's for the best, indeed
Such is my simple creed;
Still I must go and weed
   Hard in my garden.

         Frederick Locker-Lampson

THE JIM-JAM KING OF THE JOU-JOUS

AN ARABIAN LEGEND

·(*Translated from the Arabic*)

Far off in the waste of desert sand,
The Jim-jam rules in the Jou-jou land:
He sits on a throne of red-hot rocks,
And moccasin snakes are his curling locks;

And the Jou-jous have the conniption fits
In the far-off land where the Jim-jam sits —
If things are nowadays as things were then.
Allah il Allah! Oo-aye! Amen!

The country's so dry in Jou-jou land
You could wet it down with Sahara sand,
And over its boundaries the air
Is hotter than 'tis — no matter where:
A camel drops down completely tanned
When he crosses the line into Jou-jou land —
If things are nowadays as things were then.
Allah il Allah! Oo-aye! Amen!

A traveller once got stuck in the sand
On the fiery edge of Jou-jou land;
The Jou-jous they confiscated him,
And the Jim-jam tore him limb from limb;
But, dying, he said: "If eaten I am,
I'll disagree with this Dam-jim-jam!
He'll think his stomach's a Hoodoo's den!"
Allah il Allah! Oo-aye! Amen!

Then the Jim-jam felt so bad inside,
It just about humbled his royal pride.
He decided to physic himself with sand,
And throw up his job in the Jou-jou land.
He descended his throne of red-hot rocks,
And hired a barber to cut his locks:
The barber died of the got-'em-again.
Allah il Allah! Oo-aye! Amen!

And now let every good Mussulman
Get all the good from this tale he can.
If you wander off on a Jamboree,
Across the stretch of the desert sea,
Look out that right at the height of your booze
You don't get caught by the Jou-jou-jous!
You may, for the Jim-jam's at it again.
Allah il Allah! Oo-aye! Amen!
                              Alaric Bertrand Start

BEHOLD THE DEEDS!

(*Chant Royal*)

I would that all men my hard case might know;
  How grievously I suffer for no sin:
I, Adolphe Culpepper Furguson, for lo!
  I, of my landlady, am lockèd in,
For being short on this sad Saturday,
Nor having shekels of silver wherewith to pay;
  She has turned and is departed with my key;
  Wherefore, not even as other boarders free,
    I sing (as prisoners to their dungeon stones
  When for ten days they expiate a spree) :
    Behold the deeds that are done of Mrs. Jones!

One night and one day have I wept my woe;
  Nor wot I when the morrow doth begin,
If I shall have to write to Briggs & Co.,
  To pray them to advance the requisite tin
For ransom of their salesman, that he may
Go forth as other boarders go alway —
  As those I hear now flocking from their tea,
  Led by the daughter of my landlady
    Piano-ward. This day for all my moans,
  Dry bread and water have been servèd me.
    Behold the deeds that are done of Mrs. Jones!

Miss Amabel Jones is musical, and so
  The heart of the young he-boardèr doth win,
Playing " The Maiden's Prayer," *adagio* —
  That fetcheth him, as fetcheth the banco skin
The innocent rustic. For my part, I pray:
That Badarjewska maid may wait for aye
  Ere sits she with a lover, as did we
  Once sit together, Amabel! Can it be
    That all that arduous wooing not atones
  For Saturday shortness of trade dollars three?
    Behold the deeds that are done of Mrs. Jones!

Yea! she forgets the arm was wont to go
  Around her waist. She wears a buckle whose pin
Galleth the crook of the young man's elbòw;
  I forget not, for I that youth have been.
Smith was aforetime the Lothario gay.
Yet once, I mind me, Smith was forced to stay
  Close in his room. Not calm, as I, was he;
  But his noise brought no pleasaunce, verily.
    Small ease he gat of playing on the bones,
  Or hammering on his stovepipe, that I see.
    Behold the deeds that are done of Mrs. Jones!

Thou, for whose fear the figurative crow
  I eat, accursed be thou and all thy kin!
Thee will I show up — yea, up will I show
  Thy too thick buckwheats, and thy tea too thin.
Ay! here I dare thee, ready for the fray!
Thou dost *not* " keep a first-class house," I say!
  It does not with the advertisements agree.
  Thou lodgest a Briton with a puggaree,
    And thou hast harbored Jacobses and Cohns,
  Also a Mulligan. Thus denounce I thee!
    Behold the deeds that are done of Mrs. Jones!

Envoy

  Boarders! the worst I have not told to ye:
  She hath stolen my trousers, that I may not flee
    Privily by the window. Hence these groans,
  There is no fleeing in a *robe de nuit.*
    Behold the deeds that are done of Mrs. Jones!
                Henry Cuyler Bunner

HER LITTLE FEET

  Her little feet! . . . Beneath us ranged the sea,
    She sat, from sun and wind umbrella-shaded,
  One shoe above the other danglingly,
    And lo! a Something exquisitely graded,
  Brown rings and white, distracting — to the knee!

The band was loud. A wild waltz melody
   Flowed rhythmic forth. The nobodies paraded.
And thro' my dream went pulsing fast and free:
      Her little feet.

Till she made room for some one. It was He!
   A port-wine flavored He, a He who traded,
Rich, rosy, round, obese to a degree!
A sense of injury overmastered me.
   Quite bulbously his ample boots upbraided
      Her little feet.
            William Ernest Henley

JABBERWOCKY

'Twas brillig, and the slithy toves
   Did gyre and gimble in the wabe:
All mimsy were the borogoves,
   And the mome raths outgrabe.

" Beware the Jabberwock, my son!
   The jaws that bite, the claws that catch!
Beware the Jubjub bird, and shun
   The frumious Bandersnatch! "

He took his vorpal sword in hand;
   Long time the manxome foe he sought.
So rested he by the Tumtum tree,
   And stood awhile in thought.

And as in uffish thought he stood,
   The Jabberwock with eyes of flame,
Came whiffling through the tulgey wood,
   And burbled as it came!

One, two! One, two! And through, and through,
   The vorpal blade went snicker-snack!
He left it dead, and with its head
   He went galumphing back.

" And hast thou slain the Jabberwock?
   Come to my arms, my beamish boy!

Oh, frabjous day! Callooh! Callay!"
  He chortled in his joy.

'Twas brillig, and the slithy toves
  Did gyre and gimble in the wabe:
All mimsy were the borogoves
  And the mome raths outgrabe.

Lewis Carroll

LITTLE MAMMA

• Why is it the children don't love me
          As they do Mamma?
That they put her ever above me —
      "Little Mamma?"
I'm sure I do all that I can do,
What more can a rather big man do,
      Who can't be Mamma —
          Little Mamma?

Any game that the tyrants suggest,
"Logomachy," — which I detest, —
Doll-babies, hop-scotch, or baseball,
I'm always on hand at the call.
When Noah and the others embark,
I'm the elephant saved in the ark.
I creep, and I climb, and I crawl —
By turns am the animals all.
        For the show on the stair
        I'm always the bear,
Chimpanzee, camel, or kangaroo.
        It is never, " Mamma, —
            Little Mamma, —
            Won't *you?* "

My umbrella's the pony, if any —
None ride on Mamma's parasol:
I'm supposed to have always the penny
For bonbons, and beggars, and all.
My room is the one where they clatter —
Am I reading, or writing, what matter!
My knee is the one for a trot,
My foot is the stirrup for Dot.

If his fractions get into a snarl
Who straightens the tangles for Karl?
Who bounds Massachusetts and Maine,
And tries to bound flimsy old Spain?
   Why,
  It is *I*,
    Papa, —
  Not Little Mamma!

That the youngsters are ingrates don't say.
I think they love me — in a way —
As one does the old clock on the stair, —
Any curious, cumbrous affair
That one's used to having about,
And would feel rather lonely without.
I think that they love me, I say,
In a sort of a tolerant way;
   But it's plain that Papa
   Isn't Little Mamma.

Thus when twilight comes stealing anear,
When things in the firelight look queer;
And shadows the playroom enwrap,
They never climb into my lap
And toy with *my* head, smooth and bare,
As they do with Mamma's shining hair;
Nor feel round my throat and my chin
For dimples to put fingers in;
Nor lock my neck in a loving vise,
And say they're " mousies " — that's mice —
   And will nibble my ears,
   Will nibble and bite
With their little mice-teeth, so sharp and so white,
If I do not kiss them this very minute —
Don't-wait-a-bit-but-at-once-begin-it —
   Dear little Papa!
That's what they say and do to Mamma.

If, mildly hinting, I quietly say that
Kissing's a game that more can play at,
They turn up at once those innocent eyes,
And I suddenly learn to my great surprise
   That my face has " prickles " —
   My moustache tickles.

If, storming their camp, I seize a pert shaver,
And take as a right what was asked as a favor,
  It is, " Oh, Papa,
  How horrid you are —
You taste exactly like a cigar! "

But though the rebels protest and pout,
And make a pretence of driving me out,
I hold, after all, the main redoubt, —
Not by force of arms nor the force of will,
But the power of love, which is mightier still.
And very deep in their hearts, I know,
Under the saucy and petulant " Oh,"
The doubtful " Yes," or the naughty " No,"
  They love Papa.

And down in the heart that no one sees,
Where I hold my feasts and my jubilees,
I know that I would not abate one jot
Of the love that is held by my little Dot
Or my great big boy for their little Mamma,
Though out in the cold it crowded Papa.
I would not abate it the tiniest whit,
And I am not jealous the least little bit;
For I'll tell you a secret: Come, my dears,
And I'll whisper it — right-into-your-ears —
  I, too, love Mamma,
  Little Mamma!

      Charles Henry Webb

THE INVENTOR'S WIFE

It's easy to talk of the patience of Job. Humph! Job hed
 nothin' to try him!
Ef *he'd* been married to 'Bijah Brown, folks wouldn't have
 dared come nigh him.
Trials, indeed! Now, I'll tell you what — ef you want to
 be sick of your life,
Jest come and change places with me a spell — for I'm an
 inventor's wife.

And sech inventions! I'm never sure, when I take up my
 coffee-pot,
That 'Bijah hain't ben " improvin' " it, and it mayn't go off
 like a shot.
Why, didn't he make me a cradle once, that would keep
 itself a-rockin';
And didn't it pitch the baby out, and wasn't his head bruised
 shockin'?
And there was his " Patent Peeler," too — a wonderful
 thing, I'll say;
But it hed one fault, — it never stopped till the apple was
 peeled away.
As for locks, and clocks, and mowin' machines, and reapers,
 and all sech trash,
Why, 'Bijah's invented heaps of 'em, but they don't bring in
 no *cash*.
Law! that don't worry him — not at all; he's the aggravatin'est man —
He'll set in his little workshop there, and whistle, and
 think, and plan,
Inventin' a Jew's-harp to go by steam, or a new-fangled
 powder-horn,
While the children's goin' barefoot to schocl, and the weeds
 is chokin' our corn.
When 'Bijah and me kep' company, he warn't like this, you
 know;
Our folks all thought he was dreadful smart — but that was
 years ago.
He was handsome as any pictur then, and he had such a
 glib, bright way —
I never thought that a time would come when I'd rue my
 weddin' day;
But when I've been forced to chop the wood, and tend to
 the farm beside,
And look at 'Bijah a-settin' there, I've jest dropped down
 and cried.
We lost the hull of our turnip crop while he was inventin'
 a gun;
But I counted it one of my marcies when it bu'st before
 'twas done.
So he turned it into a " burglar alarm." It ought to give
 thieves a fright —
'Twould scare an honest man out of his wits ef he sot it
 off at night.

Sometimes I wonder ef 'Bijah's crazy, he does sech cur'ous
    things.
Hev I told you about his bedstead yit? — 'Twas full of
    wheels and springs;
It hed a key to wind it up, and a clock face at the head;
All you did was to turn them hands, and at any hour you
    said,
That bed got up and shook itself, and bounced you on the
    floor,
And then shet up, jest like a box, so you couldn't sleep
    no more.
Wa'al, 'Bijah he fixed it all complete, and he sot it at half-
    past five,
But he hadn't more'n got into it when — dear me! sakes
    alive!
Them wheels began to whizz and whirr. I heerd a fearful
    snap!
And there was that bedstead, with 'Bijah inside, shet up
    jest like a trap!
I screamed, of course, but 'twan't no use, then I worked
    that hull long night
A-tryin' to open the pesky thing. At last I got in a fright;
I couldn't hear his voice inside, and I thought he might be
    dyin';
So I took a crowbar and smashed it in. — There was
    'Bijah, peacefully lyin',
Inventin' a way to git out agin. That was all very well to
    say,
But I don't b'lieve he'd have found it out if I'd left him in
    all day.
Now, sence I've told you my story, do you wonder I'm tired
    of life?
Or think it strange I often wish I warn't an inventor's wife?
                                 Mrs. E. R. Corbett

FATHER WILLIAM

"You are old, Father William," the young man said,
  "And your hair has become very white;
And yet you incessantly stand on your head —
  Do you think, at your age, it is right?"

"In my youth," Father William replied to his son,
  "I feared it might injure the brain;
But now that I'm perfectly sure I have none,
  Why, I do it again and again."

"You are old," said the youth, "as I mentioned before,
  And have grown most uncommonly fat;
Yet you turned a back somersault in at the door —
  Pray, what is the reason of that?"

"In my youth," said the sage, as he shook his gray locks,
  "I kept all my limbs very supple
By the use of this ointment — one shilling the box —
  Allow me to sell you a couple."

"You are old," said the youth, "and your jaws are too weak
  For anything tougher than suet;
Yet you finished the goose, with the bones and the beak;
  Pray, how did you manage to do it?"

"In my youth," said his father, "I took to the law,
  And argued each case with my wife;
And the muscular strength which it gave to my jaw,
  Has lasted the rest of my life."

"You are old," said the youth; "one would hardly suppose
  That your eye was as steady as ever;
Yet you balanced an eel on the end of your nose —
  What made you so awfully clever?"

"I have answered three questions, and that is enough,"
  Said his father; "don't give yourself airs!
Do you think I can listen all day to such stuff?
  Be off, or I'll kick you down-stairs!"

Lewis Carroll

THE AMATEUR ORLANDO

THE RESULT OF THE HUNKY KID'S PLAYING CHARLES THE
WRESTLER

It was an Amateur Dram. Ass.
  (Kind reader, although your
Knowledge of French is not first-class,
  Don't call that Amature),
It was an Amateur Dram. Ass.,
  The which did warfare wage
On the dramatic works of this
  And every other age.

It had a walking gentleman,
  A leading juvenile,
First lady in book-muslin dressed
  With a galvanic smile;
Thereto a singing chambermaid,
  Benignant heavy pa,
And, oh, heavier still was the heavy vill-
  Ain, with his fierce " Ha ! Ha ! "

There wasn't an author from Shakespeare down
  — Or up — to Boucicault,
These amateurs weren't competent
  (S. Wegg) to collar and throw.
And when the winter time came round —
" Season's " a stagier phrase —
The Am. Dram. Ass. assaulted one
  Of the Bard of Avon's plays.

'Twas " As You Like It " that they chose,
  For the leading lady's heart
Was set on playing *Rosalind,*
  Or some other page's part.
And the President of the Am. Dram. Ass.,
  A stalwart dry-goods clerk,
Was cast for *Orlando,* in which rôle
  He felt he'd make his mark.

"I mind me," said the President
   (All thoughtful was his face),
"When *Orlando* was taken by Thingummy
   That *Charles* was played by Mace.
Charles hath not many lines to speak;
   Nay, not a single length —
Oh, if find we can a Mussulman,
   (That is, a man of strength),
And bring him on the stage as *Charles* —
   But, alas, it can't be did —"
"It can," replied the Treasurer;
   "Let's get The Hunky Kid."

This Hunky Kid, of whom they spoke,
   Belonged to the P. R.;
He always had his hair cut short,
   And always had catarrh.
His voice was gruff, his language rough,
   His forehead villainous low,
And 'neath his broken nose a vast
   Expanse of jaw did show.
He was forty-eight about the chest,
   And his forearm at the mid-
Dle measured twenty-one and a half —
   Such was The Hunky Kid!

The Am. Dram. Ass. they have engaged
   This pet of the P. R.;
As *Charles the Wrestler,* he's to be
   A bright particular star.
And when they put the programme out,
   Announce him thus they did, —
Orlando . . . Mr. Romeo Jones
Charles . . . . Mr. T. H. Kidd

. . . The night has come; the house is packed
   From pit to gallery;
As those who through the curtain peep
   Quake inwardly to see.
A squeak's heard in the orchestra,
   The leader draws across
Th' intestines of the agile cat
   The tail of the noble hoss.

All is at sea behind the scenes,
  Why do they fear and funk?
Alas, alas, The Hunky Kid
  Is lamentably drunk!
He's in that most unlovely stage
  Of half intoxication,
When men resent the hint they're tight
  As a personal imputation.

"Ring up! Ring up!" *Orlando* cried,
  " Or we must cut the scene;
For *Charles the Wrestler* is imbued
  With poisonous benzine,
And every moment gets more drunk
  Than he before has been."

. . . The wrestling scene has come, and *Charles*
  Is much disguised in drink;
The stage to him's an inclined plane,
  The footlights make him blink.
Still strives he to act well his part
  Where all the honor lies,
Though Shakespeare would not in his lines
  His language recognize.
Instead of, " Come, where is this young — ? "
  This man of bone and brawn,
He squares himself, and bellows, " Time!
  Fetch your *Orlandos* on! "

" Now Hercules be thy speed, young man,"
  Fair *Rosalind,* said she,
As the two wrestlers in the ring
  They grappled furiously;
But *Charles the Wrestler* had no sense
  Of dramatic propriety.

He seized on Mr. Romeo Jones,
  In Græco-Roman style;
He got what they call a grapevine lock
  On that leading juvenile.
He flung him into the orchestra,
  And the man with the ophicleide,
On whom he fell, he just said — well,
  No matter what, and died!

When once the tiger has tasted blood,
    And found that it is sweet,
He has a habit of killing more
    Than he can possibly eat.
And thus it was that The Hunky Kid
    In his homicidal blindness,
He lifted his hand against *Rosalind*
    Not in the way of kindness.
He chased poor *Celia* off at L.,
    At R. U. E., *Le Beau,*
And he put such a head upon *Duke Fred,*
    In fifteen seconds or so,
That never one of the courtly train
    Might his haughty master know.

.   .   .   .

And that's precisely what came to pass
    Because the luckless carls
Belonging to the Am. Dram. Ass.
    Cast The Hunky Kid for *Charles!*
                    George Thomas Lanigan

AUNT SHAW'S PET JUG

Now there was Uncle Elnathan Shaw,
— Most regular man you ever saw!
Just half-past four in the afternoon
He'd start and whistle that old jig tune,
Take the big blue jug from the but'ry shelf
And trot down cellar, to draw himself
Old cider enough to last him through
The winter ev'nin'. Two quarts would do.
— Just as regular as half-past four
Come round, he'd tackle that cellar door,
As he had for thutty years or more.

And as regular, too, as he took that jug
Aunt Shaw would yap through her old cross mug,
" Now, Nathan, for goodness' sake, take care!
You allus trip on the second stair;

It seems as though you were just possessed
To break that jug. It's the very best
There is in town and you know it, too,
And 'twas left to me by my great-aunt Sue.
For goodness' sake, why don't yer lug
A tin dish down, for ye'll break that jug?"
Allus the same, suh, for thutty years,
Allus the same old twits and jeers
Slammed for the nineteenth thousand time
And still we wonder, my friend, at crime.
But Nathan took it meek's a pup
And the worst he said was, " Please shut up."
You know what the Good Book says befell
The pitcher that went to the old-time well;
Wal, whether 'twas that or his time had come,
Or his stiff old limbs got weak and numb,
Or whether his nerves at last giv' in
To Aunt Shaw's everlasting chin —
One day he slipped on that second stair,
Whirled round and grabbed at the empty air,
And clean to the foot of them stairs, ker-smack,
He bumped on the bulge of his humped old back,
And he'd hardly finished the final bump
When old Aunt Shaw she giv' a jump
And screamed down-stairs as mad's a bug,
" Dod-rot your hide, did ye break my jug?"

Poor Uncle Nathan lay there flat,
Knocked in the shape of an old cocked hat,
But he rubbed his legs, brushed off the dirt,
And found after all that he warn't much hurt.
And he'd saved the jug, for his last wild thought
Had been of that; he might have caught
At the cellar shelves and saved his fall,
But he kept his hands on the jug through all.
And now as he loosed his jealous hug,
His wife just screamed, " Did ye break my jug?"
Not a single word for his poor old bones,
Nor a word when she heard his awful groans,
But the blamed old hard-shell turkle just
Wanted to know if that jug was bust.
Old Uncle Nathan he let one roar,
And he shook his fist at the cellar door;

" Did ye break my jug? " she was yellin' still.
" No, dern yer pelt, but I swow I will."
  And you'd thought that the house was a-going to fall
When the old jug smashed on the cellar wall.

Holman F. Day

AN ELEGY ON THE DEATH OF A MAD DOG

    Good people all, of every sort,
      Give ear unto my song;
    And if you find it wond'rous short
      It cannot hold you long.

    In Islington there was a man,
      Of whom the world might say
    That still a godly race he ran,
      Whene'er he went to pray.

    A kind and gentle heart he had,
      To comfort friends and foes;
    The naked every day he clad,
      When he put on his clothes.

    And in that town a dog was found,
      As many dogs there be,
    Both mongrel, puppy, whelp, and hound,
      And curs of low degree.

    This dog and man at first were friends,
      But when a pique began,
    The dog, to gain his private ends,
      Went mad, and bit the man.

    Around from all the neighboring streets
      The wondering neighbors ran,
    And swore the dog had lost his wits
      To bite so good a man.

    The wound it seemed both sore and sad,
      To every Christian eye:
    And while they swore the dog was mad,
      They swore the man would die.

But soon a wonder came to light,
  That showed the rogues they lied:
The man recovered of the bite,
  The dog it was that died.

Oliver Goldsmith

WOMAN'S WILL

Men, dying, make their wills, but wives
  Escape a work so sad;
Why should they make what all their lives
  The gentle dames have had?

John Godfrey Saxe

A LAWYER'S DAUGHTER

"To me, I swear, you're a volume rare — "
  But she said with judicial look,
"Your oath's not valid at Common Law
  Until you've kissed the Book."

J. H. Thacher

THE ORIGIN OF IRELAND

With due condescension, I'd call your attention
To what I shall mention of Erin so green,
And without hesitation I will show how that nation
Became of creation the gem and the queen.

'Twas early one morning, without any warning,
That Vanus was born in the beautiful say,
And by the same token, and sure 'twas provoking,
Her pinions were soaking and wouldn't give play.

Old Neptune, who knew her, began to pursue her,
In order to woo her — the wicked old Jew —
And almost had caught her atop of the water —
Great Jupiter's daughter! — which never would do.

But Jove, the great janius, looked down and saw Vanus,
And Neptune so heinous pursuing her wild,
And he spoke out in thunder, he'd rend him asunder —
And sure 'twas no wonder — for tazing his child.

A star that was flying hard by him espying,
He caught with small trying, and down let it snap;
It fell quick as winking, on Neptune a-sinking,
And gave him, I'm thinking, a bit of a rap.

That star it was dry land, both low land and high land,
And formed a sweet island, the land of my birth;
Thus plain is the story, that sent down from glory,
Old Erin asthore as the gem of the earth!

Upon Erin nately jumped Vanus so stately,
But fainted, kase lately so hard she was pressed —
Which much did bewilder, but ere it had killed her
Her father distilled her a drop of the best.

That sup was victorious, it made her feel glorious —
A little uproarious, I fear it might prove —
So how can you blame us that Ireland's so famous
For drinking and beauty, for fighting and love?

Anonymous

MY LORD TOMNODDY

My Lord Tomnoddy's the son of an Earl;
His hair is straight, but his whiskers curl:
His Lordship's forehead is far from wide,
But there's plenty of room for the brains inside.
He writes his name with indifferent ease,
He's rather uncertain about the " d's; "
But what does it matter, if three or one,
To the Earl of Fitzdotterel's eldest son?

My Lord Tomnoddy to college went;
Much time he lost, much money he spent;
Rules, and windows, and heads, he broke —
Authorities wink'd — young men will joke!

He never peep'd inside of a book:
In two years' time a degree he took,
And the newspapers vaunted the honors won
By the Earl of Fitzdotterel's eldest son.

My Lord Tomnoddy came out in the world:
Waists were tighten'd and ringlets curl'd.
Virgins languish'd — and matrons smil'd —
'Tis true, his Lordship is rather wild;
In very queer places he spends his life,
There's talk of some children by nobody's wife —
But we mustn't look close into what is done
By the Earl of Fitzdotterel's eldest son.

My Lord Tomnoddy must settle down —
There's a vacant seat in the family town!
('Tis time he should sow his eccentric oats) —
He hasn't the wit to apply for votes:
He cannot e'en learn his election speech,
Three phrases he speaks, a mistake in each!
And then breaks down — but the borough is won
For the Earl of Fitzdotterel's eldest son.

My Lord Tomnoddy prefers the Guards,
(The House is a bore) so, it's on the cards!
My Lord's a Lieutenant at twenty-three,
A Captain at twenty-six is he:
He never drew sword, except on drill;
The tricks of parade he has learnt but ill;
A full-blown Colonel at thirty-one
Is the Earl of Fitzdotterel's eldest son!

My Lord Tomnoddy is thirty-four;
The Earl can last but a few years more.
My Lord in the Peers will take his place:
Her Majesty's councils his words will grace.
Office he'll hold, and patronage sway;
Fortunes and lives he will vote away;
And what are his qualifications? — ONE!
He's the Earl of Fitzdotterel's eldest son.

Robert Barnabas Brough

PALABRAS GRANDIOSAS[1]

AFTER T— B— A—

I lay i' the bosom of the sun,
Under the roses dappled and dun.
I thought of the Sultan Gingerbeer,
In his palace beside the Bendemeer,
With his Affghan guards and his eunuchs blind,
And the harem that stretched for a league behind.
The tulips bent i' the summer breeze,
Under the broad chrysanthemum-trees,
And the minstrel, playing his culverin,
Made for mine ears a merry din.
If I were the Sultan, and he were I,
Here i' the grass he should loafing lie,
And I should bestride my zebra steed,
And ride to the hunt of the centipede:
While the pet of the harem, Dandeline,
Should fill me a crystal bucket of wine,
And the kislar aga, Up-to-Snuff,
Should wipe my mouth when I sighed, " Enough ! "
And the gay court poet, Fearfulbore,
Should sit in the hall when the hunt was o'er,
And chant me songs of silvery tone,
Not from Hafiz, but — mine own!

Ah, wee sweet love, beside me here,
I am not the Sultan Gingerbeer,
Nor you the odalisque Dandeline,
Yet I am yourn, and you are mine!

Bayard Taylor

RORY O'MORE; OR, GOOD OMENS

Young Rory O'More courted Kathleen Bawn,
He was bold as a hawk, — she as soft as the dawn;
He wish'd in his heart pretty Kathleen to please,
And he thought the best way to do that was to tease.

[1] From " The Echo Club."

" Now, Rory, be aisy," sweet Kathleen would cry,
(Reproof on her lip, but a smile in her eye),
" With your tricks I don't know, in troth, what I'm about,
Faith you've teased till I've put on my cloak inside out."
" Oh, jewel," says Rory, " that same is the way
You've thrated my heart for this many a day;
And 'tis plaz'd that I am, and why not to be sure?
For 'tis all for good luck," says bold Rory O'More.

" Indeed, then," says Kathleen, " don't think of the like,
For I half gave a promise to soothering Mike;
The ground that I walk on he loves, I'll be bound."
" Faith," says Rory, " I'd rather love you than the ground."
" Now, Rory, I'll cry if you don't let me go;
Sure I drame ev'ry night that I'm hating you so!"
" Oh," says Rory, " that same I'm delighted to hear,
For drames always go by conthraries, my dear;
Oh! jewel, keep draming that same till you die,
And bright morning will give dirty night the black lie!
And 'tis plaz'd that I am, and why not, to be sure?
Since 'tis all for good luck," says bold Rory O'More.

" Arrah, Kathleen, my darlint, you've teas'd me enough,
Sure I've thrash'd for your sake Dinny Grimes and Jim
    Duff;
And I've made myself, drinking your health, quite a baste,
So I think, after that, I may talk to the praste."
Then Rory, the rogue, stole his arm round her neck,
So soft and so white, without freckle or speck,
And he look'd in her eyes that were beaming with light,
And he kiss'd her sweet lips; — don't you think he was
    right?
" Now, Rory, leave off, sir; you'll hug me no more,
That's eight times to-day you have kiss'd me before."
" Then here goes another," says he, " to make sure,
For there's luck in odd numbers," says Rory O'More.
                                        Samuel Lover

COURTING IN KENTUCKY

When Mary Ann Dollinger got the skule daown thar on
    Injun Bay,
I was glad, fer I like ter see a gal makin' her honest way.
I heerd some talk in the village abaout her flyin' high,
Tew high fer busy farmer folks with chores ter do ter fly;
But I paid no sorter attention ter all the talk ontell
She come in her reg'lar boardin' raound ter visit with us
    a spell.
My Jake an' her had been cronies ever since they could
    walk,
An' it tuk me aback to hear her kerrectin' him in his talk.

Jake ain't no hand at grammar, though he hain't his beat
    for work;
But I sez ter myself, "Look out, my gal, yer a-foolin' with
    a Turk!"
Jake bore it wonderful patient, an' said in a mournful way,
He p'sumed he was behindhand with the doin's at Injun
    Bay.
I remember once he was askin' for some o' my Injun
    buns,
An' she said he should allus say, " them air," stid o' " them
    is " the ones.
Wal, Mary Ann kep' at him stiddy mornin' an' evenin' long,
Tell he dassent open his mouth for fear o' talkin' wrong.

One day I was pickin' currants daown by the old quince-
    tree,
When I heerd Jake's voice a-sayin', " Be yer willin' ter
    marry me?"
An' Mary Ann kerrectin', " Air ye willin' yeou sh'd say; "
Our Jake he put his foot daown in a plum, decided way,
" No wimmen-folks is a-goin' ter be rearrangin' me,
Hereafter I says ' craps,' ' them is,' ' I calk'late,' an' ' I be.'
Ef folks don't like my talk they needn't hark ter what I
    say:
But I ain't a-goin' to take no sass from folks from Injun
    Bay.
I ask you free an' final, ' Be ye goin' ter marry me?' "
An' Mary Ann says, tremblin' yet anxious-like, " I be."

Florence E. Pratt

" She was cutting bread and butter."

OF A BAD SINGER

Swans sing before they die; 'twere no bad thing
Did certain persons die before they sing.
Samuel Taylor Coleridge

EPIGRAM

After such years of dissension and strife,
Some wonder that Peter should weep for his wife:
But his tears on her grave are nothing surprising, —
He's laying her dust, for fear of its rising.
Thomas Hood

SORROWS OF WERTHER

Werther had a love for Charlotte
  Such as words could never utter;
Would you know how first he met her?
  She was cutting bread and butter.

Charlotte was a married lady,
  And a moral man was Werther,
And, for all the wealth of Indies,
  Would do nothing for to hurt her.

So he sighed and pined and ogled,
  And his passion boiled and bubbled,
Till he blew his silly brains out,
  And no more was by it troubled.

Charlotte, having seen his body
  Borne before her on a shutter,
Like a well-conducted person,
  Went on cutting bread and butter.
William Makepeace Thackeray

REFLECTIONS ON CLEOPATHERA'S NEEDLE

So that's Cleopathera's Needle, bedad,
  An' a quare lookin' needle it is, I'll be bound;
What a powerful muscle the queen must have had
  That could grasp such a weapon an' wind it around!

Imagine her sittin' there stitchin' like mad
  Wid a needle like that in her hand! I declare
It's as big as the Round Tower of Slane, an', bedad,
  It would pass for a round tower, only it's square!

The taste of her, ordherin' a needle of granite!
  Begorra, the sight of it sthrikes me quite dumb!
An' look at the quare sort of figures upon it;
  I wondher can these be the thracks of her thumb!

I once was astonished to hear of the faste
  Cleopathera made upon pearls; but now
I declare, I would not be surprised in the laste
  If ye told me the woman had swallowed a cow!

It's aisy to see why bould Cæsar should quail
  In her presence, an' meekly submit to her rule;
Wid a weapon like that in her fist I'll go bail
  She could frighten the sowl out of big Finn MacCool!

But, Lord, what poor pigmies the women are now,
  Compared with the monsthers they must have been then!
Whin the darlin's in those days would kick up a row,
  Holy smoke, but it must have been hot for the men!

Just think how a chap that goes courtin' would start
  If his girl was to prod him wid that in the shins!
I have often seen needles, but bouldly assart
  That the needle in front of me there takes the pins!

O, sweet Cleopathera! I'm sorry you're dead;
  An' whin lavin' this wondherful needle behind
Had ye thought of bequathin' a spool of your thread
  An' yer thimble an' scissors, it would have been kind.

But pace to your ashes, ye plague of great men,
  Yer strength is departed, yer glory is past;
Ye'll never wield sceptre or needle again,
  An' a poor little asp did yer bizzness at last!
Cormac O'Leary

A SAILOR'S APOLOGY FOR BOW - LEGS

There's some is born with their straight legs by natur,
And some is born with bow-legs from the first —
And some that should have growed a good deal straighter,
    But they were badly nursed,
And set, you see, like Bacchus, with their pegs
    Astride of casks and kegs:
I've got myself a sort of bow to larboard,
    And starboard,
And this is what it was that warped my legs. —

'Twas all along of Poll, as I may say,
That fouled my cable when I ought to slip;
    But on the tenth of May,
    When I gets under weigh,
Down there in Hartfordshire, to join my ship,
      I sees the mail
      Get under sail,
The only one there was to make the trip.
      Well — I gives chase,
      But as she run
      Two knots to one,
There warn't no use in keeping on the race!

Well — casting round about, what next to try on,
      And how to spin,
I spies an ensign with a Bloody Lion,
And bears away to leeward for the inn,
      Beats round the gable,
And fetches up before the coach-horse stable:
Well — there they stand, four kickers in a row,
      And so
I just makes free to cut a brown 'un's cable.
But riding isn't in a seaman's natur —
So I whips out a toughish end of yarn,

And gets a kind of sort of a land-waiter
    To splice me, heel to heel,
    Under the she-mare's keel,
And off I goes, and leaves the inn a-starn!

    My eyes! how she did pitch!
And wouldn't keep her own to go in no line,
Though I kept bowsing, bowsing at her bowline,
But always making lee-way to the ditch,
And yawed her head about all sorts of ways.
    The devil sink the craft!
And wasn't she trimendous slack in stays!
We couldn't, no how, keep the inn abaft!
    Well — I suppose
We hadn't run a knot — or much beyond —
(What will you have on it?) — but off she goes,
Up to her bends in a fresh-water pond!
    There I am! — all a-back!
So I looks forward for her bridle-gears,
To heave her head round on the t'other tack;
    But when I starts,
    The leather parts,
And goes away right over by the ears!

    What could a fellow do,
Whose legs, like mine, you know, were in the bilboes,
But trim myself upright for bringing-to,
And square his yard-arms, and brace up his elbows,
    In rig all snug and clever,
Just while his craft was taking in her water?
I didn't like my berth, though, howsomdever,
Because the yarn, you see, kept getting tauter, —
Says I — I wish this job was rather shorter!

    The chase had gained a mile
Ahead, and still the she-mare stood a-drinking:
    Now, all the while
Her body didn't take of course to shrinking.
Says I, she's letting out her reefs, I'm thinking —
    And so she swelled, and swelled,
    And yet the tackle held,
Till both my legs began to bend like winkin.

My eyes! but she took in enough to founder!
And there's my timbers straining every bit,
    Ready to split,
And her tarnation hull a-growing rounder!

        Well, there — off Hartford Ness,
We lay both lashed and water-logged together,
        And can't contrive a signal of distress;
Thinks I, we must ride out this here foul weather,
Though sick of riding out — and nothing less;
When, looking round, I sees a man a-starn: —
Hollo! says I, come underneath her quarter! —
And hands him out my knife to cut the yarn.
So I gets off, and lands upon the road,
And leaves the she-mare to her own consarn,
        A-standing by the water.
If I get on another, I'll be blowed! —
And that's the way, you see, my legs got bowed!

                                    Thomas Hood

THE CHEMIST TO HIS LOVE

I love thee, Mary, and thou lovest me —
Our mutual flame is like th' affinity
That doth exist between two simple bodies:
I am Potassium to thine Oxygen.
'Tis little that the holy marriage vow
Shall shortly make us one. That unity
Is, after all, but metaphysical.
Oh, would that I, my Mary, were an acid,
A living acid; thou an alkali
Endow'd with human sense, that, brought together,
We both might coalesce into one salt,
One homogeneous crystal. Oh, that thou
Wert Carbon, and myself were Hydrogen;
We would unite to form olefiant gas,
Or common coal, or naphtha — would to heaven
That I were Phosphorus, and thou wert Lime!
And we of Lime composed a Phosphuret.
I'd be content to be Sulphuric Acid,
So that thou might be Soda. In that case
We should be Glauber's Salt. Wert thou Magnesia

Instead we'd form the salt that's named from Epsom.
Couldst thou Potassa be, I Aqua-fortis,
Our happy union should that compound form,
Nitrate of Potash — otherwise Saltpetre.
And thus our several natures sweetly blent,
We'd live and love together, until death
Should decompose the fleshly *tertium quid*,
Leaving our souls to all eternity
Amalgamated. Sweet, thy name is Briggs
And mine is Johnson. Wherefore should not we
Agree to form a Johnsonate of Briggs?

Punch

LITTLE BILLEE

There were three sailors of Bristol city
  Who took a boat and went to sea.
But first with beef and captain's biscuits
  And pickled pork they loaded she.

There was gorging Jack and guzzling Jimmy,
  And the youngest he was little Billee.
Now when they got as far as the Equator
  They'd nothing left but one split pea.

Says gorging Jack to guzzling Jimmy,
  "I am extremely hungaree."
To gorging Jack says guzzling Jimmy,
  "We've nothing left, us must eat we."

Says gorging Jack to guzzling Jimmy,
  "With one another we shouldn't agree!
There's little Bill, he's young and tender,
  We're old and tough, so let's eat he.

"Oh, Billy, we're going to kill and eat you,
  So undo the button of your chemie."
When Bill received this information
  He used his pocket-handkerchie.

"Oh, Billy, we're going to kill and eat you."

" First let me say my catechism,
    Which my poor mammy taught to me."
" Make haste, make haste," says guzzling Jimmy,
    While Jack pulled out his snickersnee.

So Billy went up to the main-topgallant mast,
    And down he fell on his bended knee.
He scarce had come to the twelfth commandment
    When up he jumps. " There's land I see:

" Jerusalem and Madagascar,
    And North and South Amerikee:
There's the British flag a-riding at anchor,
    With Admiral Napier, K. C. B."

So when they got aboard the Admiral's
    He hanged fat Jack and flogged Jimmee;
But as for little Bill he made him
    The captain of a Seventy-three.
                        William Makepeace Thackeray

THE BACHELOR'S DREAM

My pipe is lit, my grog is mixed,
My curtains drawn and all is snug;
Old Puss is in her elbow-chair,
And Tray is sitting on the rug.
Last night I had a curious dream,
Miss Susan Bates was Mistress Mogg —
What d'ye think of that, my cat?
What d'ye think of that, my dog?

She looked so fair, she sang so well,
I could but woo and she was won;
Myself in blue, the bride in white,
The ring was placed, the deed was done!
Away we went in chaise-and-four,
As fast as grinning boys could flog —
What d'ye think of that, my cat?
What d'ye think of that, my dog?

What loving tête-à-têtes to come!
But tête-à-têtes must still defer!
When Susan came to live with me,
Her mother came to live with her!
With sister Belle she couldn't part,
But all *my* ties had leave to jog —
What d'ye think of that, my cat?
What d'ye think of that, my dog?

The mother brought a pretty Poll —
A monkey too, what work he made!
The sister introduced a beau —
My Susan brought a favorite maid.
She had a tabby of her own, —
A snappish mongrel christened Gog, —
What d'ye think of that, my cat?
What d'ye think of that, my dog?

The monkey bit — the parrot screamed,
All day the sister strummed and sung;
The petted maid was such a scold!
My Susan learned to use her tongue;
Her mother had such wretched health,
She sate and croaked like any frog —
What d'ye think of that, my cat?
What d'ye think of that, my dog?

No longer Deary, Duck, and Love,
I soon came down to simple " M!"
The very servants crossed my wish,
My Susan let me down to them.
The poker hardly seemed my own,
I might as well have been a log —
What d'ye think of that, my cat?
What d'ye think of that, my dog?

My clothes they were the queerest shape!
Such coats and hats she never met!
My ways they were the oddest ways!
My friends were such a vulgar set!
Poor Tomkinson was snubbed and huffed,
She could not bear that Mister Blogg —
What d'ye think of that, my cat?
What d'ye think of that, my dog?

At times we had a spar, and then
Mamma must mingle in the song —
The sister took a sister's part —
The maid declared her master wrong —
The parrot learned to call me " Fool! "
My life was like a London fog —
What d'ye think of that, my cat?
What d'ye think of that, my dog?

My Susan's taste was superfine,
As proved by bills that had no end;
I never had a decent coat —
I never had a coin to spend!
She forced me to resign my club,
Lay down my pipe, retrench my grog —
What d'ye think of that, my cat?
What d'ye think of that, my dog?

Each Sunday night we gave a rout
To fops and flirts, a pretty list;
And when I tried to steal away,
I found my study full of whist!
Then, first to come, and last to go,
There always was a Captain Hogg —
What d'ye think of that, my cat?
What d'ye think of that, my dog?

Now was not that an awful dream
For one who single is and snug —
With Pussy in the elbow chair,
And Tray reposing on the rug? —
If I must totter down the hill,
'Tis safest done without a clog —
What d'ye think of that, my cat?
What d'ye think of that, my dog?

Thomas Hood

OULD DOCTOR MACK

Ye may tramp the world over
From Delhi to Dover,
And sail the salt say from Archangel to Arragon,
Circumvint back
Through the whole Zodiack,
But to ould Docther Mack ye can't furnish a paragon.
Have ye the dropsy,
The gout, the autopsy?
Fresh livers and limbs instantaneous he'll shape yez,
No ways infarior
In skill, but suparior,
And lineal postarior to Ould Aysculapius.

Chorus

He and his wig wid the curls so carroty,
Aigle eye, and complexion clarety:
Here's to his health,
Honor and wealth,
The king of his kind and the crame of all charity!

How the rich and the poor,
To consult for a cure,
Crowd on to his doore in their carts and their carriages,
Showin' their tongues
Or unlacin' their lungs,
For divle one symptom the docther disparages.
Troth, an' he'll tumble,
For high or for humble,
From his warm feather-bed wid no cross contrariety;
Makin' as light
Of nursin' all night
The beggar in rags as the belle of society.

Chorus — He and his wig, etc.

And as if by a meracle,
Ailments hysterical,
Dad, wid one dose of bread-pills he can smother,

And quench the love-sickness
Wid wonderful quickness,
By prescribin' the right boys and girls to aich other.
And the sufferin' childer —
Your eyes 'twould bewilder
To see the wee craythurs his coat-tails unravellin',
And aich of them fast
On some treasure at last,
Well knowin' ould Mack's just a toy-shop out travellin'.

Chorus — He and his wig, etc.

Thin, his doctherin' done,
In a rollickin' run
Wid the rod or the gun, he's the foremost to figure.
By Jupiter Ammon,
What jack-snipe or salmon
E'er rose to backgammon his tail-fly or trigger!
And hark! the view-hollo!
'Tis Mack in full follow
On black " Faugh-a-ballagh " the country-side sailin'.
Och, but you'd think
'Twas old Nimrod in pink,
Wid his spurs cryin' chink over park-wall and palin'.

Chorus

He and his wig wid the curls so carroty,
Aigle eye, and complexion clarety:
Here's to his health,
Honor and wealth!
Hip, hip, hooray! wid all hilarity,
Hip, hip, hooray! That's the way,
All at once, widout disparity!
One more cheer
For our docther dear,
The king of his kind and the crame of all charity.
Hip, hip, hooray!

Alfred Perceval Graves

THE WHITE SQUALL

On deck beneath the awning,
I dozing lay and yawning;
It was the gray of dawning,
  Ere yet the sun arose;
And above the funnel's roaring,
And the fitful wind's deploring,
I heard the cabin snoring
  With universal nose.
I could hear the passengers snorting —
I envied their disporting —
Vainly I was courting
  The pleasure of a doze!

So I lay, and wondered why light
Came not, and watched the twilight,
And the glimmer of the skylight
  That shot across the deck;
And the binnacle pale and steady,
And the dull glimpse of the dead-eye,
And the sparks in fiery eddy
  That whirled from the chimney neck.
In our jovial floating prison
There was sleep from fore to mizzen,
And never a star had risen
  The hazy sky to speck.

Strange company we harbored;
We'd a hundred Jews to larboard,
Unwashed, uncombed, unbarbered —
  Jews black, and brown, and gray;
With terror it would seize ye,
And make your souls uneasy,
To see those Rabbis greasy,
  Who did naught but scratch and pray:
Their dirty children puking —
Their dirty saucepans cooking —
Their dirty fingers hooking
  Their swarming fleas away.

To starboard, Turks and Greeks were —
Whiskered and brown their cheeks were —
Enormous wide their breeks were,
   Their pipes did puff alway;
Each on his mat allotted
In silence smoked and squatted,
Whilst round their children trotted
   In pretty, pleasant play.
He can't but smile who traces
The smiles on those brown faces,
And the pretty, prattling graces
   Of those small heathens gay.

And so the hours kept tolling,
And through the ocean rolling
Went the brave *Iberia* bowling
   Before the break of day —
When A SQUALL, upon a sudden,
Came o'er the waters scudding;
And the clouds began to gather,
And the sea was lashed to lather,
And the lowering thunder grumbled,
And the lightning jumped and tumbled,
And the ship, and all the ocean,
Woke up in wild commotion.
Then the wind set up a howling,
And the poodle dog a yowling,
And the cocks began a crowing,
And the old cow raised a lowing,
As she heard the tempest blowing;
And fowls and geese did cackle,
And the cordage and the tackle
Began to shriek and crackle;
And the spray dashed o'er the funnels,
And down the deck in runnels;
And the rushing water soaks all,
From the seamen in the fo'ksal
To the stokers whose black faces
Peer out of their bed-places;
And the captain he was bawling,
And the sailors pulling, hauling,
And the quarter-deck tarpauling
Was shivered in the squalling;

And the passengers awaken,
Most pitifully shaken;
And the steward jumps up, and hastens
For the necessary basins.

Then the Greeks they groaned and quivered,
And they knelt, and moaned, and shivered,
As the plunging waters met them,
And splashed and overset them;
And they call in their emergence
Upon countless saints and virgins;
And their marrowbones are bended,
And they think the world is ended.

And the Turkish women for'ard
Were frightened and behorror'd;
And shrieking and bewildering,
The mothers clutched their children;
The men sung "Allah! Illah!
Mashallah Bismillah!"
As the warring waters doused them
And splashed them and soused them,
And they called upon the Prophet,
And thought but little of it.

Then all the fleas in Jewry
Jumped up and bit like fury;
And the progeny of Jacob
Did on the main-deck wake up
(I wot those greasy Rabbins
Would never pay for cabins);
And each man moaned and jabbered in
His filthy Jewish gaberdine,
In woe and lamentation,
And howling consternation.
And the splashing water drenches
Their dirty brats and wenches;
And they crawl from bales and benches
In a hundred thousand stenches.

This was the White Squall famous,
Which latterly o'ercame us,
And which all will well remember
On the 28th September;

When a Prussian captain of Lancers
(Those tight-laced, whiskered prancers)
Came on the deck astonished,
By that wild squall admonished,
And wondering cried, " Potztausend,
Wie ist der Stürm jetzt brausend?"
And looked at Captain Lewis,
Who calmly stood and blew his
Cigar in all the bustle,
And scorned the tempest's tussle,
And oft we've thought thereafter
How he beat the storm to laughter;
For well he knew his vessel
With that vain wind could wrestle;
And when a wreck we thought her,
And doomed ourselves to slaughter,
How gaily he fought her,
And through the hubbub brought her,
And as the tempest caught her,
Cried, "*George! some brandy and water!*"

And when, its force expended,
The harmless storm was ended,
And as the sunrise splendid
   Came blushing o'er the sea;
I thought, as day was breaking,
My little girls were waking,
And smiling, and making
   A prayer at home for me.

William Makepeace Thackeray

MOTHERHOOD

She laid it where the sunbeams fall
Unscann'd upon the broken wall.
Without a tear, without a groan,
She laid it near a mighty stone,
Which some rude swain had haply cast
Thither in sport, long ages past,
And Time with mosses had o'erlaid,
And fenced with many a tall grass-blade,

And all about bid roses bloom
And violets shed their soft perfume.
There, in its cool and quiet bed,
She set her burden down and fled:
Nor flung, all eager to escape,
One glance upon the perfect shape,
That lay, still warm and fresh and fair,
But motionless and soundless there.

No human eye had mark'd her pass
Across the linden-shadow'd grass
Ere yet the minster clock chimed seven:
Only the innocent birds of heaven —
The magpie, and the rook whose nest
Swings as the elm-tree waves his crest —
And the lithe cricket, and the hoar
And huge-limb'd hound that guards the door,
Look'd on when, as a summer wind
That, passing, leaves no trace behind,
All unapparell'd, barefoot all,
She ran to that old ruin'd wall,
To leave upon the chill dank earth
(For ah! she never knew its worth)
'Mid hemlock rank, and fern, and ling,
And dews of night, that precious thing!

And there it might have lain forlorn
From morn till eve, from eve to morn:
But that, by some wild impulse led,
The mother, ere she turn'd and fled,
One moment stood erect and high;
Then pour'd into the silent sky
A cry so jubilant, so strange,
That Alice — as she strove to range
Her rebel ringlets at her glass —
Sprang up, and gazed across the grass;
Shook back those curls so fair to see,
Clapp'd her soft hands in childish glee,
And shriek'd — her sweet face all aglow,
   Her very limbs with rapture shaking —
"My hen has laid an egg, I know;
    And only hear the noise she's making!"

                  Charles Stuart Calverley

THE BANISHED BEJANT

FROM THE UNPUBLISHED REMAINS OF EDGAR ALLAN POE

In the oldest of our alleys,
  By good bejants tenanted,
Once a man whose name was Wallace —
  William Wallace — reared his head.
Rowdy Bejant in the College
  He was styled:
Never had these halls of knowledge
  Welcomed waster half so wild!

Tassel blue and long and silken
  From his cap did float and flow
(This was cast into the Swilcan
  Two months ago);
And every gentle air that sported
  With his red gown,
Displayed a suit of clothes, reported
  The most alarming in the town.

Wanderers in that ancient alley
  Through his luminous window saw
Spirits come continually
  From a case well packed with straw,
Just behind the chair where, sitting
  With air serene,
And in a blazer loosely fitting,
  The owner of the bunk was seen.

And all with cards and counters straying
  Was the place littered o'er,
With which sat playing, playing, playing,
  And wrangling evermore,
A group of fellows, whose chief function
  Was to proclaim,
In voices of surprising unction,
  The luck and losses in the game.

But stately things, in robes and learning,
　Discussed one day the bejant's fate:
Ah, let us mourn him unreturning,
　For they resolved to rusticate!
And now the glory he inherits
　Thus dished and doomed,
Is largely founded on the merits
　Of the Old Tom consumed.

And wanderers, now, within that alley,
　Through the half-open shutters see
Old crones, that talk continually
　In a discordant minor key:
While, with a kind of nervous shiver,
　Past the front door,
His former set go by forever,
　But knock — or ring — no more.

R. F. Murray

THE SMACK IN SCHOOL

A district school, not far away,
Mid Berkshire's hills, one winter's day,
Was humming with its wonted noise
Of threescore mingled girls and boys;
Some few upon their tasks intent,
But more on furtive mischief bent.
The while the master's downward look
Was fastened on a copy-book;
When suddenly, behind his back,
Rose sharp and clear a rousing smack!
As 'twere a battery of bliss
Let off in one tremendous kiss!
"What's that?" the startled master cries;
"That, thir," a little imp replies,
"Wath William Willith, if you pleathe, —
I thaw him kith Thuthanna Peathe!"
With frown to make a statue thrill,
The master thundered, "Hither, Will!"
Like wretch o'ertaken in his track,
With stolen chattels on his back,

Will hung his head in fear and shame,
And to the awful presence came, —
A great, green, bashful simpleton,
The butt of all good-natured fun.
With smile suppressed, and birch upraised,
The thunderer faltered, — " I'm amazed
That you, my biggest pupil, should
Be guilty of an act so rude!
Before the whole set school to boot —
What evil genius put you to't?"
" 'Twas she herself, sir," sobbed the lad,
" I did not mean to be so bad;
But when Susannah shook her curls,
And whispered, I was 'fraid of girls
And dursn't kiss a baby's doll,
I couldn't stand it, sir, at all,
But up and kissed her on the spot!
I know — boo — hoo — I ought to not,
But, somehow, from her looks — boo — hoo —
I thought she kind o' wished me to!'"

William Pitt Palmer

THE QUAKER'S MEETING

A traveller wended the wilds among,
With a purse of gold and a silver tongue;
His hat it was broad, and all drab were his clothes,
For he hated high colors — except on his nose,
And he met with a lady, the story goes.
    Heigho! *yea* thee and *nay* thee.

The damsel she cast him a merry blink,
And the traveller nothing was loth, I think,
Her merry black eye beamed her bonnet beneath,
And the Quaker, he grinned, for he'd very good teeth,
And he asked, " Art thee going to ride on the heath?"

"I hope you'll protect me, kind sir," said the maid,
" As to ride this heath over, I'm sadly afraid;
For robbers, they say, here in numbers abound,
And I wouldn't for anything I should be found,
For, between you and me, I have five hundred pound."

"If that is thee own, dear," the Quaker, he said,
"I ne'er saw a maiden I sooner would wed;
And I have another five hundred just now,
In the padding that's under my saddle-bow,
And I'll settle it all upon thee, I vow!"

The maiden she smil'd, and her rein she drew,
"Your offer I'll take, but I'll not take you,"
A pistol she held at the Quaker's head —
"Now give me your gold, or I'll give you my lead,
'Tis under the saddle, I think you said."

The damsel she ripped up the saddle-bow,
And the Quaker was never a quaker till now!
And he saw, by the fair one he wished for a bride,
His purse borne away with a swaggering stride,
And the eye that shamm'd tender, now only defied.

"The spirit doth move me, friend Broadbrim," quoth she,
"To take all this filthy temptation from thee,
For Mammon deceiveth, and beauty is fleeting,
Accept from thy maiden this right-loving greeting,
For much doth she profit by this Quaker's meeting!

"And hark! jolly Quaker, so rosy and sly,
Have righteousness, more than a wench, in thine eye;
Don't go again peeping girls' bonnets beneath,
Remember the one that you met on the heath,
Her name's Jimmy Barlow, I tell to your teeth."

"Friend James," quoth the Quaker, "pray listen to me,
For thou canst confer a great favor, d'ye see;
The gold thou hast taken is not mine, my friend,
But my master's; and truly on thee I depend,
To make it appear I my trust did defend.

"So fire a few shots thro' my clothes, here and there,
To make it appear 'twas a desp'rate affair."
So Jim he popp'd first through the skirt of his coat,
And then through his collar — quite close to his throat;
"Now one thro' my broadbrim," quoth Ephraim, "I vote."

"I have but a brace," said bold Jim, "and they're spent,
  And I won't load again for a make-believe rent." —
"Then!" — said Ephraim, producing his pistols, "just give
  My five hundred pounds back, or, as sure as you live,
  I'll make of your body a riddle or sieve."

Jim Barlow was diddled — and, tho' he was game,
He saw Ephraim's pistol so deadly in aim,
That he gave up the gold, and he took to his scrapers,
And when the whole story got into the papers,
They said that *"the thieves were no match for the
    Quakers."*
  Heigho! *yea* thee and *nay* thee.

Samuel Lover

SARY "FIXES UP" THINGS

Oh, yes, we've be'n fixin' up some sence we sold that piece
    o' groun'
Fer a place to put a golf-lynx to them crazy dudes from
    town.
(Anyway, they laughed like crazy when I had it specified,
Ef they put a golf-lynx on it, thet they'd haf to keep him
    tied.)
But they paid the price all reg'lar, an' then Sary says to me,
"Now we're goin' to fix the parlor up, an' settin'-room,"
    says she.
Fer she 'lowed she'd been a-scrimpin' an' a-scrapin' all her
    life,
An' she meant fer once to have things good as Cousin
    Ed'ard's wife.

Well, we went down to the city, an' she bought the
    blamedest mess;
An' them clerks there must 'a' took her fer a' Astoroid, I
    guess;
Fer they showed her fancy bureaus which they said was
    shiffoneers,
An' some more they said was dressers, an' some curtains
    called porteers.

An' she looked at that there furnicher, an' felt them cur-
    tains' heft;
Then she sailed in like a cyclone an' she bought 'em right
    an' left;
An' she picked a Bress'ls carpet thet was flowered like
    Cousin Ed's,
But she drawed the line com-pletely when we got to foldin'-
    beds.

Course, she said, 't 'u'd make the parlor lots more roomier,
    she s'posed;
But she 'lowed she'd have a bedstid thet was shore to stay
    un-closed;
An' she stopped right there an' told us sev'ral tales of folks
    she'd read
Bein' overtook in slumber by the " fatal foldin'-bed."
" Not ef it wuz set in di'mon's! Nary foldin'-bed fer me!
I ain't goin' to start fer glory in a rabbit-trap! " says she.
" When the time comes I'll be ready an' a-waitin'; but ez
    yet,
I sha'n't go to sleep a-thinkin' that I've got the triggers
    set."

Well, sir, shore as yo' 're a-livin', after all thet Sary said,
'Fore we started home that evenin' she hed bought a foldin'-
    bed;
An' she's put it in the parlor, where it adds a heap o' style;
An' we're sleepin' in the settin'-room at present fer a while.
Sary still maintains it's han'some, " an' them city folks 'll
    see
That we're posted on the fashions when they visit us," says
    she;
But it plagues her some to tell her, ef it ain't no other use,
We can set it fer the golf-lynx ef he ever sh'u'd get loose.

Albert Bigelow Paine

FIVE LIVES

Five mites of monads dwelt in a round drop
That twinkled on a leaf by a pool in the sun.
To the naked eye they lived invisible;
Specks, for a world of whom the empty shell
Of a mustard-seed had been a hollow sky.

One was a meditative monad, called a sage;
And, shrinking all his mind within, he thought:
" Tradition, handed down for hours and hours,
Tells that our globe, this quivering crystal world,
Is slowly dying. What if, seconds hence
When I am very old, yon shimmering doom
Comes drawing down and down, till all things end?"
Then with a wizen smirk he proudly felt
No other mote of God had ever gained
Such giant grasp of universal truth.

One was a transcendental monad; thin
And long and slim of mind; and thus he mused:
" Oh, vast, unfathomable monad-souls!
Made in the image" — a hoarse frog croaks from the pool,
" Hark! 'twas some god, voicing his glorious thought
In thunder music. Yea, we hear their voice,
And we may guess their minds from ours, their work.
Some taste they have like ours, some tendency
To wriggle about, and munch a trace of scum."
He floated up on a pin-point bubble of gas
That burst, pricked by the air, and he was gone.

One was a barren-minded monad, called
A positivist; and he knew positively;
" There was no world beyond this certain drop.
Prove me another! Let the dreamers dream
Of their faint gleams, and noises from without,
And higher and lower; life is life enough."
Then swaggering half a hair's breadth hungrily,
He seized upon an atom of bug, and fed.

One was a tattered monad, called a poet;
And with a shrill voice ecstatic thus he sang:
" Oh, little female monad's lips!
Oh, little female monad's eyes!
Ah, the little, little, female, female monad!"
The last was a strong-minded monadess,
Who dashed amid the infusoria,
Danced high and low, and wildly spun and dove,
Till the dizzy others held their breath to see.

But while they led their wondrous little lives
Æonian moments had gone wheeling by,

The burning drop had shrunk with fearful speed;
A glistening film — 'twas gone; the leaf was dry.
The little ghost of an inaudible squeak
Was lost to the frog that goggled from his stone;

Who, at the huge, slow tread of a thoughtful ox
Coming to drink, stirred sideways fatly, plunged,
Launched backward twice, and all the pool was still.

Edward Rowland Sill

THE HUNTING OF THE SNARK

"Come, listen, my men, while I tell you again
    The five unmistakable marks
By which you may know, wheresoever you go,
    The warranted genuine Snarks.

"Let us take them in order.   The first is the taste,
    Which is meagre and hollow, but crisp:
Like a coat that is rather too tight in the waist,
    With a flavor of Will-o'-the-wisp.

"Its habit of getting up late you'll agree
    That it carries too far when I say
That it frequently breakfasts at five-o'clock tea,
    And dines on the following day.

. . . .

"The fourth is its fondness for bathing-machines,
    Which it constantly carries about,
And believes that they add to the beauty of scenes —
    A sentiment open to doubt.

"The fifth is ambition.   It next will be right
    To describe each particular batch;
Distinguishing those that have feathers, and bite,
    From those that have whiskers, and scratch.

"For, although common Snarks do no manner of harm,
    Yet I feel it my duty to say
Some are Boojums —" The Bellman broke off in alarm,
    For the Baker had fainted away.

They roused him with muffins — they roused him with
    ice —
    They roused him with mustard and cress —
They roused him with jam and judicious advice —
    They set him conundrums to guess.

When at length he sat up and was able to speak,
    His sad story he offered to tell;
And the Bellman cried " Silence! Not even a shriek! "
    And excitedly tingled his bell.

There was silence supreme! Not a shriek, not a scream,
    Scarcely even a howl or a groan,
As the man they called " Ho! " told his story of woe
    In an antediluvian tone.

" My father and mother were honest, though poor — "
    " Skip all that! " cried the Bellman in haste,
" If it once becomes dark, there's no chance of a Snark,
    We have hardly a minute to waste! "

" I skip forty years," said the Baker, in tears,
    " And proceed without further remark
To the day when you took me aboard of your ship
    To help you in hunting the Snark.

" A dear uncle of mine (after whom I was named)
    Remarked, when I bade him farewell — "
" Oh, skip your dear uncle," the Bellman exclaimed,
    As he angrily tingled his bell.

" He remarked to me then," said that mildest of men,
    " ' If your Snark be a Snark, that is right;
Fetch it home by all means — you may serve it with greens
    And it's handy for striking a light.

" ' You may seek it with thimbles — and seek it with care;
    You may hunt it with forks and hope;
You may threaten its life with a railway-share;
    You may charm it with smiles and soap —

" ' But oh, beamish nephew, beware of the day,
    If your Snark be a Boojum! For then

You will softly and suddenly vanish away
   And never be met with again!'

"It is this, it is this that oppresses my soul,
   When I think of my uncle's last words:
And my heart is like nothing so much as a bowl
   Brimming over with quivering curds!

"It is this, it is this —" "We have had that before!"
   The Bellman indignantly said.
And the Baker replied, "Let me say it once more.
   It is this, it is this that I dread!

"I engage with the Snark — every night after dark —
   In a dreamy delirious fight:
I serve it with greens in those shadowy scenes,
   And I use it for striking a light:

"But if ever I meet with a Boojum, that day,
   In a moment (of this I am sure),
I shall softly and suddenly vanish away —
   And the notion I cannot endure!"

Lewis Carroll

ANY ONE WILL DO

A maiden once, of certain age,
To catch a husband did engage;
But, having passed the prime of life
In striving to become a wife
Without success, she thought it time
To mend the follies of her prime.

Departing from the usual course
Of paint and such like for resource,
With all her might this ancient maid
Beneath an oak-tree knelt and prayed;
Unconscious that a grave old owl
Was perched above — the mousing fowl!

"Oh, give! a husband give!" she cried,
"While yet I may become a bride;

Soon will my day of grace be o'er,
And then, like many maids before,
I'll die without an early love,
And none to meet me there above!

" Oh, 'tis a fate too hard to bear!
Then answer this my humble prayer,
And oh, a husband give to me! "
Just then the owl from out the tree,
In deep bass tones cried, " Who — who — who! "
" Who, Lord? And dost Thou ask me who?
Why, any one, good Lord, will do."

Anonymous

UPON BEING OBLIGED TO LEAVE A PLEASANT PARTY

FROM THE WANT OF A PAIR OF BREECHES TO DRESS FOR DINNER IN

Between Adam and me the great difference is,
    Though a paradise each has been forced to resign,
That he never wore breeches till turn'd out of his,
    While, for want of my breeches, I'm banish'd from mine.

Thomas Moore

KENTUCKY PHILOSOPHY

You Wi'yum, cum 'ere, suh, dis minute. Wut dat you
    got under dat box?
I don't want no foolin' — you hear me? Wut you say?
    Ain't nu'h'n but *rocks?*
'Peahs ter me you's owdashus perticler. S'posin' dey's uv a
    new kine.
I'll des take a look at dem rocks. Hi yi! der you think dat
    I's bline?

I calls dat a plain water-million, you scamp, en I knows
    whah it growed;
It come fum de Jimmerson cawn fiel', dah on ter side er
    de road.

You stole it, you rascal — you stole it! I watched you fum
    down in de lot.
En time I gits th'ough wid you, nigger, you won't eb'n be
    a grease spot!

I'll fix you. Mirandy! Mi*ra*ndy! go cut me a hick'ry —
    make 'ase!
En cut me de toughes' en keenes' you c'n fine anywhah on
    de place.
I'll larn you, Mr. Wi'yum Joe Vetters, ter steal en ter lie,
    you young sinner,
Disgracin' yo' ole Christian mammy, en makin' her leave
    cookin' dinner!

Now ain't you ashamed er yo'se'f, suh? I is. I's 'shamed
    you's my son!
En de holy accorjun angel he's 'shamed er wut you has
    done;
En he's tuk it down up yander in coal-black, blood-red
    letters —
"One water-million stoled by Wi'yum Josephus Vetters."

En wut you s'posin' Brer Bascom, yo' teacher at Sunday
    school,
'Ud say ef he knowed how you's broke de good Lawd's
    Gol'n Rule?
Boy, whah's de raisin' I give you? Is you boun' fuh ter
    be a black villiun?
I's s'prised dat a chile er yo' mammy 'ud steal any man's
    water-million.

En I's now gwiner cut it right open, en you shain't have
    narry bite,
Fuh a boy who'll steal water-millions — en dat in de day's
    broad light —
Ain't — *Lawdy!* it's GREEN! Mirandy! Mi-ran-dy! come
    on wi' dat switch!
Well, stealin' a g-r-e-e-n water-million! who ever heered
    tell er des sich?

"When they are on the river's brink."

Cain't tell w'en dey's ripe? W'y, you thump 'um, en w'en
    dey go pank dey is green;
But when dey go *punk,* now you mine me, dey's ripe — en
    dat's des wut I mean.
En nex' time you hook water-millions — *you* heered me, you
    ign'ant young hunk,
Ef you don't want a lickin' all over, be sho dat dey allers go
    " punk ! "

Harrison Robertson

BAIT OF THE AVERAGE FISHERMAN

This is the bait
the fisher-
men   take
the fishermen take, the fishermen take, when they start out the fish to
wake, so early in the morning. They take a nip before they go — a good one, ah! and long and slow,
for fear the chills will lay them low, so early in
the morning.   Another — when they're on the
street, which they repeat each time they meet
for " luck " — for that's the way to greet a
fisher in the morning.   And when they are
on the river's brink again they drink without a wink — to fight malaria they think
it proper in the morning. They tip a
flask with true delight when there's a
bite; if fishing's light they " smile "
the more, till jolly tight all fishing
they are scorning. Another nip as
they depart; one at the mart and
one to part; but none when in
the house they dart expecting
there'll be mourning.   This
is the bait the fishermen try,
who fishes buy at prices
high, and tell each one
a bigger lie of fishing
in the morning.

H. C. Dodge

ON THE DEATH OF A FAVORITE CAT

DROWNED IN A TUB OF GOLDFISHES

'Twas on a lofty vase's side,
Where China's gayest art had dyed
  The azure flowers that blow,
Demurest of the tabby kind,
The pensive Selima, reclined,
  Gazed on the lake below.

Her conscious tail her joy declared;
The fair round face, the snowy beard,
  The velvet of her paws,
Her coat, that with the tortoise vies,
Her ears of jet, and emerald eyes,
  She saw, and purred applause.

Still had she gaz'd; but, 'midst the tide,
Two angel forms were seen to glide,
  The Genii of the stream:
Their scaly armor's Tyrian hue,
Through richest purple, to the view
  Betrayed a golden gleam.

The hapless nymph with wonder saw;
A whisker first, and then a claw,
  With many an ardent wish,
She stretched in vain to reach the prize:
What female heart can gold despise?
  What Cat's averse to fish?

Presumptuous maid! with looks intent,
Again she stretched, again she bent,
  Nor knew the gulf between:
(Malignant Fate sat by and smiled)
The slippery verge her feet beguiled;
  She tumbled headlong in.

Eight times emerging from the flood,
She mewed to every watery god
   Some speedy aid to send.
No Dolphin came, no Nereid stirred,
Nor cruel Tom nor Susan heard:
   A fav'rite has no friend!

From hence, ye Beauties, undeceived,
Know one false step is ne'er retrieved,
   And be with caution bold:
Not all that tempts your wandering eyes,
And heedless hearts, is lawful prize,
   Nor all that glisters, gold.

Thomas Gray

HERE SHE GOES, AND THERE SHE GOES

Two Yankee wags, one summer day,
Stopped at a tavern on their way,
Supped, frolicked, late retired to rest,
And woke to breakfast on the best.
The breakfast over, Tom and Will
Sent for the landlord and the bill;
Will looked it over: — " Very right —
But hold! what wonder meets my sight?
Tom, the surprise is quite a shock!"
"What wonder? where?" "The clock, the clock!"

Tom and the landlord in amaze
Stared at the clock with stupid gaze,
And for a moment neither spoke;
At last the landlord silence broke, —

" You mean the clock that's ticking there?
I see no wonder, I declare!
Though maybe, if the truth were told,
'Tis rather ugly, somewhat old;
Yet time it keeps to half a minute;
But, if you please, what wonder's in it?"

" Tom, don't you recollect," said Will,
" The clock at Jersey, near the mill,
  The very image of this present,
  With which I won the wager pleasant? "
  Will ended with a knowing wink;
  Tom scratched his head and tried to think.
" Sir, begging pardon for inquiring,"
  The landlord said, with grin admiring,
" What wager was it? "

           " You remember
It happened, Tom, in last December:
In sport I bet a Jersey Blue
That it was more than he could do
To make his finger go and come
In keeping with the pendulum,
Repeating, till the hour should close,
Still, — '*Here she goes, and there she goes.*'
He lost the bet in half a minute."

" Well, if I would, the deuce is in it! "
  Exclaimed the landlord; " try me yet,
  And fifty dollars be the bet."
" Agreed, but we will play some trick,
  To make you of the bargain sick! "
" I'm up to that! "

           " Don't make us wait, —
Begin, — the clock is striking eight."
He seats himself, and left and right
His finger wags with all its might,
And hoarse his voice and hoarser grows,
With — "*Here she goes, and there she goes!*"

" Hold! " said the Yankee, " Plank the ready! "
  The landlord wagged his finger steady,
  While his left hand, as well as able,
  Conveyed a purse upon the table.
" Tom! with the money let's be off! "
  This made the landlord only scoff.

He heard them running down the stair,
But was not tempted from his chair;
Thought he, " The fools! I'll bite them yet!
So poor a trick sha'n't win the bet."
And loud and long the chorus rose
Of — *" Here she goes, and there she goes!"*
While right and left his finger swung,
In keeping to his clock and tongue.

His mother happened in to see
Her daughter: " Where is Mrs. B—— ? "
" When will she come, do you suppose?
Son!" —
   " Here she goes, and there she goes!"
" Here! — where? " — the lady in surprise
His finger followed with her eyes:
" Son! why that steady gaze and sad?
Those words, — that motion, — are you mad?
But here's your wife, perhaps she knows,
And — "
   " Here she goes, and there she goes!"

His wife surveyed him with alarm,
And rushed to him, and seized his arm;
He shook her off, and to and fro
His finger persevered to go;
While curled his very nose with ire
That *she* against him should conspire;
And with more furious tone arose
The — *" Here she goes, and there she goes!"*

⬤

" Lawks! " screamed the wife, " I'm in a whirl!
Run down and bring the little girl;
She is his darling, and who knows
But — "
   " Here she goes, and there she goes!"

" Lawks! he is mad! What made him thus?
Good Lord! what will become of us?
Run for a doctor, — run, run, run, —
For Doctor Brown and Doctor Dun,
And Doctor Black and Doctor White,
And Doctor Gray, with all your might! "

The doctors came, and looked, and wondered,
And shook their heads, and paused and pondered.
Then one proposed he should be bled, —
" No, leeched you mean," the other said,
" Clap on a blister ! " roared another, —
" No ! cup him," — " No, trepan him, brother."
A sixth would recommend a purge,
The next would an emetic urge ;
The last produced a box of pills,
A certain cure for earthly ills :
" I had a patient yesternight,"
Quoth he, " and wretched was her plight,
And as the only means to save her,
Three dozen patent pills I gave her ;
And by to-morrow I suppose
That — "
        " Here she goes, and there she goes !"

" You are all fools ! " the lady said, —
" The way is just to shave his head.
Run ! bid the barber come anon."
" Thanks, mother ! " thought her clever son ;
" You help the knaves that would have bit me,
But all creation sha'n't outwit me ! "
Thus to himself while to and fro
His finger perseveres to go,
And from his lips no accent flows
But, — *" Here she goes, and there she goes !"*
The barber came — " Lord help him ! what
A queerish customer I've got ;
But we must do our best to save him, —
So hold him, gemmen, while I shave him ! "
But here the doctors interpose, —
" A woman never — "
        " There she goes !"

" A woman is no judge of physic,
Not even when her baby is sick.
He must be bled," — " No, cup him," — " Pills ! "
And all the house the uproar fills.

What means that smile ? what means that shiver ?
The landlord's limbs with rapture quiver,

And triumph brightens up his face,
His finger yet will win the race;
The clock is on the stroke of nine,
And up he starts, — "'Tis mine! 'tis mine!"
"What do you mean?"
                              "I mean the fifty;
I never spent an hour so thrifty.
But you who tried to make me lose,
Go, burst with envy, if you choose!
But how is this? where are they?"
                                        "Who?"
"The gentlemen, — I mean the two
Came yesterday, — are they below?"
"They galloped off an hour ago."
"Oh, dose me! blister! shave and bleed!
For, hang the knaves, I'm mad indeed!"

> *James Nack*

COLOGNE

In Köln, a town of monks and bones,
And pavements fanged with murderous stones,
And rags, and hags, and hideous wenches,
I counted two-and-seventy stenches,
All well defined, and separate stinks!
Ye nymphs that reign o'er sewers and sinks,
The river Rhine, it is well known,
Doth wash your city of Cologne;
But tell me, nymphs, what power divine
Shall henceforth wash the river Rhine?

> *Samuel Taylor Coleridge*

IN THE CATACOMBS

Sam Brown was a fellow from way down East,
Who never was "staggered" in the least.
No tale of marvellous beast or bird
Could match the stories he had heard;
No curious place or wondrous view
"Was ekil to Podunk, I tell yu."

If they told him of Italy's sunny clime,
"Maine kin beat it, every time!"
If they marvelled at Ætna's fount of fire,
They roused his ire:
With an injured air
He'd reply, "I swear
I don't think much of a smokin' hill;
We've got a moderate little rill
Kin make yer old volcaner still;
Jes' pour old Kennebec down the crater,
'N' I guess it'll cool her fiery nater!"

They showed him a room where a queen had slept;
"'Twan't up to the tavern daddy kept."
They showed him Lucerne; but he had drunk
From the beautiful Molechunkamunk.
They took him at last to ancient Rome,
And inveigled him into a catacomb:

Here they plied him with draughts of wine,
Though he vowed old cider was twice as fine,
Till the fumes of Falernian filled his head,
And he slept as sound as the silent dead;
They removed a mummy to make him room,
And laid him at length in the rocky tomb.

They piled old skeletons round the stone,
Set a "dip" in a candlestick of bone,
And left him to slumber there alone;
Then watched from a distance the taper's gleam,
Waiting to jeer at his frightened scream,
When he should wake from his drunken dream.

After a time the Yankee woke,
But instantly saw through the flimsy joke;
So never a cry or shout he uttered,
But solemnly rose, and slowly muttered:
"I see how it is. It's the judgment day,
We've all been dead and stowed away;
All these stone furreners sleepin' yet,
An' I'm the fust one up, you bet!
Can't none o' you Romans start, I wonder?
United States ahead, by thunder!"

Harlan Hoge Ballard

MY FAMILIAR

Again I hear that creaking step —
  He's rapping at the door! —
Too well I know the boding sound
  That ushers in a bore.
I do not tremble when I meet
  The stoutest of my foes,
But Heaven defend me from the friend
  Who comes — but never goes!

He drops into my easy chair,
  And asks about the news;
He peers into my manuscript,
  And gives his candid views;
He tells me where he likes the line,
  And where he's forced to grieve;
He takes the strangest liberties, —
  But never takes his leave!

He reads my daily paper through
  Before I've seen a word;
He scans the lyric that I wrote
  And thinks it quite absurd;
He calmly smokes my last cigar,
  And coolly asks for more;
He opens everything he sees —
  Except the entry door!

He talks about his fragile health,
  And tells me of his pains;
He suffers from a score of ills
  Of which he ne'er complains;
And how he struggled once with death
  To keep the fiend at bay;
On themes like those away he goes —
  But never goes away!

He tells me of the carping words
  Some shallow critic wrote;

And every precious paragraph
    Familiarly can quote;
He thinks the writer did me wrong;
    He'd like to run him through!
He says a thousand pleasant things —
    But never says " Adieu!"

Whene'er he comes — that dreadful man —
    Disguise it as I may,
I know that, like an autumn rain,
    He'll last throughout the day.
In vain I speak of urgent tasks;
    In vain I scowl and pout;
A frown is no extinguisher, —
    It does not put him out!

I mean to take the knocker off,
    Put crape upon the door,
Or hint to John that I am gone
    To stay a month or more.
I do not tremble when I meet
    The stoutest of my foes,
But Heaven defend me from the friend
    Who never, never goes!

John Godfrey Saxe

THE MODEST COUPLE

When man and maiden meet, I like to see a drooping eye,
I always droop my own — I am the shyest of the shy,
I'm also fond of bashfulness, and sitting down on thorns,
And modesty's a quality that womankind adorns.

Whenever I am introduced to any pretty maid,
My knees they knock together, just as if I were afraid;
I flutter, and I stammer, and I turn a pleasing red,
For to laugh, and flirt, and ogle, I consider most ill-bred.

Some persons, when they're introduced to maidens young
        and fair,
Begin at once by begging for a little lock of hair;

Or when they meet a strange young girl, they'll take her
    round the waist;
Perhaps I am old-fashioned, but it argues want of taste.

But still in all these matters, as in other things below,
There is a proper medium, as I'm about to show.
I do not recommend a newly-married pair to try
To carry on as Peter carried on with Sarah Bligh.

Betrothed they were when very young — before they'd
    learnt to speak
(For Sarah was but six days old, and Peter was a week);
Though little more than babies at those early ages, yet
They bashfully would faint when they occasionally met.

They blushed, and flushed, and fainted, till they reached the
    age of nine,
When Peter's good Papa (he was a Baron of the Rhine)
Determined to endeavor some sound argument to find
To bring these shy young people to a proper frame of
    mind.

He told them that as Sarah was to be his Peter's bride,
They might at least consent to sit at table side by side;
He begged that they would now and then shake hands, till
    he was hoarse,
Which Sarah thought indelicate, and Peter very coarse.

And Peter in a tremble to the blushing maid would say,
"You must excuse Papa, Miss Bligh, — it is his mountain
    way."
Says Sarah, "His behavior I'll endeavor to forget,
But your Pa's the very coarsest person that I ever met.

"He plighted us without our leave, when we were very
    young,
Before we had begun articulating with the tongue.
His underbred suggestions fill your Sarah with alarm;
Why, gracious me! he'll ask us next to walk out arm in
    arm!"

At length, when Sarah reached the legal age of twenty-one,
The Baron he determined to unite her to his son;

And Sarah in a fainting fit for weeks unconscious lay,
And Peter blushed so hard you might have heard him miles
    away.

And when the time arrived for taking Sarah to his heart,
They were married in two churches half a dozen miles
    apart
(Intending to escape all public ridicule and chaff),
And the service was conducted by electric telegraph.

And when it was concluded, and the priest had said his say,
Until the time arrived when they were both to drive away,
They never spoke or offered for to fondle or to fawn,
For *he* waited in the attic, and *she* waited on the lawn.

At length, when four o'clock arrived, and it was time to go,
The carriage was announced, but decent Sarah answered
    "No!
Upon my word, I'd rather sleep my everlasting nap
Than go and ride alone with Mister Peter in a trap."

And Peter's ever sensitive and highly-polished mind
Wouldn't suffer him to sanction a proceeding of the kind;
And further, he declared he suffered overwhelming shocks
At the bare idea of having any coachman on the box.

So Peter in one chariot incontinently rushed,
While Sarah in a second trap sat modestly and blushed;
And Mister Newman's coachman, on authority I've heard,
Deposited himself upon the coach-box of a third.

Now, though this modest couple in the matter of the car
Were very very likely carrying a principle too far,
I hold their shy behavior was more laudable in them
Than that of Peter's brother with Miss Sarah's sister Em.

Alphonso, who in cool assurance all creation licks,
He up and said to Emmie (who had impudence for six),
"Miss Emily, I love you — will you marry?   Say the
    word!"
And Emily said, "Certainly, Alphonso, like a bird!"

I do not recommend a newly-married pair to try
To carry on as Peter carried on with Sarah Bligh,
But still their shy behavior was more laudable in them
Than that of Peter's brother 'with Miss Sarah's sister Em.
William S. Gilbert

REV. GABE TUCKER'S REMARKS

You may notch it on de palin's as a mighty resky plan
To make your judgment by de clo'es dat kivers up a man;
For I hardly needs to tell you how you often come across
A fifty-dollar saddle on a twenty-dollar hoss;
An', wukin' in de low-groun's, you diskiver, as you go,
Dat de fines' shuck may hide de meanes' nubbin in a row.

I think a man has got a mighty slender chance for heben
Dat holds on to his piety but one day out o' seben;
Dat talks about de sinners wid a heap o' solemn chat,
And nebber draps a nickle in de missionary hat;
Dat's foremost in de meetin'-house for raisin' all de chunes,
But lays aside his 'ligion wid his Sunday pantaloons.

I nebber judge o' people dat I meets along de way
By de places whar dey come fum an' de houses whar dey
    stay;
For de bantam chicken's awful fond o' roostin' pretty high,
An' de turkey buzzard sails above de eagle in de sky;
Dey ketches little minners in de middle ob de sea,
An' you finds de smalles' possum up de bigges' kind o' tree!
Anonymous

BELAGCHOLLY DAYS

Chilly Dovebber with his boadigg blast
    Dow cubs add strips the beddow add the lawd,
Eved October's suddy days are past —
        Add Subber's gawd!

I kdow dot what it is to which I cligg
  That stirs to sogg add sorrow, yet I trust
That still I sigg, but as the liddets sigg —
    Because I bust.

Add dow, farewell to roses add to birds,
  To larded fields and tigkligg streablets eke;
Farewell to all articulated words
    I faid would speak.

Farewell, by cherished strolliggs od the sward,
  Greed glades add forest shades, farewell to you;
With sorrowing heart I, wretched add forlord,
    Bid you — achew!!!

                                        Anonymous

THE BALLAD OF CHARITY

It was in a pleasant deepô, sequestered from the rain,
That many weary passengers were waitin' for the train;
Piles of quite expensive baggage, many a gorgeous port-
    mantó,
Ivory-handled umberellas made a most touristic show.

Whereunto there came a person, very humble was his mien,
Who took an observation of the interestin' scene;
Closely scanned the umberellas, watched with joy the mighty
    trunks,
And observed that all the people were securin' Pullman
    bunks:

Who was followed shortly after by a most unhappy tramp,
Upon whose features poverty had jounced her iron stamp;
And to make a clear impression as bees sting you while
    they buzz,
She had hit him rather harder than she generally does.

For he was so awful ragged, and in parts so awful bare,
That the folks were quite repulsioned to behold him begging
    there;

And instead of drawing currency from out their pocket-
  books,
They drew themselves asunder with aversionary looks.

Sternly gazed the first newcomer on the unindulgent crowd,
Then in tones which pierced the deepô he sililicussed
  aloud : —
"I hev trevelled o'er this cont'nent from Quebec to Bogo-
  táw,
But sech a set of scallawags as these I never saw.

" Ye are wealthy, ye are gifted, ye have house and lands and
  rent,
Yet unto a suff'rin' mortal ye will not donate a cent ;
Ye expend your missionaries to the heathen and the Jew,
But there isn't any heathen that is half as small as you.

" Ye are lucky — ye hev cheque-books and deeposits in the
  bank,
And ye squanderate your money on the titled folks of rank ;
The onyx and the sardonyx upon your garments shine,
An' ye drink at every dinner p'r'aps a dollar's wuth of wine.

" Ye are goin' for the summer to the islands by the sea,
Where it costs four dollars daily — setch is not for setch as
  me ;
Iv'ry-handled umberellas do not come into my plan,
But I kin give a dollar to this suff'rin' fellow-man.

"Hand-bags made of Rooshy leather are not truly at my
  call,
Yet in the eyes of Mussy I am richer 'en you all,
For I kin give a dollar wher' you dare not stand a dime,
And never miss it nother, nor regret it ary time."

Sayin' this he drew a wallet from the inner of his vest,
And gave the tramp a daddy, which it was his level best ;
Other people havin' heard him soon to charity inclined —
One giver soon makes twenty if you only get their wind.

The first who gave the dollar led the other one about,
And at every contribution he a-raised a joyful shout,
Exclaimin' how 'twas noble to relieviate distress,
And remarkin' that our duty is our present happiness.

Thirty dollars altogether were collected by the tramp,
When he bid 'em all good evenin' and went out into the
damp,
And was followed briefly after by the one who made the
speech,
And who showed by good example how to practise as to
preach.

Which soon around the corner the couple quickly met,
And the tramp produced the specie for to liquidate his debt;
And the man who did the preachin' took his twenty of the
sum,
Which you see that out of thirty left a tenner for the bum.

And the couple passed the summer at Bar Harbor with the
rest,
Greatly changed in their appearance and most elegantly
dressed.
Any fowl with change of feathers may a brilliant bird become:
Oh, how hard is life for many! oh, how sweet it is for
some!

Charles Godfrey Leland

MR. MOLONY'S ACCOUNT OF THE BALL

GIVEN TO THE NEPAULESE AMBASSADOR BY THE PENINSULAR AND ORIENTAL COMPANY

O will ye choose to hear the news,
  Bedad I cannot pass it o'er:
I'll tell you all about the Ball
  To the Naypaulase Ambassador.
Begor! this fête all balls does bate
  At which I've worn a pump, and I
Must here relate the splendthor great
  Of th' Oriental Company.

These men of sinse dispoised expinse,
  To fête these black Achilleses.
"We'll show the blacks," says they, "Almack's,
  And take the rooms at Willis's."

With flags and shawls, for these Nepauls,
  They hung the rooms of Willis up,
And decked the walls, and stairs, and halls,
  With roses and with lilies up.

And Jullien's band it tuck its stand,
  So sweetly in the middle there,
And soft bassoons played heavenly chunes,
  And violins did fiddle there.
And when the Coort was tired of spoort,
  I'd lave you, boys, to think there was
A nate buffet before them set,
  Where lashins of good dhrink there was.

At ten before the ballroom door,
  His moighty Excellincy was,
He smoiled and bowed to all the crowd,
  So gorgeous and imminse he was.
His dusky shuit, sublime and mute,
  Into the doorway followed him;
And O the noise of the blackguard boys,
  As they hurrood and hollowed him!

The noble Chair stud at the stair,
  And bade the dthrums to thump; and he
Did thus evince to that Black Prince,
  The welcome of his Company.
O fair the girls, and rich the curls,
  And bright the oys you saw there, was;
And fixed each oye, ye there could spoi,
  On Gineral Jung Behawther, was!

This Gineral great then tuck his sate,
  With all the other ginerals
(Bedad his troat, his belt, his coat,
  All bleezed with precious minerals);
And as he there, with princely air,
  Recloinin on his cushion was,
All round about his royal chair
  The squeezin and the pushin was.

O Pat, such girls, such Jukes, and Earls,
  Such fashion and nobilitee!

Just think of Tim, and fancy him
    Amidst the hoigh gentilitee!
There was Lord de L'Huys, and the Portygeese
    Ministher and his lady there,
And I reckonized, with much surprise,
    Our messmate, Bob O'Grady, there;

There was Baroness Brunow, that looked like Juno,
    And Baroness Rehausen there,
And Countess Roullier, that looked peculiar
    Well, in her robes of gauze in there.
There was Lord Crowhurst (I knew him first,
    When only Misther Pips he was),
And Mick O'Toole, the great big fool,
    That after supper tipsy was.

There was Lord Fingall, and his ladies all,
    And Lords Killeen and Dufferin,
And Paddy Fife, with his fat wife:
    I wondther how he could stuff her in.
There was Lord Belfast, that by me passed,
    And seemed to ask how should *I* go there?
And the Widow Macrae, and Lord A. Hay,
    And the Marchioness of Sligo there.

Yes, Jukes, and Earls, and diamonds, and pearls,
    And pretty girls, was sporting there;
And some beside (the rogues!) I spied,
    Behind the windies, coorting there.
O there's one I know, bedad would show
    As beautiful as any there,
And I'd like to hear the pipers blow,
    And shake a fut with Fanny there!
        William Makepeace Thackeray

KITTY OF COLERAINE

As beautiful Kitty one morning was tripping,
    With a pitcher of milk from the fair of Coleraine,
When she saw me she stumbled, the pitcher it tumbled,
    And all the sweet buttermilk water'd the plain.

" O, what shall I do now, 'twas looking at you now,
  Sure, sure, such a pitcher I'll ne'er meet again!
'Twas the pride of my dairy: O Barney M'Cleary!
  You're sent as a plague to the girls of Coleraine."

I sat down beside her, — and gently did chide her,
  That such a misfortune should give her such pain;
A kiss then I gave her, — and ere I did leave her,
  She vow'd for such pleasure she'd break it again.

'Twas hay-making season, I can't tell the reason,
  Misfortunes will never come single, — that's plain,
For, very soon after poor Kitty's disaster,
  The devil a pitcher was whole in Coleraine.

Edward Lysaght

REASONS FOR DRINKING

If all be true that I do think,
There are five reasons we should drink;
Good wine — a friend — or being dry —
Or lest we should be by and by —
Or any other reason why.

Dr. Henry Aldrich

TALE OF THE KENNEBEC MARINER

Guess I've never told you, sonny, of the strändin' and the
    wreck
Of the steamboat *Ezry Johnson* that run up the Kennebec.
That was 'fore the time of steam-cars, and the *Johnson*
    filled the bill
On the route between Augusty and the town of Water-
    ville.

She was built old-fashioned model, with a bottom's flat's
    your palm,
With a paddle-wheel behind her, druv' by one great churn-
    in' arm.

Couldn't say that she was speedy — sploshed along and
    made a touse,
But she couldn't go much faster than a man could tow a
    house.
Still, she skipped and skived tremendous, dodged the rocks
    and skun the shoals,
In a way the boats of these days couldn't do to save their
    souls.
Didn't draw no 'mount of water, went on top instead of
    through.
This is how there ccme to happen what I'm going to tell
    to *you.*
— Hain't no need to keep you guessing, for I know you
    won't suspect
How that thunderin' old *Ez. Johnson* ever happened to get
    wrecked.

She was overdue one ev'nin', fog come down most awful
    thick;
'Twas about like navigating round inside a feather tick.
Proper caper was to anchor, but she seemed to run all
    right,
And we humped her — though 'twas resky —kept her slosh-
    ing through the night.

Things went on all right till morning, but along 'bout half-
    past three
Ship went dizzy, blind, and crazy — waves seemed wust I
    ever see.
Up she went and down she scuttered; sometimes seemed
    to stand on end,
Then she'd wallopse, sideways, crossways, in a way, by
    gosh, to send
Shivers down your spine. She'd teeter, fetch a spring, and
    take a bounce,
Then squat down, sir, on her haunches with a most
    je-roosly jounce.
Folks got up and run a-screaming, forced the wheelhouse,
    grabbed at me,
— Thought we'd missed Augusty landin' and had gone plum
    out to sea.
— Fairly shot me full of questions, but I said 'twas jest a
    blow;

Still, that didn't seem to soothe 'em, for there warn't no
  wind, you know!
Yas, sir, spite of all that churnin', warn't a whisper of a
  breeze
— No excuse for all that upset and those strange and
  dretful seas.
Couldn't spy a thing around us — every way 'twas pitchy
  black,
And I couldn't seem to comfort them poor critters on my
  back.
Couldn't give 'em information, for 'twas dark's a cellar
  shelf;
— Couldn't tell 'em nothing 'bout it — for I didn't know myself.

So I gripped the *Johnson's* tiller, kept the rudder riggin'
  taut,
Kept a-praying, chawed tobacker, give her steam, and let
  her swat.
Now, my friend, jest listen stiddy: when the sun come out
  at four,
We warn't tossin' in the breakers off no stern and rock-
  bound shore;
But I'd missed the gol-durned river, and I swow this 'ere
  is true,
I had sailed eight miles 'cross country in a heavy autumn
  dew.
There I was clear up in Sidney, and the tossings and the
  rolls
Simply happened 'cause we tackled sev'ral miles of cradle
  knolls.
Sun come out and dried the dew up; there she was a
  stranded wreck,
And they soaked me eighteen dollars' cartage to the Kennebec.

Holman F. Day

THE MODERN BELLE

She sits in a fashionable parlor,
  And rocks in her easy chair;
She is clad in silks and satins,
  And jewels are in her hair;

She winks and giggles and simpers,
  And simpers and giggles and winks;
And though she talks but little,
  'Tis a good deal more than she thinks.

She lies abed in the morning
  Till nearly the hour of noon,
Then comes down snapping and snarling
  Because she was called so soon;
Her hair is still in papers,
  Her cheeks still fresh with paint, —
Remains of her last night's blushes,
  Before she intended to faint.

She dotes upon men unshaven,
  And men with " flowing hair; "
She's eloquent over mustaches,
  They give such a foreign air.
She talks of Italian music,
  And falls in love with the moon;
And, if a mouse were to meet her,
  She would sink away in a swoon.

Her feet are so very little,
  Her hands are so very white,
Her jewels so very heavy,
  And her head so very light;
Her color is made of cosmetics
  (Though this she will never own),
Her body is mostly of cotton,
  Her heart is wholly of stone.

She falls in love with a fellow
  Who swells with a foreign air;
He marries her for her money,
  She marries him for his hair!
One of the very best matches, —
  Both are well-mated in life;
She's got a fool for a husband,
  He's got a fool for a wife!

                                    Anonymous

TWO FISHERS

One morning when Spring was in her teens —
  A morn to a poet's wishing,
All tinted in delicate pinks and greens —
  Miss Bessie and I went fishing.

I in my rough and easy clothes,
  With my face at the sun-tan's mercy;
She with her hat tipped down to her nose,
  And her nose tipped — *vice versa.*

I with my rod, my reel, and my hooks,
  And a hamper for lunching recesses;
She with the bait of her comely looks,
  And the seine of her golden tresses.

So we sat us down on the sunny dike,
  Where the white pond-lilies teeter,
And I went to fishing like quaint old Ike,
  And she like Simon Peter.

All the noon I lay in the light of her eyes,
  And dreamily watched and waited,
But the fish were cunning and would not rise,
  And the baiter alone was baited.

And when the time of departure came,
  My bag hung flat as a flounder;
But Bessie had neatly hooked her game —
  A hundred-and-fifty-pounder.

Anonymous

JOB

Sly Beelzebub took all occasions
To try Job's constancy and patience.
He took his honor, took his health;
He took his children, took his wealth,
His servants, horses, oxen, cows, —
But cunning Satan did *not* take his spouse.

But Heaven, that brings out good from evil,
And loves to disappoint the devil,
Had predetermined to restore
Twofold all he had before;
His servants, horses, oxen, cows —
Short-sighted devil, *not* to take his spouse!

Samuel Taylor Coleridge

FALSE LOVE AND TRUE LOGIC

THE DISCONSOLATE

My heart will break — I'm sure it will:
My lover, yes, my favorite — he
Who seemed my own through good and ill —
Has basely turned his back on me.

THE COMFORTER

Ah! silly sorrower, weep no more;
Your lover's turned his back, we see;
But you had turned his head before,
And now he's as he ought to be.

Laman Blanchard

A WIFE

Lord Erskine, at women presuming to rail,
Calls a wife "a tin canister tied to one's tail;"
And fair Lady Anne, while the subject he carries on,
Seems hurt at his Lordship's degrading comparison.
But wherefore degrading? consider'd aright,
A canister's useful, and polish'd, and bright:
And should dirt its original purity hide,
That's the fault of the puppy to whom it is tied.

Richard Brinsley Sheridan

GRAMPY SINGS A SONG

Row-diddy, dow 'de, my little sis,
Hush up your teasin' and listen to this:
'Tain't much of a jingle, 'tain't much of a tune,
But it's spang-fired truth about Chester Cahoon.

The thund'rinest fireman Lord ever made
Was Chester Cahoon of the Tuttsville Brigade.
He was boss of the tub and the foreman of hose;
When the 'larm rung he'd start, sis, a-sheddin' his clothes,
— Slung cote and slung wes'cote and kicked off his shoes,
A-runnin' like fun, for he'd no time to lose.
And he'd howl down the ro'd in a big cloud of dust,
For he made it his brag he was allus there fust.
— Allus there fust, with a whoop and a shout,
And he never shut up till the fire was out.
And he'd knock out the winders and save all the doors,
And tear off the clapboards, and rip up the floors,
For he allus allowed 'twas a tarnation sin
To 'low 'em to burn, for you'd want 'em agin.
He gen'rally stirred up the most of his touse
In hustling to save the outside of the house.
And after he'd wrassled and hollered and pried,
He'd let up and tackle the stuff 'twas inside.
To see him you'd think he was daft as a loon,
But that was jest habit with Chester Cahoon.

Row diddy-iddy, my little sis,
Now see what ye think of a doin' like this:
The time of the fire at Jenkins' old place
It got a big start — was a desprit case;
The fambly they didn't know which way to turn.
And by gracious, it looked like it all was to burn.
But Chester Cahoon — oh, that Chester Cahoon,
He sailed to the roof like a reg'lar balloon;
Donno how he done it, but done it he did,
— Went down through the scuttle and shet down the lid.
And five minutes later that critter he came
To the second floor winder surrounded by flame.
He lugged in his arms, sis, a stove and a bed,
And balanced a bureau right square on his head.
His hands they was loaded with crockery stuff,
China and glass; as if that warn't enough,
He'd rolls of big quilts round his neck like a wreath,
And carried Mis' Jenkins' old aunt with his teeth.
You're right — gospel right, little sis, — didn't seem
The critter'd git down, but he called for the stream,
And when it come strong and big round as my wrist,
He stuck out his legs, sis, and give 'em a twist;

And he hooked round the water jes' if 'twas a rope,
And down he come easin' himself on the slope,
— So almighty spry that he made that 'ere stream
As fit for his pupp'us' as if 'twas a beam.
Oh, the thund'rinest fireman Lord ever made
Was Chester Cahoon of the Tuttsville Brigade.

Holman F. Day

LINES ON DOCTOR JOHNSON

I own I like not Johnson's turgid style,
That gives an inch th' importance of a mile;
Casts of manure a wagon-load around
To raise a simple daisy from the ground;
Uplifts the club of Hercules — for what? —
To crush a butterfly or brain a gnat;
Creates a whirlwind from the earth, to draw
A goose's feather or exalt a straw;
Sets wheels on wheels in motion — such a clatter:
To force up one poor pipperkin of water;
Bids ocean labor with tremendous roar,
To heave a cockle-shell upon the shore;
Alike in every theme his pompous art,
Heaven's awful thunder, or a rumbling cart!

John Wolcot ("Peter Pindar")

OFFICER BRADY

(THE MODERN RECRUIT)

I.

Sez Alderman Grady
To Officer Brady:
"G'wan! Ye're no lady!
    Luk here what ye've done:
Ye've run in Red Hogan,
Ye've pulled Paddy Grogan,
Ye've fanned Misther Brogan
    An' called him a 'gun'!

" 'Way up in Tammany Hall
  They's a gintleman layin' f'r you!
' An' what,' sez he, ' t' 'ell,' sez he,
' Does the villyun mane to do?
  Lock up the ass in his shtall!
  He'll rue the day I rue,
  F'r he's pulled the dive that kapes me alive,
  An' he'll go to the goats!¹ Whurroo!'"

II.

       Sez Alderman Grady
       To Officer Brady:
    " Ye pinched young Mullady
          F'r crackin' a safe!
       An' Sinitor Moran
       An' Alderman Doran
       Is inside, a-roarin'
          F'r justice, ye thafe!

" 'Way up in Tammany Hall
  They's a gintleman layin' f'r you!
' What's this,' sez he, ' I hear?' sez he —
  An' the air, bedad, grew blue!
' Well, I nivver did hear av such gall!
  But if phwat ye say is thrue,
  He's pulled a fri'nd av a fri'nd av me fri'nd,
  An' he'll go to the goats! Whurroo!'"

III.

       Sez Alderman Grady
       To Officer Brady:
    " Here's Sullivan's lady
          Cavoortin' an' riled;
       She lifted a locket
       From Casey's coat pocket,
       An' it goes to the docket,
          An' Sullivan's wild!

" 'Way up in Tammany Hall
  They's a gintleman layin' f'r you!

¹ "Going to the goats," that is, to an undesirable post in the suburbs.

' 'Tis a shame,' sez he, ' f'r to blame,' sez he,
' A lady so fair an' thrue,
An' so divinely tall ' —
'Tis po'ms he talked, ye Jew!
An' ye've cooked yere goose, an' now ye're loose
F'r to folly the goats! Whurroo!"

IV.

Sez Alderman Grady
To Officer Brady:
" Where's Katie Macready,
    The Confidence Queen?
She's niece to O'Lafferty's
Cousins, the Caffertys —
Sinitor Rafferty's
    Steady colleen!

" 'Way up in Tammany Hall
They's a gintleman layin' f'r you!
' He's pinched,' sez he, ' an' cinched,' sez he,
' A lady tray comme eel foo!
Go dangle th' tillyphone call,
An' gimme La Mulberry Roo,
F'r the town is too warrm f'r this gendarme,
An' he'll go to the goats, mon Dieu! ' "

V.

Sez Alderman Grady
To Officer Brady:
" McCabe is afraid he
    Can't open to-night,
F'r throuble's a-brewin',
An' mischief's a-stewin',
Wid nothin' a-doin'
    An' everything tight!
There's Register Ronnell,
Commissioner Donnell,
An' Congressman Connell
    Preparin' f'r flight;

The Dhistrict Attorney
Told Magistrate Kearny
That Captain McBurney
Was dyin' o' fright!

"Oh!
'Way up in Tammany Hall
They's a gintleman lookin' f'r you!
'Bedad,' sez he, 'he's mad,' sez he.
'So turrn on the screw f'r Bellevue,
An' chain 'im ag'in' the wall,
An' lather 'im wan or two,
An' tether 'im out on the Bloomin'dale route
Like a loonytick goat! Whurroo!'"

Robert William Chambers

PRESTO FURIOSO

AFTER WALT WHITMAN

Spontaneous Us!
O my Camarados! I have no delicatesse as a diplomat, but
    I go blind on Libertad!
Give me the flap-flap of the soaring Eagle's pinions!
Give me the tail of the British lion tied in a knot inextrica-
    ble, not to be solved anyhow!
Give me a standing army (I say "give me," because just at
    present we want one badly, armies being often useful in
    time of war).

I see our superb fleet (I take it that we are to have a superb
    fleet built almost immediately);
I observe the crews prospectively; they are constituted of
    various nationalities, not necessarily American;
I see them sling the slug and chew the plug;
I hear the drum begin to hum;

Both the above rhymes are purely accidental, and contrary
    to my principles.
We shall wipe the floor of the mill-pond with the scalps of
    able-bodied British tars!

I see Professor Edison about to arrange for us a torpedo-
    hose on wheels, likewise an infernal electro-semaphore;
I see Henry Irving dead sick and declining to play Corporal
    Brewster;
Cornell, I yell! I yell Cornell!

I note the Manhattan boss leaving his dry-goods store and
    investing in a small Gatling-gun and a ten-cent banner;
I further note the Identity evolved out of forty-four spa-
    cious and thoughtful States;
I note Canada as shortly to be merged in that Identity;
    similarly Van Diemen's Land, Gibraltar, and Stratford-
    on-Avon;
Briefly, I see creation whipped!

O ye Colonels! I am with you (I too am a Colonel and on
    the pension-list);
I drink to the lot of you; to Colonels Cleveland, Hitt, Van-
    derbilt, Chauncey M. Depew, O'Donovan Rossa, and the
    late Colonel Monroe;
I drink an egg-flip, a morning-caress, an eye-opener, a
    maiden-bosom, a vermuth-cocktail, three sherry-cob-
    blers, and a gin-sling!
Good old Eagle!

Owen Seaman

CAREY, OF CARSON

The night-mist dim and darkling,
    As o'er the roads we pass,
Lies in the morning sparkling
    As dewdrops on the grass.
E'en so the deeds of darkness,
    Which come like midnight dews,
Appear as sparkling items
    Next morning in the news.

Away in Carson City,
    Far in the Silver Land,
There lives one Justice Carey,
    A man of head and hand;

And as upon his table
　The Judge a-smoking sat,
There rowdied in a rougher
　Who wore a gallows hat.

He looked upon the Justice,
　But Justice did not budge
Until the younger warbled,
　" Say — don't you know me, Judge? "
" I think," said Carey, meekly,
　" Your face full well I know, —
I sent you up for stealing
　A horse a year ago."

" Ay, that is just the hairpin
　I am, and that's my line;
And here is twenty dollars
　I've brought to pay the fine."
" You owe no fine," said Carey,
　" Your punishment is o'er."
" Not yet," replied the rover,
　" I've come to have some more.

" Fust-rate assault and batt'ry
　I'm goin' to commit,
And you're the mournful victim
　That I intend to hit,
And give you such a scrampin'
　As never was, nohow;
And so, to save the lawin',
　I guess I'll settle now."

Up rose the Court in splendor;
　" Young man, your start is fair,
Sail in, my son, sail over,
　And we will call it square!
Go in upon your chances, —
　Perhaps you may not miss;
I like to see young heroes
　Ambitionin' like this."

The young one at the older
  Went in with all his heft,
And, like a flyin' boulder,
  At once let out his left;
The Court, in haste, ducked under
  Its head uncommon spry,
Then lifted the intruder
  With a puncher in the eye, —

A regular right-hander;
  And like a cannon-ball,
The young man, when percussioned,
  Went over on the wall.
In just about a second,
  The Court, with all its vim,
Like squash-vines o'er a meadow,
  Went climbing over him.

Yea, as the pumpkin clambers
  Above an Indian grave,
Or as the Mississippi
  Inunders with its wave,
And merrily slops over
  A town in happy sport,
E'en so that man was clambered
  All over by the Court.

And in about a minute
  That party was so raw,
He would have seemed a stranger
  Unto his dearest squaw;
Till he was soft and tender,
  This morsel once so tough,
And then, in sad surrender,
  He moaned aloud, "Enough!"

He rose: and Justice Carey
  Said to him ere he went,
"I do not think the fightin'
  You did was worth a cent.
I charge for time two dollars,
  As lawyers should, 'tis plain;
The balance of the twenty
  I give you back again.

" At church, in silks and satins new,
With hoop of monstrous size."

" I like to be obligin'
    To folks with all my powers,
So when you next want fightin'
    Don't come in office hours;
I only make my charges
    For what's in legal time, —
Drop in, my son, this evenin',
    And I'll not charge a dime."

The young man took the guerdon,
    As he had ta'en the scars;
Then took himself awayward
    To the 'Ginia City cars.
'Tis glorious when heroes
    Go in to right their wrongs;
But if you're only hairpins,
    Oh, then beware of tongs!

                    Charles Godfrey Leland

AN ELEGY

ON THE GLORY OF HER SEX, MRS. MARY BLAIZE

Good people all, with one accord,
    Lament for Madam Blaize,
Who never wanted a good word —
    From those who spoke her praise.

The needy seldom pass'd her door,
    And always found her kind;
She freely lent to all the poor —
    Who left a pledge behind.

She strove the neighborhood to please
    With manners wondrous winning;
And never follow'd wicked ways —
    Unless when she was sinning.

At church, in silks and satins new,
    With hoop of monstrous size,
She never slumber'd in her pew —
    But when she shut her eyes.

Her love was sought, I do aver,
  By twenty beaux and more;
The King himself has follow'd her —
  When she has walk'd before.

But now, her wealth and finery fled,
  Her hangers-on cut short all;
The doctors found, when she was dead —
  Her last disorder mortal.

Let us lament, in sorrow sore,
  For Kent Street well may say,
That had she lived a twelvemonth more
  She had not died to-day.

Oliver Goldsmith

LODGINGS FOR SINGLE GENTLEMEN

Who has e'er been in London, that overgrown place,
Has seen "Lodgings to let" stare him full in the face:
Some are good, and let dearly; while some, 'tis well known,
Are so dear, and so bad, they are best let alone.

Will Waddle, whose temper was studious and lonely,
Hired lodgings that took single gentlemen only;
But Will was so fat he appear'd like a ton,
Or like two single gentlemen roll'd into one.

He enter'd his room, and to bed he retreated;
But, all the night long, he felt fever'd and heated;
And, though heavy to weigh as a score of fat sheep,
He was not, by any means, heavy to sleep.

Next night 'twas the same. And the next. And the next:
He perspired like an ox; he was nervous and vex'd;
Week pass'd after week; till, by weekly succession,
His weakly condition was past all expression.

In six months, his acquaintance began much to doubt him:
For his skin, like a lady's loose gown, hung about him.

He sent for a doctor; and cried, like a ninny,
"I have lost many pounds. Make me well. There's a
   guinea."

The doctor look'd wise: — "A slow fever," he said:
Prescribed sudorifics, — and going to bed.
"Sudorifics in bed," exclaim'd Will, "are humbugs!
I've enough of them there, without paying for drugs!"

Will kick'd out the doctor: — but, when ill indeed,
E'en dismissing the doctor don't always succeed;
So, calling his host, he said: — "Sir, do you know,
I'm the fat single gentleman, six months ago?

"Look'e, landlord, I think," argued Will, with a grin,
"That with honest intentions you first took me in:
But from the first night — and to say it I'm bold —
I have been so d——d hot, that I'm sure I caught cold."

Quoth the landlord, "Till now, I ne'er had a dispute;
I've let lodgings ten years; I'm a baker, to boot;
In airing your sheets, sir, my wife is no sloven;
And your bed is immediately over my oven."

"The oven!" says Will. Says the host, "Why this pas-
   sion?
In that excellent bed died three people of fashion.
Why so crusty, good sir?" — "Zounds!" cried Will, in a
   taking,
"Who wouldn't be crusty with half a year's baking?"

Will paid for his rooms: — cried the host, with a sneer,
"Well, I see you've been going away half a year."
"Friend, we can't well agree, — yet no quarrel" — Will
   said; —
"But I'd rather not perish while you make your bread."
                        George Colman the Younger

MAUD

Nay, I cannot come into the garden just now,
    Tho' it vexes me much to refuse:
But I *must* have the next set of waltzes, I vow,
    With Lieutenant de Boots of the Blues.

I am sure you'll be heartily pleas'd when you hear
    That our ball has been quite a success.
As for *me* — I've been looking a monster, my dear,
    In that old-fashion'd guy of a dress.

You had better at once hurry home, dear, to bed;
    It is getting so dreadfully late.
You may catch the bronchitis or cold in the head
    If you linger so long at our gate.

Don't be obstinate, Alfy; come, take my advice —
    For I know you're in want of repose:
Take a basin of gruel (you'll find it *so* nice),
    And remember to tallow your nose.

No, I tell you I can't and I sha'n't get away,
    For De Boots has implor'd me to sing.
As to *you* — if you like it, of course you can stay,
    You were always an obstinate thing.

If you feel it a pleasure to talk to the flow'rs
    About " babble and revel and wine,"
When you might have been snoring for two or three hours,
    Why, it's not the least business of mine.

Henry S. Leigh

EVE'S DAUGHTER

I waited in the little sunny room:
    The cool breeze waved the window-lace, at play,
The white rose on the porch was all in bloom,
    And out upon the bay
I watched the wheeling sea-birds go and come.

"Such an old friend, — she would not make me stay
  While she bound up her hair." I turned, and lo,
Danaë in her shower! and fit to slay
  All a man's hoarded prudence at a blow:
Gold hair, that streamed away
  As round some nymph a sunlit fountain's flow.
"She would not make me wait!" — but well I know
She took a good half-hour to loose and lay
  Those locks in dazzling disarrangement so!

Edward Rowland Sill

THE RELIGION OF HUDIBRAS

For his religion it was fit
To match his learning and his wit:
'Twas Presbyterian true blue;
For he was of that stubborn crew
Of errant saints, whom all men grant
To be the true church militant;
Such as do build their faith upon
The holy text of pike and gun;
Decide all controversies by
Infallible artillery;
And prove their doctrine orthodox,
By apostolic blows and knocks;
Call fire, and sword, and desolation,
A godly, thorough reformation,
Which always must be carried on,
And still be doing, never done;
As if religion were intended
For nothing else but to be mended:
A sect whose chief devotion lies
In odd perverse antipathies;
In falling out with that or this,
And finding somewhat still amiss;
More peevish, cross, and splenetic,
Than dog distract, or monkey sick;
That with more care keep holy-day
The wrong, than others the right way,
Compound for sins they are inclin'd to,
By damning those they have no mind to:
Still so perverse and opposite,
As if they worshipped God for spite:
The self-same thing they will abhor

One way, and long another for:
Free-will they one way disavow,
Another, nothing else allow:
All piety consists therein
In them, in other men all sin:
Rather than fail, they will defy
That which they love most tenderly;
Quarrel with minc'd pies and disparage
Their best and dearest friend, plum porridge,
Fat pig and goose itself oppose,
And blaspheme custard through the nose.

Samuel Butler

THE PILGRIMS AND THE PEAS

A brace of sinners, for no good,
  Were order'd to the Virgin Mary's shrine,
Who at Loretto dwelt, in wax, stone, wood,
  And in a fair white wig look'd wondrous fine.

Fifty long miles had those sad rogues to travel,
With something in their shoes much worse than gravel;
In short, their toes so gentle to amuse,
The priest had order'd peas into their shoes:

A nostrum, famous in old popish times,
For purifying souls that stunk with crimes;
  A sort of apostolic salt,
  Which popish parsons for its powers exalt,
For keeping souls of sinners sweet,
Just as our kitchen salt keeps meat.

The knaves set off on the same day,
Peas in their shoes, to go and pray:
  But very different was their speed, I wot:
One of the sinners gallop'd on,
Swift as a bullet from a gun;
  The other limp'd, as if he had been shot.

One saw the Virgin soon — *peccavi* cried —
  Had his soul whitewash'd all so clever;

Then home again he nimbly hied,
  Made fit with saints above to live forever.

In coming back, however, let me say,
He met his brother rogue about half-way,
Hobbling, with outstretch'd arms and bended knees,
Damning the souls and bodies of the peas;
His eyes in tears, his cheeks and brow in sweat,
Deep sympathizing with his groaning feet.

"How now," the light-toed, white-wash'd pilgrim broke,
  "You lazy lubber!"
"Odds curse it!" cried the other, "'tis no joke;
My feet, once hard as any rock,
  Are now as soft as blubber.

"Excuse me, Virgin Mary, that I swear:
As for Loretto, I shall not go there;
No! to the Devil my sinful soul must go,
For damme if I ha'n't lost every toe.
But, brother sinner, pray explain
How 'tis that you are not in pain?
  What power hath work'd a wonder for your toes?
Whilst I, just like a snail, am crawling,
Now swearing, now on saints devoutly bawling,
  Whilst not a rascal comes to ease my woes?

"How is't that *you* can like a greyhound go,
  Merry as if that naught had happen'd, burn ye!"
"Why," cried the other, grinning, "you must know,
That, just before I ventured on my journey,
  To walk a little more at ease,
  I took the liberty to boil *my* peas."
                    John Wolcot (*"Peter Pindar"*)

CASEY AT THE BAT

It looked extremely rocky for the Mudville nine that day,
The score stood four to six with but an inning left to play.
And so, when Cooney died at first, and Burrows did the
    same,
A pallor wreathed the features of the patrons of the game.

A straggling few got up to go, leaving there the rest,
With that hope which springs eternal within the human
  breast.
For they thought if only Casey could get a whack at that,
They'd put up even money with Casey at the bat.
But Flynn preceded Casey, and likewise so did Blake,
And the former was a pudding and the latter was a fake;
So on that striken multitude a death-like silence sat,
For there seemed but little chance of Casey's getting to the
  bat.
But Flynn let drive a single to the wonderment of all,
And the much despisèd Blakey tore the cover off the ball,
And when the dust had lifted and they saw what had
  occurred,
There was Blakey safe on second, and Flynn a-hugging
  third.
Then from the gladdened multitude went up a joyous yell,
It bounded from the mountain top and rattled in the dell,
It struck upon the hillside, and rebounded on the flat,
For Casey, mighty Casey, was advancing to the bat.
There was ease in Casey's manner as he stepped into his
  place,
There was pride in Casey's bearing and a smile on Casey's
  face,
And when responding to the cheers he lightly doffed his
  hat.
No stranger in the crowd could doubt, 'twas Casey at the
  bat.
Ten thousand eyes were on him as he rubbed his hands with
  dirt,
Five thousand tongues applauded as he wiped them on his
  shirt;
And while the writhing pitcher ground the ball into his
  hip —
Defiance gleamed from Casey's eye — a sneer curled
  Casey's lip.
And now the leather-covered sphere came hurtling through
  the air,
And Casey stood. a-watching it in haughty grandeur there;
Close by the sturdy batsman the ball unheeded sped —
"That hain't my style," said Casey — "Strike one," the
  Umpire said.
From the bleachers black with people there rose a sullen
  roar,

Like the beating of the storm waves on a stern and distant
    shore,
"Kill him! kill the Umpire!" shouted some one from the
    stand —
And it's likely they'd have done it had not Casey raised his
    hand.
With a smile of Christian charity great Casey's visage
    shone,
He stilled the rising tumult and he bade the game go on;
He signalled to the pitcher and again the spheroid flew,
But Casey still ignored it and the Umpire said "Strike
    two."
"Fraud!" yelled the maddened thousands, and the echo an-
    swered "Fraud,"
But one scornful look from Casey and the audience was
    awed;
They saw his face grow stern and cold; they saw his mus-
    cles strain,
And they knew that Casey would not let that ball go by
    again.
The sneer is gone from Casey's lip; his teeth are clenched
    with hate,
He pounds with cruel violence his bat upon the plate;
And now the pitcher holds the ball, and now he lets it go,
And now the air is shattered by the force of Casey's blow.
Oh! somewhere in this favored land the sun is shining
    bright,
The band is playing somewhere, and somewhere hearts are
    light,
And somewhere men are laughing, and somewhere children
    shout;
But there is no joy in Mudville — mighty Casey has "Struck
    Out."

                      Joseph Quinlan Murphy

NONGTONGPAW

John Bull for pastime took a prance,
Some time ago, to peep at France;
To talk of sciences and arts,
And knowledge gain'd in foreign parts.

Monsieur, obsequious, heard him speak,
And answer'd John in heathen Greek:
To all he ask'd, 'bout all he saw,
'Twas, *Monsieur, je vous n'entends pas.*

John, to the Palais-Royal come,
Its splendor almost struck him dumb.
"I say, whose house is that there here?"
"House! *Je vous n'entends pas, Monsieur.*"
"What, Nongtongpaw again!" cries John;
"This fellow is some mighty Don:
No doubt he's plenty for the maw,
I'll breakfast with this Nongtongpaw."

John saw Versailles from Marli's height,
And cried, astonish'd at the sight,
"Whose fine estate is that there here?"
"State! *Je vous n'entends pas, Monsieur.*"
"His? what! the land and houses, too?
The fellow's richer than a Jew:
On *everything* he lays his claw!
I'd like to dine with Nongtongpaw."

Next tripping came a courtly fair,
John cried, enchanted with her air,
"What lovely wench is that there here?"
"Ventch! *Je vous n'entends pas, Monsieur.*"
"What, he again? Upon my life!
A palace, lands, and then a wife
Sir Joshua might delight to draw!
I'd like to sup with Nongtongpaw."

"But hold! whose funeral's that?" cries John.
"*Je vous n'entends pas.*" — "What! is he gone?
Wealth, fame, and beauty could not save
Poor Nongtongpaw then from the grave!
His race is run, his game is up, —
I'd with him breakfast, dine, and sup;
But since he chooses to withdraw,
Good night t'ye, Mounseer Nongtongpaw!"

Charles Dibdin

THE LITERARY LADY

What motley cares Corilla's mind perplex,
Whom maids and metaphors conspire to vex!
In studious dishabille behold her sit,
A letter'd gossip and a household wit;
At once invoking, though for different views,
Her gods, her cook, her milliner, and muse.
Round her strew'd room a frippery chaos lies,
A chequer'd wreck of notable and wise,
Bills, books, caps, couplets, combs, a varied mass,
Oppress the toilet and obscure the glass;
Unfinish'd here an epigram is laid,
And there a mantua-maker's bill unpaid.
There new-born plays foretaste the town's applause,
There dormant patterns pine for future gauze.
A moral essay now is all her care,
A satire next, and then a bill of fare.
A scene she now projects, and now a dish;
Here Act the First, and here Remove with Fish.
Now, while this eye in a fine frenzy rolls,
That soberly casts up a bill for coals;
Black pins and daggers in one leaf she sticks,
And tears, and threads, and bowls, and thimbles mix.
                                   Richard Brinsley Sheridan

OLD GRIMES

Old Grimes is dead; that good old man
    We never shall see more:
He used to wear a long, black coat,
    All button'd down before.

His heart was open as the day,
    His feelings all were true;
His hair was some inclined to gray —
    He wore it in a queue.

Whene'er he heard the voice of pain,
  His breast with pity burn'd;
The large, round head upon his cane
  From ivory was turn'd.

Kind words he ever had for all;
  He knew no base design:
His eyes were dark and rather small,
  His nose was aquiline.

He lived at peace with all mankind,
  In friendship he was true:
His coat had pocket-holes behind,
  His pantaloons were blue.

Unharm'd, the sin which earth pollutes
  He pass'd securely o'er,
And never wore a pair of boots
  For thirty years or more.

But good old Grimes is now at rest,
  Nor fears misfortune's frown:
He wore a double-breasted vest —
  The stripes ran up and down.

He modest merit sought to find,
  And pay it its desert:
He had no malice in his mind,
  No ruffles on his shirt.

His neighbors he did not abuse —
  Was sociable and gay:
He wore large buckles on his shoes,
  And changed them every day.

His knowledge, hid from public gaze,
  He did not bring to view,
Nor made a noise, town-meeting days,
  As many people do.

His worldly goods he never threw
  In trust to fortune's chances,
But lived (as all his brothers do)
  In easy circumstances.

Thus undisturb'd by anxious cares,
  His peaceful moments ran;
And everybody said he was
  A fine old gentleman.

Albert Gorton Greene

WIDOW BEDOTT TO ELDER SNIFFLES [1]

O reverend sir, I do declare
  It drives me most to frenzy,
To think of you a-lying there
  Down sick with influenzy.

A body'd thought it was enough
  To mourn your wife's departer,
Without sich trouble as this ere
  To come a-follerin' arter.

But sickness and affliction
  Are sent by a wise creation,
And always ought to be underwent
  By patience and resignation.

O, I could to your bedside fly,
  And wipe your weeping eyes,
And do my best to cure you up,
  If 'twouldn't create surprise.

It's a world of trouble we tarry in,
  But, Elder, don't despair;
That you may soon be movin' again
  Is constantly my prayer.

Both sick and well, you may depend
  You'll never be forgot
By your faithful and affectionate friend,

PRISCILLA POOL BEDOTT.
Frances Miriam Whitcher

[1] From "The Widow Bedott Papers."

DORA *VERSUS* ROSE

"The case is proceeding."
From the tragic-est novels at Mudie's —
   At least, on a practical plan —
To the tales of mere Hodges and Judys,
   One love is enough for a man.
But no case that I ever yet met is
   Like mine: I am equally fond
Of Rose, who a charming brunette is,
                  And Dora, a blonde.

Each rivals the other in powers —
   Each waltzes, each warbles, each paints —
Miss Rose, chiefly tumble-down towers;
   Miss Do., perpendicular saints.
In short, to distinguish is folly;
   'Twixt the pair I am come to the pass
Of Macheath, between Lucy and Polly, —
                  Or Buridan's ass.

If it happens that Rosa I've singled
   For a soft celebration in rhyme,
Then the ringlets of Dora get mingled
   Somehow with the tune and the time;
Or I painfully pen me a sonnet
   To an eyebrow intended for Do.'s,
And behold I am writing upon it
                  The legend, "To Rose."

Or I try to draw Dora (my blotter
   Is all overscrawled with her head),
If I fancy at last that I've got her,
   It turns to her rival instead;
Or I find myself placidly adding
   To the rapturous tresses of Rose
Miss Dora's bud-mouth, and her madding
                  Ineffable nose.

Was there ever so sad a dilemma?
   For Rose I would perish (pro tem.);

For Dora I'd willingly stem a —
  (Whatever might offer to stem);
But to make the invidious election, —
  To declare that on either one's side
I've a scruple, — a grain, more affection,
          I *cannot* decide.

And, as either so hopelessly nice is,
  My sole and my final resource
Is to wait some indefinite crisis, —
  Some feat of molecular force,
To solve me this riddle conducive
  By no means to peace or repose,
Since the issue can scarce be inclusive
        Of Dora *and* Rose.

(*Afterthought*)

But, perhaps, if a third (say a Nora),
  Not quite so delightful as Rose, —
Not wholly so charming as Dora, —
  Should appear, is it wrong to suppose, —
As the claims of the others are equal, —
  And flight — in the main — is the best, —
That I might . . . But no matter, — the sequel
        Is easily guessed.
                Austin Dobson

HOME THEY BROUGHT HER LAP-DOG DEAD

Home they brought her lap-dog dead,
  Just run over by a fly;
Jeames to Buttons, winking, said,
  "Won't there be a row, O my!"

Then they call'd the flyman low,
  Said his baseness could be proved;
How she to the Beak should go —
  Yet she neither spoke nor moved.

Said her maid (and risked her place),
  "In the 'ouse it should have kept;

Flymen drives at such a pace " —
Still the lady's anger slept.

Rose her husband, best of dears,
Laid a bracelet on her knee,
Like a playful child she boxed his ears —
" Sweet old pet! — let's have some tea."
Charles Shirley Brooks

THE RECOGNITION

Home they brought her sailor son,
Grown a man across the sea,
Tall and broad and black of beard,
And hoarse of voice as man may be.

Hand to shake and mouth to kiss,
Both he offered ere he spoke ;
But she said — " What man is this
Comes to play a sorry joke? "

Then they praised him — call'd him " smart,"
" Tightest lad that ever stept ; "
But her son she did not know,
And she neither smiled nor wept.

Rose a nurse of ninety years,
Set a pigeon-pie in sight ;
She saw him eat — " 'Tis he! 'tis he! "
She knew him — by his appetite!
William Sawyer

THE MASHER

It was in the Indian summer-time, when life is tender
    brown,
And people in the country talk of going into town,
When the nights are crisp and cooling, though the sun is
    warm by day,
In the homelike town of Glasgow, in the State of Iowa;

It was in the railroad deepô of that greatly favored zone,
That a young man met a stranger, who was still not all
    unknown,
For they had run-countered casual in riding in the car,
And the latter to the previous had offered a cigar.

Now as the primal gentleman was nominated Gale,
It follows that the secondary man was Mr. Dale;
This is called poetic justice when arrangements fit in time,
And Fate allows the titles to accommodate in rhyme.

And a lovely sense of autumn seemed to warble in the air;
Boys with baskets selling peaches were vibratin' everywhere,
While in the mellow distance folks were gettin' in their
    corn,
And the biggest yellow punkins ever seen since you were
    born.

Now a gradual sensation emotioned this our Gale,
That he'd seldom seen so fine a man for cheek as Mr. Dale:
Yet simultaneous he felt that he was all the while
The biggest dude and cock-a-hoop within a hundred mile.

For the usual expression of his quite enormous eyes
Was that of two ripe gooseberries who've been decreed a
    prize;
Like a goose apart from berries, too — though not removed
    from sauce —
He conversed on lovely Woman as if he were all her boss.

Till, in fact, he stated plainly that, between his face and
    cash,
There was not a lady living whom he was not sure to mash;
The wealthiest, the loveliest, of families sublime,
At just a single look from him must all give in in time.

Now when our Dale had got along so far upon the strain,
They saw a Dream of Loveliness descending from the
    train,
A proud and queenly beauty of a transcendental face,
With gloves unto her shoulders, and the most expensive
    lace.

All Baltimore and New Orleans seemed centred into one,
As if their stars of beauty had been fused into a sun;
But, oh! her frosty dignity expressed a kind of glow
Like sunshine when thermometers show thirty grades
  below.

But it flashed a gleam of shrewdness into the head of Gale,
And with aggravatin' humor he explained to Mr. Dale,
"Since every girl's a cricket-ball and you're the only bat,
If you want to show you're champion, go in and mash on
  that.

"I will bet a thousand dollars, and plank them on the rub,
That if you try it thither, you will catch a lofty snub.
I don't mean but what a lady may reply to what you say,
But I bet you cannot win her into wedding in a day."

A singular emotion enveloped Mr. Dale;
One would say he seemed confuseled, for his countenance
  was pale:
At first there came an angry look, and when that look did
  get,
He larft a wild and hollow larf, and said, "I take the bet.

"The brave deserve the lovely — every woman may be won;
What men have fixed before us may by other men be done.
You will lose your thousand dollars. For the first time in
  my life
I have gazed upon a woman whom I wish to make my
  wife."

Like a terrier at a rabbit, with his hat upon his eyes,
Mr. Dale, the awful masher, went head-longing at the
  prize,
Looking rather like a party simply bent to break the peace.
Mr. Gale, with smiles, expected just a yell for the police.

Oh! what are women made of? Oh! what can women be?
From Eves to Jersey Lilies what bewildering sights we see!
One listened on the instant to all the Serpent said;
The other paid attention right away to Floral Ned.

With a blow as with a hammer the intruder broke the ice,
And the proud and queenly beauty seemed to think it
    awful nice.
Mr. Gale, as he beheld it, with a trembling heart began
To realize he really was a most astonished man.

Shall I tell you how he wooed her? Shall I tell you how
    he won?
How they had a hasty wedding ere the evening was done?
For when all things were considered, the fond couple
    thought it best —
Such things are not uncommon in the wild and rapid West.

Dale obtained the thousand dollars, and then vanished with
    the dream.
Gale stayed in town with sorrow, like a spoon behind the
    cream;
Till one morning in the paper he read, though not in
    rhymes,
How a certain blooming couple had been married fifty
    times!

How they wandered o'er the country; how the bridegroom
    used to bet
He would wed the girl that evening, — how he always
    pulled the debt;
How his eyes were large and greensome; how, in fact, to
    end the tale,
Their very latest victim was a fine young man named Gale.
                    Charles Godfrey Leland

CONSTANCY

"You gave me the key of your heart, my love;
    Then why do you make me knock?"
"Oh, that was yesterday, Saints above!
    And last night — I changed the lock!"
                    John Boyle O'Reilly

THE RETORT

Old Nick, who taught the village school,
  Wedded a maid of homespun habit;
He was as stubborn as a mule,
  She was as playful as a rabbit.

Poor Jane had scarce become a wife,
  Before her husband sought to make her
The pink of country-polished life,
  And prim and formal as a Quaker.

One day the tutor went abroad,
  And simple Jenny sadly missed him;
When he returned, behind her lord
  She slyly stole, and fondly kissed him!

The husband's anger rose!—and red
  And white his face alternate grew!
"Less freedom, ma'am!" Jane sighed and said,
  "*Oh, dear! I didn't know 'twas you!*"
                              George Pope Morris

THE RECRUIT

Sez Corporal Madden to Private McFadden:
  "Bedad, yer a bad 'un!
  Now turn out yer toes!
  Yer belt is unhookit,
  Yer cap is on crookit,
  Ye may not be dhrunk,
  But, be jabers, ye look it!
      Wan—two!
      Wan—two!
Ye monkey-faced divil, I'll jolly ye through!
      Wan—two!—
      Time! Mark!
Ye march like the aigle in Cintheral Parrk!"

Sez Corporal Madden to Private McFadden:
    "A saint it ud sadden
      To dhrill such a mug!
    Eyes front! — ye baboon, ye! —
    Chin up! — ye gossoon, ye!
    Ye've jaws like a goat —
    Halt! ye leather-lipped loon, ye!
        Wan — two!
        Wan — two!
Ye whiskered orang-outang, I'll fix you!
        Wan — two! —
        Time! Mark!
Ye've eyes like a bat! — can ye see in the dark?"

Sez Corporal Madden to Private McFadden:
    "Yer figger wants padd'n' —
      Sure, man, ye've no shape!
    Behind ye yer shoulders
    Stick out like two boulders;
    Yer shins is as thin
    As a pair of pen-holders!
        Wan — two!
        Wan — two!
Yer belly belongs on yer back, ye Jew!
        Wan — two! —
        Time! Mark!
I'm dhry as a dog — I can't shpake but I bark!"

Sez Corporal Madden to Private McFadden:
    "Me heart it ud gladden
      To blacken your eye.
    Ye're gettin' too bold, ye
    Compel me to scold ye, —
    'Tis halt! that I say, —
    Will ye heed what I told ye?
        Wan — two'
        Wan — two!
Be jabers, I'm dhryer than Brian Boru!
        Wan — two! —
        Time! Mark!
What's wur-ruk for chickens is sport for the lark!"

Sez Corporal Madden to Private McFadden:
    "I'll not stay a gaddin'

Wid dagoes like you!
I'll travel no farther,
I'm dyin' for — wather; —
Come on, if ye like, —
Can ye loan me a quather?
Ya-as, you —
What, — two?
And ye'll pay the potheen? Ye're a daisy! Whurroo!
You'll do!
Whist! Mark!
The Rigiment's flattered to own ye, me spark!"

Robert William Chambers

THE JUMBLIES

From "Nonsense Songs"

They went to sea in a sieve, they did;
In a sieve they went to sea;
In spite of all their friends could say,
On a winter's morn, on a stormy day,
In a sieve they went to sea.
And when the sieve turn'd round and round,
And every one cried, "You'll be drown'd!"
They call'd aloud, "Our sieve ain't big:
But we don't care a button; we don't care a fig:
In a sieve we'll go to sea!"
Far and few, far and few,
Are the lands where the Jumblies live:
Their heads are green, and their hands are blue;
And they went to sea in a sieve.

They sail'd away in a sieve, they did,
In a sieve they sail'd so fast,
With only a beautiful pea-green veil
Tied with a ribbon, by way of a sail,
To a small tobacco-pipe mast.
And every one said who saw them go,
"Oh, won't they be soon upset, you know:
For the sky is dark, and the voyage is long;

And, happen what may, it's extremely wrong
   In a sieve to sail so fast."

The water it soon came in, it did;
   The water it soon came in:
So, to keep them dry, they wrapp'd their feet
In a pinky paper all folded neat:
   And they fasten'd it down with a pin.
And they pass'd the night in a crockery-jar;
And each of them said, "How wise we are!
Though the sky be dark, and the voyage be long,
Yet we never can think we were rash or wrong,
   While round in our sieve we spin."

And all night long they sail'd away;
   And, when the sun went down,
They whistled and warbled a moony song
To the echoing sound of a coppery gong,
   In the shade of the mountains brown,
"O Timballoo! how happy we are
When we live in a sieve and a crockery-jar!
And all night long, in the moonlight pale,
We sail away with a pea-green sail
   In the shade of the mountains brown."

They sail'd to the Western Sea, they did —
   To a land all cover'd with trees:
And they bought an owl, and a useful cart,
And a pound of rice, and a cranberry-tart,
   And a hive of silvery bees;
And they bought a pig, and some green jackdaws,
And a lovely monkey with lollipop paws,
And forty bottles of ring-bo-ree,
   And no end of Stilton cheese:

And in twenty years they all came back, —
   In twenty years or more;
And every one said, "How tall they've grown!
For they've been to the Lakes, and the Torrible Zone,
   And the hills of the Chankly Bore."
And they drank their health, and gave them a feast
Of dumplings made of beautiful yeast;

And every one said, "If we only live,
We, too, will go to sea in a sieve,
    To the hills of the Chankly Bore."
      Far and few, far and few,
    Are the lands where the Jumblies live:
      Their heads are green, and their hands are blue;
    And they went to sea in a sieve.

Edward Lear

MY ANGELINE

From "The Wizard of the Nile"

She kept her secret well, oh, yes,
    Her hideous secret well.
We together were cast, I knew not her past;
    For how was I to tell?
I married her, guileless lamb I was;
    I'd have died for her sweet sake.
How could I have known that my Angeline
    Had been a Human Snake?
Ah, we had been wed but a week or two
    When I found her quite a wreck:
Her limbs were tied in a double bow-knot
    At the back of her swan-like neck.
No curse there sprang to my pallid lips,
    Nor did I reproach her then;
I calmly untied my bonny bride
    And straightened her out again.

Refrain

My Angeline! My Angeline!
Why didst disturb my mind serene?
My well-belovèd circus queen,
My Human Snake, my Angeline!

At night I'd wake at the midnight hour,
    With a weird and haunted feeling,
And there she'd be, in her *robe de nuit*,
    A-walking upon the ceiling.

She said she was being " the human fly,"
  And she'd lift me up from beneath
By a section slight of my garb of night,
  Which she held in her pearly teeth.
For the sweet, sweet sake of the Human Snake
  I'd have stood this conduct shady;
But she skipped in the end with an old, old friend,
  An eminent bearded lady.
But, oh, at night, when my slumber's light,
  Regret comes o'er me stealing;
For I miss the sound of those little feet,
  As they pattered along the ceiling.

Refrain

  My Angeline! My Angeline!
  Why didst disturb my mind serene?
  My well-belovèd circus queen,
  My Human Snake, my Angeline!

                    Harry B. Smith

LOVERS, AND A REFLECTION

IN IMITATION OF JEAN INGELOW

In moss-prankt dells which the sunbeams flatter
  (And Heaven it knoweth what that may mean;
Meaning, however, is no great matter)
  Where woods are a-tremble, with rifts atween;

Thro' God's own heather we wonn'd together,
  I and my Willie (O love my love):
I need hardly remark it was glorious weather,
  And flitterbats waver'd alow, above:

Boats were curtseying, rising, bowing,
  (Boats in that climate are so polite),
And sands were a ribbon of green endowing,
  And O the sundazzle on bark and bight!

Thro' the rare red heather we danced together
  (O love my Willie!) and smelt for flowers:
I must mention again it was gorgeous weather,
  Rhymes are so scarce in this world of ours: —

By rises that flush'd with their purple flavors,
  Thro' becks that brattled o'er grasses sheen,
We walked and waded, we two young shavers,
  Thanking our stars we were both so green.

We journeyed in parallels, I and Willie,
  In fortunate parallels! Butterflies,
Hid in weltering shadows of daffodilly
  Or marjoram, kept making peacock eyes:

Songbirds darted about, some inky
  As coal, some snowy (I ween) as curds;
Or rosy as pinks, or as roses pinky —
  They reck of no eerie To-come, those birds!

But they skim over bents which the millstream washes,
  Or hang in the lift 'neath a white cloud's hem;
They need no parasols, no goloshes;
  And good Mrs. Trimmer she feedeth them.

Then we thrid God's cowslips (as erst his heather)
  That endowed the wan grass with their golden blooms;
And snapt — (it was perfectly charming weather) —
  Our fingers at Fate and her goddess-glooms:

And Willie 'gan sing (O, his notes were fluty;
  Wafts fluttered them out to the white-wing'd sea) —
Something made up of rhymes that have done much duty,
  Rhymes (better to put it) of "ancientry:"

Bowers of flowers encounter'd showers
  In William's carol — (O love my Willie!)
Then he bade sorrow borrow from blithe to-morrow
  I quite forget what — say a daffodilly:

A nest in a hollow, "with buds to follow,"
  I think occurred next in his nimble strain;
And clay that was "kneaden" of course in Eden —
  A rhyme most novel, I do maintain:

Mists, bones, the singer himself, love-stories,
  And all least furlable things got " furled ; "
Not with any design to conceal their " glories,"
  But simply and solely to rhyme with " world."

   .   .   .   .

O if billows and pillows and hours and flowers,
  And all the brave rhymes of an elder day,
Could be furled together, this genial weather,
  And carted, or carried on " wafts " away,
Nor ever again trotted out — ah me !
How much fewer volumes of verse there'd be !
Charles Stuart Calverley

THE IDEAL HUSBAND TO HIS WIFE

We've lived for forty years, dear wife,
  And walked together side by side,
And you to-day are just as dear
  As when you were my bride.
I've tried to make life glad for you,
  One long, sweet honeymoon of joy,
A dream of marital content,
  Without the least alloy.
I've smoothed all boulders from our path,
  That we in peace might toil along,
By always hastening to admit
  That I was right and you were wrong.

No mad diversity of creed
  Has ever sundered me from thee;
For I permit you evermore
  To borrow your ideas of me.
And thus it is, through weal or woe,
  Our love forevermore endures;
For I permit that you should take
  My views and creeds, and make them yours.
And thus I let you have my way,
  And thus in peace we toil along,
For I am willing to admit
  That I am right and you are wrong.

And when our matrimonial skiff
  Strikes snags in love's meandering stream,
I lift our shallop from the rocks,
  And float as in a placid dream.
And well I know our marriage bliss
  While life shall last will never cease;
For I shall always let thee do,
  In generous love, just what I please.
Peace comes, and discord flies away,
  Love's bright day follows hatred's night;
For I am ready to admit
  That you are wrong and I am right.

Sam Walter Foss

THE HUNTING SEASON

BY A MATCH - SCHEMING MAMMA

Don't talk of September! — a lady
  Must think it of all months the worst;
The men are preparing already
  To take themselves off on the First.
I try to arrange a small party,
  The girls dance together; how tame!
I'd get up a game of écarté,
  But they go to bring down *their* game!

Last month, their attention to quicken,
  A supper I knew was the thing;
But now from my turkey and chicken
  They're tempted by birds on the wing!
They shoulder their terrible rifles,
  (It's really too much for my nerves!)
And slighting my sweets and my trifles,
  Prefer my Lord Harry's preserves!

Miss Lovemore, with great consternation,
  Now hears of the terrible plan,
And fears that her little flirtation
  Was only a flash in the pan!
O! marriage is hard of digestion,
  And men are all sparing of words;

And now, 'stead of popping the question,
   They set off to pop at the birds.

Go, false ones, your aim is so horrid,
   That love at the sight of you dies;
You care not for locks on the forehead,
   The *locks* made by Manton you prize.
All thoughts sentimental exploding,
   Like *flints* I behold you depart;
You heed not, when priming and loading,
   The load you have left on my heart!

They talk about patent percussions,
   And all preparations for sport;
And those double-barrel discussions
   Exhaust double bottles of port!
The dearest is deaf to my summons,
   As off on his pony he jogs;
A doleful condition is woman's, —
   The men are all gone to the dogs.
               Thomas Haynes Bayly

THE CONFESSION

There's somewhat on my breast, father,
   There's somewhat on my breast!
The livelong day I sigh, father,
   And at night I cannot rest.
I cannot take my rest, father,
   Though I would fain do so;
A weary weight oppresseth me —
   This weary weight of woe!

'Tis not the lack of gold, father,
   Nor want of worldly gear;
My lands are broad, and fair to see,
   My friends are kind and dear.
My kin are leal and true, father,
   They mourn to see my grief;
But, oh! 'tis not a kinsman's hand
   Can give my heart relief!

'Tis not that Janet's false, father,
  'Tis not that she's unkind;
Though busy flatterers swarm around,
  I know her constant mind.
'Tis not *her* coldness, father,
  That chills my laboring breast;
It's that confounded cucumber
  I ate, and can't digest.

         Richard Harris Barham

THE EDITOR'S WOOING

We love thee, Ann Maria Smith,
  And in thy condescension
We see a future full of joys
  Too numerous to mention.

There's Cupid's arrow in thy glance,
  That by thy love's coercion
Has reached our melting heart of hearts,
  And asked for one insertion.

With joy we feel the blissful smart;
  And ere our passion ranges,
We freely place thy love upon
  The list of our exchanges.

There's music in thy lowest tone,
  And silver in thy laughter:
And truth — but we will give the full
  Particulars hereafter.

Oh, we could tell thee of our plans
  All obstacles to scatter;
But we are full just now, and have
  A press of other matter.

Then let us marry, Queen of Smiths,
  Without more hesitation:
The very thought doth give our blood
  A larger circulation.

         Robert H. Newell
        (" Orpheus C. Kerr ")

OUR TRAVELLER

If thou would'st stand on Etna's burning brow,
With smoke above, and roaring flame below;
And gaze adown that molten gulf reveal'd,
Till thy soul shudder'd and thy senses reel'd:
If thou wouldst beard Niag'ra in his pride,
Or stem the billows of Propontic tide;
Scale all alone some dizzy Alpine *haut,*
And shriek "Excelsior!" among the snow:
Would'st tempt all deaths, all dangers that may be —
Perils by land, and perils on the sea;
This vast round world, I say, if thou wouldst view it —
Then, why the dickens don't you go and do it?
                    Henry Cholmondeley Pennell

IF YOU HAVE SEEN

Good reader! if you e'er have seen,
    When Phœbus hastens to his pillow,
The mermaids, with their tresses green,
    Dancing upon the western billow:
If you have seen, at twilight dim,
When the lone spirit's vesper hymn
    Floats wild along the winding shore:
If you have seen, through mist of eve,
The fairy train their ringlets weave,
Glancing along the spangled green; —
    If you have seen all this, and more,
God bless me! what a deal you've seen!
                    Thomas Moore

A DIRGE

Concerning the Late Lamented King of the Cannibal Islands

And so our royal relative is dead!
    And so he rests from gustatory labors!
The white man was his choice, but when he fed
    He'd sometimes entertain his tawny neighbors.

He worshipped, as he said, his " Fe-fo-fum,"
The goddess of the epigastrium.

And missionaries graced his festive board,
  Solemn and succulent, in twos and dozens,
And smoked before their hospitable lord,
  Welcome as if they'd been his second cousins.
When cold, he warmed them as he would his kin —
They came as strangers, and he took them in.

And generous! — oh, wasn't he? I have known him
  Exhibit a celestial amiability: —
He'd eat an enemy, and then would own him
  Of flavor excellent, despite hostility.
The cruelest captain of the Turkish navy
He buried in an honorable grave — y.

He had a hundred wives. To make things pleasant
  They found it quite judicious to adore him; —
And when he dined, the nymphs were always present —
  Sometimes beside him and sometimes — before him.
When he was tired of one, he called her " sweet,"
And told her she was " good enough to eat."

He was a man of taste — and justice, too;
  He oped his mouth for e'en the humblest sinner,
And three weeks stall-fed an emaciate Jew
  Before they brought him to the royal dinner.
With preacher-men he shared his board and wallet
And let them nightly occupy his palate!

We grow like what we eat. Bad food depresses;
  Good food exalts us like an inspiration,
And missionary on the *menu* blesses
  And elevates the Feejee population.
A people who for years, saints, bairns, and women ate
Must soon their vilest qualities eliminate.

But the deceased could never hold a candle
  To those prim, pale-faced people of propriety
Who gloat o'er gossip and get fat on scandal —
  The cannibals of civilized society;
They drink the blood of brothers with their rations,
And crunch the bones of living reputations.

They kill the soul; he only claimed the dwelling.
    They take the sharpened scalpel of surmises
And cleave the sinews when the heart is swelling,
    And slaughter Fame and Honor for their prizes.
They make the spirit in the body quiver;
They quench the Light! He only took the — Liver!

I've known some hardened customers, I wot,
    A few tough fellows — pagans beyond question —
I wish had got into his dinner-pot;
    Although I'm certain they'd defy digestion,
And break his jaw, and ruin his esophagus,
Were he the chief of beings anthropophagous!

How fond he was of children! To his breast
    The tenderest nurslings gained a free admission.
Rank he despised, nor, if they came well dressed,
    Cared if they were plebeian or patrician.
Shade of Leigh Hunt! Oh, guide this laggard pen
To write of one who loved his fellow men!
                    William Augustus Croffut

THE BIRTH OF SAINT PATRICK

On the eighth day of March it was, some people say,
That Saint Pathrick at midnight he first saw the day;
While others declare 'twas the ninth he was born,
And 'twas all a mistake between midnight and morn;
For mistakes *will* occur in a hurry and shock,
And some blam'd the baby — and some blam'd the clock —
Till with all their cross-questions sure no one could know,
If the child was too fast — or the clock was too slow.

Now the first faction fight in ould Ireland, they say,
Was all on account of Saint Pathrick's birthday,
Some fought for the eighth — for the ninth more would
    die,
And who wouldn't see right, sure they blacken'd his eye!
At last, both the factions so positive grew,
That *each* kept a birthday, so Pat then had *two*,
Till Father Mulcahy, who showed them their sins,
Said, " No one could have two birthdays but a *twins*."

Says he, "Boys, don't be fightin' for eight or for nine,
Don't be always dividin' — but sometimes combine;
Combine eight with nine, and seventeen is the mark,
So let that be his birthday." — "Amen," says the clerk.
"If he wasn't a *twins,* sure our hist'ry will show —
That, at least, he's worth any *two* saints that we know!"
Then they all got blind dhrunk — which complated their
    bliss,
And we keep up the practice from that day to this.

Samuel Lover

THE MEETING OF THE CLABBERHUSES

I.

He was the Chairman of the Guild
    Of Early Pleiocene Patriarchs;
He was chief Mentor of the Lodge
    Of the Oracular Oligarchs;
He was the Lord High Autocrat
    And Vizier of the Sons of Light,
And Sultan and Grand Mandarin
    Of the Millennial Men of Might.

He was Grand Totem and High Priest
    Of the Independent Potentates;
Grand Mogul of the Galaxy
    Of the Illustrious Stay-out-lates;
The President of the Dandydudes,
    The Treasurer of the Sons of Glee;
The Leader of the Clubtown Band
    And Architects of Melody.

II.

She was Grand Worthy Prophetess
    Of the Illustrious Maids of Mark;
Of Vestals of the Third Degree
    She was Most Potent Matriarch;
She was High Priestess of the Shrine
    Of Clubtown's Culture Coterie,
And First Vice-President of the League
    Of the Illustrious G. A. B.

She was the First Dame of the Club
  For teaching Patagonians Greek;
She was Chief Clerk and Auditor
  Of Clubtown's Anti-Bachelor Clique;
She was High Treasurer of the Fund
  For Borrioboolaghalians,
And the Fund for Sending Browning's Poems
  To Native-born Australians.

III.

Once to a crowded social fête
  Both these much-titled people came,
And each perceived, when introduced,
  They had the selfsame name.
Their hostess said, when first they met:
" Permit me now to introduce
My good friend Mr. Clabberhuse
  To Mrs. Clabberhuse."

" 'Tis very strange," said she to him,
  " Such an unusual name! —
A name so very seldom heard,
  That we should bear the same."
" Indeed, 'tis wonderful," said he,
  " And I'm surprised the more,
Because I never heard the name
  Outside my home before.

" But now I come to look at you,"
  Said he, " upon my life,
If I am not indeed deceived,
  You are — you are — my wife."
She gazed into his searching face
  And seemed to look him through;
" Indeed," said she, " it seems to me
  You are my husband, too.

" I've been so busy with my clubs
  And in my various spheres
I have not seen you now," she said,
  " For over fourteen years."

"That's just the way it's been with me,
These clubs demand a sight"—
And then they both politely bowed,
And sweetly said "Good night."
Sam Walter Foss

DIDO

IMPROMPTU EPIGRAM ON THE LATIN GERUNDS

When Dido found Æneas would not come,
She mourn'd in silence, and was *Di-do-dum* (*b*).
Richard Porson

ON HEARING A LADY PRAISE A CERTAIN REV. DOCTOR'S EYES

I cannot praise the Doctor's eyes;
I never saw his glance divine;
He always shuts them when he prays,
And when he preaches he shuts mine.
George Outram

EPITAPH INTENDED FOR HIS WIFE

Here lies my wife: here let her lie!
Now she's at rest, and so am I.
John Dryden

A FAREWELL TO TOBACCO

May the Babylonish curse
Straight confound my stammering verse,
If I can a passage see
In this word-perplexity,
Or a fit expression find,
Or a language to my mind,
(Still the phrase is wide or scant)
To take leave of thee, *great plant!*

Gilbert   Burns

Moore

Calverley   Hood

Or in any terms relate
Half my love, or half my hate:
For I hate, yet love thee so,
That, whichever thing I show,
The plain truth will seem to be
A constrain'd hyperbole,
And the passion to proceed
More from a mistress than a weed.

Sooty retainer to the vine,
Bacchus' black servant, negro fine;
Sorcerer, that mak'st us dote upon
Thy begrimed complexion,
And, for thy pernicious sake,
More and greater oaths to break
Than reclaimèd lovers take
'Gainst women: thou thy siege dost lay
Much too in the female way,
While thou suck'st the laboring breath
Faster than kisses or than death.

Thou in such a cloud dost bind us
That our worst foes cannot find us,
And ill-fortune, that would thwart us,
Shoots at rovers, shooting at us;
While each man, through thy height'ning steam,
Does like a smoking Etna seem,
And all about us does express
(Fancy and wit in richest dress)
A Sicilian fruitfulness.

Thou through such a mist dost show us
That our best friends do not know us,
And, for those allowèd features,
Due to reasonable creatures,
Liken'st us to fell Chimeras,
Monsters, — that who see us, fear us;
Worse than Cerberus or Geryon,
Or, who first loved a cloud, Ixion.

Bacchus we know, and we allow
His tipsy rites. But what art thou
That but by reflex canst show
What his deity can do,

As the false Egyptian spell
Aped the true Hebrew miracle?
Some few vapors thou may'st raise,
The weak brain may serve to amaze,
But to the reins and nobler heart
Canst nor life nor heat impart.

Brother of Bacchus, later born,
The old world was sure forlorn
Wanting thee, that aidest more
The god's victories than, before,
All his panthers, and the brawls
Of his piping Bacchanals.
These, as stale, we disallow,
Or judge of *thee* meant: only thou
His true Indian conquest art;
And, for ivy round his dart,
The reformèd god now weaves
A finer thyrsus of thy leaves.

Scent to match thy rich perfume
Chemic art did ne'er presume
Through her quaint alembic strain,
None so sov'reign to the brain;
Nature, that did in thee excel,
Framed again no second smell.
Roses, violets, but toys
For the smaller sort of boys,
Or for greener damsels meant;
Thou art the only manly scent.

Stinkingest of the stinking kind!
Filth of the mouth and fog of the mind!
Africa, that brags her foison,
Breeds no such prodigious poison!
Henbane, nightshade, both together,
Hemlock, aconite —

                    Nay, rather,
Plant divine, of rarest virtue;
Blisters on the tongue would hurt you!
'Twas but in a sort I blamed thee;
None e'er prosper'd who defamed thee;

Irony all, and feign'd abuse,
Such as perplex'd lovers use,
At a need, when, in despair
To paint forth their fairest fair,
Or in part but to express
That exceeding comeliness
Which their fancies doth so strike,
They borrow language of dislike;
And, instead of Dearest Miss,
Jewel, Honey, Sweetheart, Bliss,
And those forms of old admiring,
Call her Cockatrice and Siren,
Basilisk, and all that's evil,
Witch, Hyena, Mermaid, Devil,
Ethiop, Wench, and Blackamoor,
Monkey, Ape, and twenty more;
Friendly Trait'ress, loving Foe —
Not that she is truly so,
But no other way they know
A contentment to express,
Borders so upon excess,
That they do not rightly wot
Whether it be from pain or not.

Or, as men constrain'd to part
With what's nearest to their heart,
While their sorrow's at the height,
Lose discrimination quite,
And their hasty wrath let fall,
To appease their frantic gall,
On the darling thing whatever,
Whence they feel it death to sever
Though it be, as they, perforce,
Guiltless of the sad divorce.

For I must (nor let it grieve thee,
Friendliest of plants, that I must) leave thee.
For thy sake, TOBACCO, I
Would do anything but die,
And but seek to extend my days
Long enough to sing thy praise.
But, as she who once hath been
A king's consort is a queen

Ever after, nor will bate
Any tittle of her state
Though a widow, or divorced,
So I, from thy converse forced,
The old name and style retain,
A right Katherine of Spain;
And a seat, too, 'mongst the joys
Of the blest Tobacco Boys;
Where, though I, by sour physician,
Am debarr'd the full fruition
Of thy favors, I may catch
Some collateral sweets, and snatch
Sidelong odors, that give life
Like glances from a neighbor's wife;
And still live in the by-places
And the suburbs of thy graces;
And in thy borders take delight,
An unconquer'd Canaanite.

Charles Lamb

IF I SHOULD DIE TO-NIGHT

If I should die to-night
And you should come to my cold corpse and say,
Weeping and heartsick o'er my lifeless clay —
    If I should die to-night,
And you should come in deepest grief and woe —
And say: "Here's that ten dollars that I owe,"
    I might arise in my large white cravat
    And say, "What's that?"

If I should die to-night
And you should come to my cold corpse and kneel,
Clasping my bier to show the grief you feel,
    I say, if I should die to-night
And you should come to me, and there and then
Just even hint 'bout payin' me that ten,
    I might arise the while,
    But I'd drop dead again.

Ben King

TOO GREAT A SACRIFICE

The maid, as by the papers doth appear,
Whom fifty thousand dollars made so dear,
To test Lothario's passion, simply said:
" Forego the weed before we go to wed.
For smoke take flame; I'll be that flame's bright fanner:
To have your Anna, give up your Havana."
But he, when thus she brought him to the scratch,
Lit his cigar, and threw away his match.

Anonymous

BEN BLUFF

Ben Bluff was a whaler, and many a day
Had chased the huge fish about Baffin's old Bay;
But time brought a change his diversion to spoil,
And that was when Gas took the shine out of Oil.

He turned up his nose at the fumes of the coke,
And swore the whole scheme was a bottle of smoke;
As to London, he briefly delivered his mind,
" Sparma-city," said he, — but the city declined.

So Ben cut his line in a sort of a huff,
As soon as his whales had brought profits enough,
And hard by the Docks settled down for his life,
But, true to his text, went to Wales for a wife.

A big one she was, without figure or waist,
More bulky than lovely, but that was his taste;
In fat she was lapped from her sole to her crown,
And, turned into oil, would have lighted a town.

But Ben, like a whaler, was charmed with the match,
And thought, very truly, his spouse a great catch;
A flesh-and-blood emblem of Plenty and Peace,
And would not have changed her for Helen of Greece!

For Greenland was green in his memory still;
He'd quitted his trade, but retained the good-will;
And often when softened by bumbo and flip,
Would cry till he blubbered about his old ship.

No craft like the *Grampus* could work through a floe,
What knots she could run, and what tons she could stow!
And then that rich smell he preferred to the rose,
By just nosing the hold without holding his nose.

Now Ben he resolved, one fine Saturday night,
A snug arctic circle of friends to invite;
Old tars in the trade, who related old tales,
And drank, and blew clouds that were "very like whales."

Of course with their grog there was plenty of chat,
Of canting, and flenching, and cutting up fat;
And how gun-harpoons into fashion had got,
And if they were meant for the gun-whale or not?

At last they retired, and left Ben to his rest,
By fancies cetaceous and drink well possessed,
When, lo! as he lay by his partner in bed,
He heard something blow through two holes in its head!

"A start!" muttered Ben, in the *Grampus* afloat,
And made but one jump from the deck to the boat!
"Huzza! pull away for the blubber and bone, —
I look on that whale as already my own!"

Then groping about by the light of the moon,
He soon laid his hand on his trusty harpoon;
A moment he poised it, to send it more pat,
And then made a plunge to imbed it in fat!

"Starn all!" he sang out, "as you care for your lives, —
Starn all! as you hope to return to your wives, —
Stand by for the flurry! she throws up the foam!
Well done, my old iron; I've sent you right home!"

And scarce had he spoken, when lo! bolt upright
The leviathan rose in a great sheet of white,
And swiftly advanced for a fathom or two,
As only a fish out of water could do.

"Starn all!" echoed Ben, with a movement aback,
But too slow to escape from the creature's attack;
If flippers it had, they were furnished with nails, —
"You willin, I'll teach you that women ain't whales!"

"Avast!" shouted Ben, with a sort of a screech,
"I've heard a whale spouting, but here is a speech!"
"A-spouting, indeed! — very pretty," said she;
"But it's you I'll blow up, not the froth of the sea!

"To go to pretend to take *me* for a fish!
You great polar bear — but I know what you wish;
You're sick of a wife that your hankering balks,
You want to go back to some young Esquimaux!"

"O dearest," cried Ben, frightened out of his life,
"Don't think I would go for to murder a wife
I must long have bewailed!" But she only cried, "Stuff!"
Don't name it, you brute, you've *be-whaled* me enough!"

"Lord, Polly!" said Ben, "such a deed could I do?
I'd rather have murdered all Wapping than you!
Come, forgive what is past." "O you monster!" she cried,
"It was none of your fault that it passed off one side!"

However, at last she inclined to forgive;
"But, Ben, take this warning as long as you live, —
If the love of harpooning so strong must prevail,
Take a whale for a wife, — not a wife for a whale!"

Thomas Hood

THE WALRUS AND THE CARPENTER

The sun was shining on the sea,
　　Shining with all his might:
He did his very best to make
　　The billows smooth and bright —
And this was odd, because it was
　　The middle of the night.

The moon was shining sulkily,
　　Because she thought the sun

Had got no business to be there
After the day was done —
"It's very rude of him," she said,
"To come and spoil the fun!"

The sea was wet as wet could be,
The sands were dry as dry.
You could not see a cloud, because
No cloud was in the sky:
No birds were flying overhead —
There were no birds to fly.

The Walrus and the Carpenter
Were walking close at hand:
They wept like anything to see
Such quantities of sand:
"If this were only cleared away,"
They said, "it would be grand!"

"If seven maids with seven mops
Swept it for half a year,
Do you suppose," the Walrus said,
"That they could get it clear?"
"I doubt it," said the Carpenter,
And shed a bitter tear.

"O Oysters come and walk with us!"
The Walrus did beseech.
"A pleasant walk, a pleasant talk,
Along the briny beach:
We cannot do with more than four,
To give a hand to each."

The eldest Oyster looked at him,
But never a word he said:
The eldest Oyster winked his eye,
And shook his heavy head —
Meaning to say he did not choose
To leave the oyster-bed.

But four young Oysters hurried up,
All eager for the treat:
Their coats were brushed, their faces washed,
Their shoes were clean and neat —

And this was odd, because, you know,
  They hadn't any feet.

Four other Oysters followed them,
  And yet another four;
And thick and fast they came at last,
  And more, and more, and more —
All hopping through the frothy waves,
  And scrambling to the shore.

The Walrus and the Carpenter
  Walked on a mile or so,
And then they rested on a rock
  Conveniently low:
And all the little Oysters stood
  And waited in a row.

"The time has come," the Walrus said,
  "To talk of many things:
Of shoes — and ships — and sealing-wax —
  Of cabbages — and kings —
And why the sea is boiling hot —
  And whether pigs have wings."

"But wait a bit," the Oysters cried,
  "Before we have our chat:
For some of us are out of breath,
  And all of us are fat!"
"No hurry!" said the Carpenter.
  They thanked him much for that.

"A loaf of bread," the Walrus said,
  "Is what we chiefly need:
Pepper and vinegar besides
  Are very good indeed —
Now if you're ready, Oysters dear,
  We can begin to feed."

"But not on us!" the Oysters cried,
  Turning a little blue.
"After such kindness that would be
  A dismal thing to do!"
"The night is fine," the Walrus said,
  "Do you admire the view?"

"It was so kind of you to come!
    And you are very nice!"
The Carpenter said nothing but
    "Cut us another slice:
I wish you were not quite so deaf —
    I've had to ask you twice!"

"It seems a shame," the Walrus said,
    "To play them such a trick,
After we've brought them out so far,
    And made them trot so quick!"
The Carpenter said nothing but
    "The butter's spread too thick!"

"I weep for you," the Walrus said;
    "I deeply sympathise."
With sobs and tears he sorted out
    Those of the largest size,
Holding his pocket-handkerchief
    Before his streaming eyes.

"O Oysters," said the Carpenter,
    "You've had a pleasant run!
Shall we be trotting home again?"
    But answer came there none —
And this was scarcely odd, because
    They'd eaten every one.

                                Lewis Carroll

"FUZZY - WUZZY"

(SOUDAN EXPEDITIONARY FORCE)

We've fought with many men acrost the seas,
    An' some of 'em was brave an' some was not,
The Paythan an' the Zulu an' Burmese;
    But the Fuzzy was the finest o' the lot.
We never got a ha'porth's change of 'im:
    'E squatted in the scrub an' 'ocked our 'orses,
'E cut our sentries up at Sua*kim,*
    An' 'e played the cat an' banjo with our forces.

So 'ere's *to* you, Fuzzy-Wuzzy, at your 'ome in the Soudan;
You're a pore benighted 'eathen but a first-class fightin'
    man;
We gives you your certificate, an' if you want it signed
We'll come an' 'ave a romp with you whenever you're in-
    clined.

   We took our chanst among the Kyber 'ills,
      The Boers knocked us silly at a mile,
   The Burman give us Irriwaddy chills,
      An' a Zulu *impi* dished us up in style:
   But all we ever got from such as they
      Was pop to what the Fuzzy made us swaller;
   We 'eld our bloomin' own, the papers say,
      But man for man the Fuzzy knocked us 'oller.
Then 'ere's *to* you, Fuzzy-Wuzzy, an' the missis an' the
    kid;
Our orders was to break you, an' of course we went an'
    did.
We sloshed you with Martinis, an' it wasn't 'ardly fair;
But for all the odds agin' you, Fuzzy-Wuz, you broke the
    square.

   'E 'asn't got no papers of 'is own,
      'E 'asn't got no medals nor rewards,
   So we must certify the skill 'e's shown
      In usin' of 'is long two-'anded swords:
   When 'e's 'oppin' in an' out among the bush,
      With 'is coffin-'eaded shield an' shovel-spear,
   An 'appy day with Fuzzy on the rush
      Will last an 'ealthy Tommy for a year.
So 'ere's *to* you, Fuzzy-Wuzzy, an' your friends which are
    no more,
If we 'adn't lost some messmates we would 'elp you to
    deplore;
But give an' take's the gospel, an' we'll call the bargain
    fair,
For if you 'ave lost more than us, you crumpled up the
    square!

   'E rushes at the smoke when we let drive,
      An', before we know, 'e's 'ackin' at our 'ead;
   'E's all 'ot sand an' ginger when alive,
      An' 'e's generally shammin' when 'e's dead.

'E's a daisy, 'e's a ducky, 'e's a lamb!
  'E's a injia-rubber idiot on the spree,
'E's the on'y thing that doesn't give a damn
  For a Regiment o' British Infantree!
So 'ere's *to* you, Fuzzy-Wuzzy, at your 'ome in the Sou-
  dan;
You're a pore benighted 'eathen but a first-class fightin'
  man;
An' 'ere's *to* you, Fuzzy-Wuzzy, with your 'ayrick 'ead of
  'air —
You big black boundin' beggar — for you broke a British
  square!

Rudyard Kipling

MY MISTRESS'S BOOTS

They nearly strike me dumb,
And I tremble when they come
    Pit-a-pat:
This palpitation means
These boots are Geraldine's —
    Think of that!

Oh, where did hunter win
So delectable a skin
    For her feet?
You lucky little kid,
You perished, so you did,
    For my sweet!

The faëry stitching gleams
On the sides, and in the seams,
    And it shows
The Pixies were the wags
Who tipt those funny tags
    And these toes.

What soles to charm an elf!
Had Crusoe, sick of self,
    Chanced to view

One printed near the tide,
Oh, how hard he would have tried
    For the two!

For Gerry's debonair
And innocent, and fair
    As a rose;
She's an angel in a frock,
With a fascinating cock
    To her nose.

The simpletons who squeeze
Their extremities to please
    Mandarins,
Would positively flinch
From venturing to pinch
    Geraldine's.

Cinderella's *lefts and rights,*
To Geraldine's were frights;
    And I trow,
The damsel, deftly shod,
Has dutifully trod
    Until now.

Come, Gerry, since it suits
Such a pretty Puss (in Boots)
    These to don;
Set this dainty hand awhile
On my shoulder, dear, and I'll
    Put them on.
                Frederick Locker-Lampson

SYMPATHY

A knight and a lady once met in a grove
While each was in quest of a fugitive love;
A river ran mournfully murmuring by,
And they wept in its waters for sympathy.

"Oh, never was knight such a sorrow that bore!"
"Oh, never was maid so deserted before!"
"From life and its woes let us instantly fly,
And jump in together for company!"

They searched for an eddy that suited the deed,
But here was a bramble and there was a weed;
"How tiresome it is!" said the fair, with a sigh;
So they sat down to rest them in company.

They gazed at each other, the maid and the knight;
How fair was her form, and how goodly his height!
"One mournful embrace," sobbed the youth, "ere we die!"
So kissing and crying kept company.

"Oh, had I but loved such an angel as you!"
"Oh, had but my swain been a quarter as true!"
"To miss such perfection how blinded was I!"
Sure now they were excellent company!

At length spoke the lass, 'twixt a smile and a tear,
"The weather is cold for a watery bier;
When summer returns we may easily die,
Till then let us sorrow in company."

Reginald Heber

THE MILLENIUM

TO R. K.

As long I dwell on some stupendous
And tremendous (Heaven defend us!)
Monstr'-inform'-ingens-horrendous
Demoniaco-seraphic
Penman's latest piece of graphic.
                    Browning

Will there never come a season
    Which shall rid us from the curse
Of a prose which knows no reason
    And an unmelodious verse:
When the world shall cease to wonder
    At the genius of an Ass,

And a boy's eccentric blunder
  Shall not bring success to pass:

When mankind shall be delivered
  From the clash of magazines,
And the inkstand shall be shivered
  Into countless smithereens:
When there stands a muzzled stripling,
  Mute, beside a muzzled bore:
When the Rudyards cease from Kipling
  And the Haggards Ride no more?
                James Kenneth Stephen

ON TAKING A WIFE

" Come, come," said Tom's father, " at your time of life,
  There's no longer excuse for thus playing the rake. —
It is time you should think, boy, of taking a wife." —
  " Why, so it is, father, — whose wife shall I take? "
                Thomas Moore

THE REMEDY WORSE THAN THE DISEASE

I sent for Radcliffe; was so ill,
  That other doctors gave me over:
He felt my pulse, prescribed his pill,
  And I was likely to recover.

But when the wit began to wheeze,
  And wine had warm'd the politician,
Cured yesterday of my disease,
  I died last night of my physician.
                Matthew Prior

CLAM - SOUP

First catch your clams: along the ebbing edges
Of saline coves you'll find the precious wedges
With backs up lurking in the sandy bottom;
Pull in your iron rake, and lo! you've got 'em.

Take thirty large ones, put a basin under,
And deftly cleave their stony jaws asunder.
Add water (three quarts) to the native liquor,
Bring to a boil (and, by the way, the quicker
It boils the better, if you'd do it cutely),
Now add the clams, chopped up and minced minutely,
Allow a longer boil of just three minutes,
And while it bubbles, quickly stir within its
Tumultuous depths, where still the mollusks mutter,
Four tablespoons of flour and four of butter,
A pint of milk, some pepper to your notion,
And clams need salting, although born of ocean.
Remove from fire (if much boiled it will suffer —
You'll find that India-rubber isn't tougher);
After 'tis off add three fresh eggs, well beaten,
Stir once more, and it's ready to be eaten.
Fruit of the wave! Oh, dainty and delicious!
Food for the gods! Ambrosia for Apicius!
Worthy to thrill the soul of sea-born Venus
Or titillate the palate of Silenus!

William Augustus Croffut

GOLD

Some take their gold
In minted mold,
And some in harps hereafter,
But give me mine
In tresses fine,
And keep the change in laughter!

Oliver Herford

MISTER WILLIAM

Oh, listen to the tale of Mister William, if you please,
Whom naughty, naughty judges sent away beyond the seas.
He forged a party's will, which caused anxiety and strife,
Resulting in his getting penal servitude for life.

He was a kindly, goodly man, and naturally prone,
Instead of taking others' gold, to give away his own.
But he had heard of Vice, and longed for only once to
    strike —
To plan *one* little wickedness — to see what it was like.

He argued with himself, and said, " A spotless man am I;
I can't be more respectable, however hard I try;
For six and thirty years I've always been as good as gold,
And now for half an hour I'll plan infamy untold!

" A baby who is wicked at the early age of one,
And then reforms — and dies at thirty-six a spotless son,
Is never, never saddled with his babyhood's defect,
But earns from worthy men consideration and respect.

" So one who never revelled in discreditable tricks
Until he reached the comfortable age of thirty-six,
May then for half an hour perpetrate a deed of shame,
Without incurring permanent disgrace, or even blame.

" That babies don't commit such crimes as forgery is true,
But little sins develop, if you leave 'em to accrue;
And he who shuns all vices as successive seasons roll,
Should reap at length the benefit of so much self-control.

" The common sin of babyhood — objecting to be drest —
If you leave it to accumulate at compound interest,
For anything you know, may represent, if you're alive,
A burglary or murder at the age of thirty-five.

" Still I wouldn't take advantage of this fact, but be con-
    tent
With some pardonable folly — it's a mere experiment.
The greater the temptation to go wrong, the less the sin;
So with something that's particularly tempting I'll begin.

" I would not steal a penny, for my income's very fair —
I do not want a penny — I have pennies and to spare —
And if I stole a penny from a money-bag or till,
The sin would be enormous — the temptation being *nil.*

" But if I broke asunder all such pettifogging bounds,
And forged a party's Will for (say) Five Hundred Thou-
    sand Pounds,
With such an irresistible temptation to a haul,
Of course the sin must be infinitesimally small.

" There's Wilson who is dying — he has wealth from Stock
    and rent —
If I divert his riches from their natural descent,
I'm placed in a position to indulge each little whim."
So he diverted them — and they, in turn, diverted him.

Unfortunately, though, by some unpardonable flaw,
Temptation isn't recognized by Britain's Common Law;
Men found him out by some peculiarity of touch,
And William got a " lifer," which annoyed him very much.

For, ah! he never reconciled himself to life in gaol,
He fretted and he pined, and grew dispirited and pale;
He was numbered like a cabman, too, which told upon
    him so
That his spirits, once so buoyant, grew uncomfortably low.

And sympathetic gaolers would remark, " It's very true,
He ain't been brought up common, like the likes of me and
    you."
So they took him into hospital, and gave him mutton chops,
And chocolate, and arrowroot, and buns, and malt, and
    hops.

Kind clergymen, besides, grew interested in his fate,
Affected by the details of his pitiable state.
They waited on the Secretary, somewhere in Whitehall,
Who said he would receive them any day they liked to call.

" Consider, sir, the hardship of this interesting case:
A prison life brings with it something very like disgrace;
It's telling on young William, who's reduced to skin and
    bone —
Remember he's a gentleman, with money of his own.

"He had an ample income, and of course he stands in need
Of sherry with his dinner, and his customary weed;
No delicacies now can pass his gentlemanly lips —
He misses his sea-bathing, and his continental trips.

"He says the other prisoners are commonplace and rude;
He says he cannot relish uncongenial prison food.
When quite a boy they taught him to distinguish Good from
    Bad,
And other educational advantages he's had.

"A burglar, or garotter, or, indeed, a common thief
Is very glad to batten on potatoes and on beef,
Or anything, in short, that prison kitchens can afford, —
A cut above the diet in a common workhouse ward.

"But beef and mutton-broth don't seem to suit our Will-
    iam's whim,
A boon to other prisoners — a punishment to him.
It never was intended that the discipline of gaol
Should dash a convict's spirits, sir, or make him thin or
    pale."

"Good Gracious Me!" that sympathetic Secretary cried,
"Suppose in prison fetters Mister William should have
    died!
Dear me, of course! Imprisonment for *Life* his sentence
    saith:
I'm very glad you mentioned it — it might have been for
    Death!

"Release him with a ticket — he'll be better then, no doubt,
And tell him I apologize." So Mister William's out.
I hope he will be careful in his manuscripts, I'm sure,
And not begin experimentalizing any more.
                              William S. Gilbert

LOVE IN A COTTAGE

They may talk of love in a cottage,
  And bowers of trellised vine —
Of nature bewitchingly simple,
  And milkmaids half divine;
They may talk of the pleasure of sleeping
  In the shade of a spreading tree,
And a walk in the fields at morning,
  By the side of a footstep free!

But give me a sly flirtation
  By the light of a chandelier —
With music to play in the pauses,
  And nobody very near;
Or a seat on a silken sofa,
  With a glass of pure old wine,
And mamma too blind to discover
  The small white hand in mine.

Your love in a cottage is hungry,
  Your vine is a nest for flies —
Your milkmaid shocks the Graces,
  And simplicity talks of pies!
You lie down to your shady slumber
  And wake with a bug in your ear,
And your damsel that walks in the morning
  Is shod like a mountaineer.

True love is at home on a carpet,
  And mightily likes his ease —
And true love has an eye for a dinner,
  And starves beneath shady trees.
His wing is the fan of a lady,
  His foot's an invisible thing,
And his arrow is tipp'd with a jewel
  And shot from a silver string.

Nathaniel Parker Willis

GIFTS RETURNED

"You must give back," her mother said,
To a poor sobbing little maid,
"All the young man has given you,
Hard as it now may seem to do."
"'Tis done already, mother dear!"
Said the sweet girl, "So never fear."
   Mother. Are you quite certain? Come, recount
(There was not much) the whole amount.
   Girl. The locket; the kid gloves.
   Mother.   Go on.
   Girl. Of the kid gloves I found but one.
   Mother. Never mind that. What else? Proceed.
You gave back all his trash?
   Girl.   Indeed.
   Mother. And was there nothing you would save?
   Girl. Everything I could give I gave.
   Mother. To the last tittle?
   Girl.   Even to that.
   Mother. Freely?
   Girl.   My heart went pit-a-pat
At giving up . . . ah me! ah me!
I cry so I can hardly see . . .
All the fond looks and words that past,
And all the kisses, to the last.
                    Walter Savage Landor

THAT GENTLE MAN FROM BOSTON TOWN

AN IDYL OF OREGON

Taken from the Complete Poetical Works of Joaquin Miller (copyrighted), by permission of the publishers, The Whitaker & Ray Company, of San Francisco.

Two webfoot brothers loved a fair
   Young lady, rich and good to see;
And oh, her black abundant hair!
   And oh, her wondrous witchery!
Her father kept a cattle farm,
These brothers kept her safe from harm:

From harm of cattle on the hill;
  From thick-necked bulls loud bellowing
The livelong morning, loud and shrill,
  And lashing sides like anything;
From roaring bulls that tossed the sand
And pawed the lilies from the land.

There came a third young man. He came
  From far and famous Boston town.
He was not handsome, was not "game,"
  But he could "cook a goose" as brown
As any man that set foot on
The sunlit shores of Oregon.

This Boston man he taught the school,
  Taught gentleness and love alway,
Said love and kindness, as a rule,
  Would ultimately "make it pay."
He was so gentle, kind, that he
Could make a noun and verb agree.

So when one day the brothers grew
  All jealous and did strip to fight,
He gently stood between the two,
  And meekly told them 'twas not right.
"I have a higher, better plan,"
Outspake this gentle Boston man.

"My plan is this: Forget this fray
  About that lily hand of hers;
Go take your guns and hunt all day
  High up yon lofty hill of firs,
And while you hunt, my loving doves,
Why, I will learn which one she loves."

The brothers sat the windy hill,
  Their hair shone yellow, like spun gold,
Their rifles crossed their laps, but still
  They sat and sighed and shook with cold.
Their hearts lay bleeding far below;
Above them gleamed white peaks of snow.

Their hounds lay couching, slim and neat;
  A spotted circle in the grass.
The valley lay beneath their feet;
  They heard the wide-winged eagles pass.
The eagles cleft the clouds above;
Yet what could they but sigh and love?

"If I could die," the elder sighed,
  "My dear young brother here might wed."
"Oh, would to Heaven I had died!"
  The younger sighed, with bended head.
Then each looked each full in the face
And each sprang up and stood in place.

"If I could die," — the elder spake, —
  "Die by your hand, the world would say
'Twas accident; — and for her sake,
  Dear brother, be it so, I pray."
"Not that!" the younger nobly said;
Then tossed his gun and turned his head.

And fifty paces back he paced!
  And as he paced he drew the ball;
Then sudden stopped and wheeled and faced
  His brother to the death and fall!
Two shots rang wild upon the air!
But lo! the two stood harmless there!

An eagle poised high in the air;
  Far, far below the bellowing
Of bullocks ceased, and everywhere
  Vast silence sat all questioning.
The spotted hounds ran circling round
Their red, wet noses to the ground.

And now each brother came to know
  That each had drawn the deadly ball;
And for that fair girl far below
  Had sought in vain to silent fall.
And then the two did gladly "shake,"
And thus the elder bravely spake:

" Now let us run right hastily
        And tell the kind schoolmaster all!
Yea! yea! and if she choose not me,
        But all on you her favors fall,
This valiant scene, till all life ends,
Dear brother, binds us best of friends."

The hounds sped down, a spotted line,
        The bulls in tall, abundant grass,
Shook back their horns from bloom and vine,
        And trumpeted to see them pass —
They loved so good, they loved so true,
These brothers scarce knew what to do.

They sought the kind schoolmaster out
        As swift as sweeps the light of morn;
They could but love, they could not doubt
        This man so gentle, " in a horn,"
They cried, " Now whose the lily hand —
That lady's of this webfoot land? "

They bowed before that big-nosed man,
        That long-nosed man from Boston town;
They talked as only lovers can,
        They talked, but he could only frown;
And still they talked, and still they plead;
It was as pleading with the dead.

At last this Boston man did speak —
        " Her father has a thousand ceows,
An hundred bulls, all fat and sleek;
        He also had this ample heouse."
The brothers' eyes stuck out thereat,
So far you might have hung your hat.

" I liked the looks of this big heouse —
        My lovely boys, won't you come in?
Her father has a thousand ceows,
        He also had a heap of tin.
The guirl? Oh yes, the guirl, you see —
The guirl, just neow she married me."
                              Joaquin Miller

IRELAND

Ireland never was contented.
Say you so? You are demented.
Ireland was contented when
All could use the sword and pen,
And when Tara rose so high
That her turrets split the sky,
And about her courts were seen
Liveried angels robed in green,
Wearing, by St. Patrick's bounty,
Emeralds big as half a county.

Walter Savage Landor

NORTHERN FARMER

NEW STYLE

Dosn't thou 'ear my 'erse's legs, as they canters awaäy?
Proputty, proputty, proputty — that's what I 'ears 'em saäy.
Proputty, proputty, proputty — Sam, thou's an ass for thy
    paaïns :
Theer's moor sense i' one o' 'is legs nor in all thy braaïns.

Woä — theer's a craw to pluck wi' tha, Sam : yon's parson's
    'ouse —
Dosn't thou knaw that a man mun be eäther a man or a
    mouse?
Time to think on it, then; for thou'll be twenty to weeäk.
Proputty, proputty — woä then, woä — let ma 'ear mysén
    speäk.

Me an' thy muther, Sammy, 'as beän a-talkin' o' thee;
Thou's been talkin' to muther, an' she beän a-tellin' it me.
Thou'll not marry for munny — thou's sweet upo' parson's
    lass —
Noä — thou'll marry for luvv — an' we boäth of us thinks
    tha an ass.

Seeä'd her to-daäy goä by — Saäint's-daäy — they was ring-
    ing the bells.
She's a beauty, thou thinks — an' soä is scoors o' gells,

Them as 'as munny an' all — wot's a beauty? — the flower
    as blaws.
But proputty, proputty sticks, an' proputty, proputty graws.

Do'ant be stunt: taäke time: I knaws what maäkes tha
    sa mad.
Warn't I craäzed fur the lasses mysén when I wur a lad?
But I knaw'd a Quaäker feller as often 'as towd ma this:
" Do'ant thou marry for munny, but goä wheer munny is! "

An' I went wheer munny war: an' thy mother coom to
    'and,
Wi' lots o' munny laaïd by, an' a nicetish bit o' land.
Maäybe she warn't a beauty: — I niver giv it a thowt —
But warn't she as good to cuddle an' kiss as a lass as 'ant
    nowt?

Parson's lass 'ant nowt, an' she weänt 'a nowt when 'e's
    deäd,
Mun be a guvness, lad, or summut, and addle her breäd:
Why? fur 'e's nobbut a curate, an' weänt niver git naw
    'igher;
An' 'e's maäde the bed as 'e ligs on afoor 'e coom'd to the
    shire.

An' thin 'e coom'd to the parish wi' lots o' 'Varsity debt,
Stook to his taäil they did, an' 'e 'ant got shut on 'em yet.
An' 'e ligs on 'is back i' the grip, wi' noän to lend 'im a
    shove,
Woorse nor a far-welter'd yowe: fur, Sammy, 'e married
    fur luvv.

Luvv? what's luvv? thou can luvv thy lass an' 'er munny
    too,
Maäkin' 'em goä togither, as they've good right to do.
Couldn't I luvv thy muther by cause o' 'er munny laaïd by?
Naäy — fur I luvv'd her a vast sight moor fur it: reäson
    why.

Ay, an' thy muther says thou wants to marry the lass,
Cooms of a gentleman burn: an' we boäth on us thinks tha
    an ass.

Woä then, proputty, wiltha? — an ass as near as mays
    nowt —
Woä then, wiltha? dangtha! — the bees is as fell as owt.

Breäk me a bit o' the esh for his 'eäd, lad, out o' the fence!
Gentleman burn! What's gentleman burn? Is it shillins
    an' pence?
Proputty, proputty's ivrything 'ere, an', Sammy, I'm blest
If it isn't the saäme oop yonder, fur them as 'as it's the
    best.

'Tisn' them as 'as munny as breäks into 'ouses an' steäls,
Them as 'as coöts to their backs an' taäkes their regular
    meäls.
Noä, but it's them as niver knaws wheer a meäl's to be 'ad.
Taäke my word for it, Sammy, the poor in a loomp is bad.

Them or thir feythers, tha sees, mun 'a beän a laäzy lot.
Fur work mun 'a gone to the gittin' whiniver munny was
    got.
Feyther 'ad ammost nowt; leästways 'is munny was 'id.
But 's tued an' moil'd 'issén deäd, an' 'e died a good un, 'e
    did.

Looök thou theer wheer Wrigglesby beck cooms out by the
    'ill!
Feyther run oop to the farm, an' I runs oop to the mill;
An' I'll run oop to the brig, an' that thou'll live to see;
And if thou marries a good un I'll leäve the land to thee.

Thim's my noätions, Sammy, wheerby I meäns to stick;
But if thou marries a bad un, I'll leäve the land to Dick. —
Coom oop, proputty, proputty — that's what I 'ears 'im
    saäy —
Proputty, proputty, proputty — canter an' canter awaäy.
                      Alfred Tennyson

THE REJECTED "NATIONAL HYMNS"

I.

BY H - - - Y W. L - NGF - - - - W

Back in the years when Phlagstaff, the Dane, was monarch
  Over the sea-ribb'd land of the fleet-footed Norsemen,
Once there went forth young Ursa to gaze at the heavens —
  Ursa — the noblest of all the Vikings and horsemen.

Musing, he sat in his stirrups and viewed the horizon,
  Where the Aurora lapt stars in a North-polar manner,
Wildly he started, — for there in the heavens before him
  Flutter'd and flam'd the original Star Spangled Banner.

II.

BY J - HN GR - - NL - - F WH - - T - - R

My Native Land, thy Puritanic stock
Still finds its roots firm-bound in Plymouth Rock,
And all thy sons unite in one grand wish —
To keep the virtues of Preservèd Fish.

Preservèd Fish, the Deacon stern and true,
Told our New England what her sons should do,
And if they swerve from loyalty and right,
Then the whole land is lost indeed in night.

III.

BY DR. OL - V - R W - ND - L H - LMES

A diagnosis of our hist'ry proves
Our native land a land its native loves;
Its birth a deed obstetric without peer,
Its growth a source of wonder far and near.

To love it more behold how foreign shores
Sink into nothingness beside its stores;
Hyde Park at best — though counted ultra-grand —
The " Boston Common " of Victoria's land.

IV.

BY R - LPH W - LDO EM - R - - N

Source immaterial of material naught,
   Focus of light infinitesimal,
Sum of all things by sleepless Nature wrought,
   Of which the normal man is decimal.

Refract, in prism immortal, from thy stars
   To the stars bent incipient on our flag,
The beam translucent, neutrifying death,
   And raise to immortality the rag.

V.

BY W - LL - - M C - LL - N B - Y - NT

The sun sinks softly to his Ev'ning Post,
   The sun swells grandly to his morning crown;
Yet not a star our Flag of Heav'n has lost,
   And not a sunset stripe with him goes down.

So thrones may fall, and from the dust of those
   New thrones may rise, to totter like the last;
But still our Country's nobler planet glows
   While the eternal stars of Heaven are fast.

VI.

BY N. P. W - LL - IS

One hue of our Flag is taken
   From the cheeks of my blushing Pet,
And its stars beat time and sparkle
   Like the studs on her chemisette.

Its blue is the ocean shadow
  That hides in her dreamy eyes,
It conquers all men, like her,
  And still for a Union flies.

VII.

BY TH - M - S B - IL - Y ALD - - CH

The little brown squirrel hops in the corn,
  The cricket quaintly sings,
The emerald pigeon nods his head,
  And the shad in the river springs,
The dainty sunflow'r hangs its head
  On the shore of the summer sea;
And better far that I were dead,
  If Maud did not love me.

I love the squirrel that hops in the corn,
  And the cricket that quaintly sings;
And the emerald pigeon that nods his head,
  And the shad that gaily springs.
I love the dainty sunflow'r, too,
  And Maud with her snowy breast;
I love them all; — but I love — I love —
  I love my country best.

                    Robert Henry Newell
                    ("Orpheus C. Kerr")

EARTH

If this little world to-night
  Suddenly should fall through space
In a hissing, headlong flight,
  Shrivelling from off its face,
As it falls into the sun,
  In an instant every trace
Of the little crawling things —
  Ants, philosophers, and lice,

Cattle, cockroaches, and kings,
  Beggars, millionaires, and mice,
Men and maggots, — all as one
  As it falls into the sun, —
Who can say but at the same
  Instant from some planet far
A child may watch us and exclaim:
  "See the pretty shooting star!"

Oliver Herford

UNCLE TASCUS AND THE DEED

Uncle Peter Tascus Runnels has been feeble some of late;
He has allus been a worker, and he sartinly did hate
To confess he couldn't tussle with the spryest any more,
That he wasn't fit for nothin' but to fub around an' chore.
When he climbed the stable scaffold t'other day he had a
    spell,
— Kind o' heart-disease or somethin' — an' I heard he like
    to fell.
Guess the prospect sort o' scared him; so, that ev'nin'
    after tea,
— After he had smoked a pipeful — pretty solemn, then,
    says he,
"Reckin, son, ye've noticed lately that your dad is gittin'
    old,
An' your marm is nigh as feeble; — much as ever she can
    scold!"
Uncle Tascus said so grinnin'; for the folks around here
    know
That no better-natured woman ever lived than old Aunt
    Jo.
"Now, my son," said Uncle Tascus, "you've been good to
    me an' marm,
An' you know we allus told ye, ye was sure to have the
    farm.
An' we like your wife Lucindy; there. has never been no
    touse
As is gen'ly apt to happen with two famblys in the house.
I can't manage as I used to; mother's gittin' pretty slim,
An' to hold our prop'ty longer is a whim, bub, jest a
    whim!

So I'll tell ye what I'm plannin', an' I know that marm
    agrees,
We'll sign off an' make it over; then we'll sort o' take
    our ease.
So, hitch up to-morrer mornin' — drive us down to Lawyer
    True,
Me an' marm will sign the papers, an' we'll deed the place
    to you."

Lawyer True looked kind o' doubtful when they told him
    what was on.
"I'll admit," said he, "that no one's got a better boy than
    John.
Now, don't think I'm interferin', or am prophesyin' harm,
When I warn ye not to do it; don't ye deed away your
    farm.
I have seen so many cases — heard 'em tried most ev'ry
    term —
Where a deed has busted fam'lies, that, I swow, it makes
    me squirm
If I'm asked to write a transfer to a relative or son.
Tascus, please excuse my meddlin', but — ye hold it till
    ye're done."

Uncle Tascus, though, insisted. He was allus rather sot.
He allowed he'd show the neighbors jest the kind of son
    he'd got.
— Said he'd show 'em how a Runnels allus stuck by kith
    an' kin,
So the lawyer drew the papers — an' they started home
    agin;
Uncle Tascus held the webbin's — he has allus driv' the
    hoss —
John he chuckled kind o' nervous. Then said he, "Wal,
    pa, I'm boss!
Now ye've never got to worry — I'm the one to take the
    lead,
Things were gettin' kind o' logy — guess I'll have to put
    on speed.
An' as now I head the fam'ly, an' you're sort of on the
    shelf,
Guess I'll " — John he took the webbin's — " guess I'd
    better drive, myself."

Wal, s'r, Uncle Tascus pondered, pondered, pondered all
    that day.
An' that evenin' still was pond'rin', as he rocked an'
    smoked away.
John, he set clus up t' table, underneath the hangin' lamp,
Ciph'rin' out that legal paper with its seal an' rev'nue
    stamp.
Then he folded it an' chuckled. "That's all right an'
    tight," he said,
"Lawyers tie things tighter'n Jehu. Dad, ye'd better go
    to bed.
You an' marm are gettin' feeble; mustn't have ye up so
    late!
I'm the boss" — John sort o' tee-heed, — "so I'll have to
    keep ye straight.
'Sides, I'll need ye bright an' early. In the mornin' hitch
    the mare,
Take that paper down t' court-house. Have it put on
    record there."

Uncle Tascus took the writin', pulled his specs down on
    his nose,
Read it over very careful. Then says he, "My son, I
    s'pose
You are jest as good's they make 'em; I hain't got no
    fault to find,
You are thrifty, smart, an' stiddy; rather bluff, but allus
    kind,
An' I guess you'd prob'ly use us jest as well's ye really
    knew,
But I hain't so awful sartin that I'm done an' out an'
    through!
— Tell ye, son, I've been a-thinkin' since ye took an' driv'
    that hoss,
— Since ye sort o' throwed your shoulders an' allowed that
    you was boss!
Hate to act so whiffle-minded, but my father used to say,
'Men would sometimes change opinions; mules would
    stick the same old way.'"
Uncle Tascus tore the paper twice acrost, then calmly
    threw
On the fire the shriv'lin' pieces. Poof! They vanished up
    the flue.

"There, bub, run to bed," said Tascus, with his sweet,
   old-fashioned smile.
"These old hands are sort of shaky, but I guess I'll drive
   awhile."

Holman F. Day

ODE FOR A SOCIAL MEETING

WITH SLIGHT ALTERATIONS BY A TEETOTALER

Come! fill a fresh bumper, — for why should we go
  logwood
While the ~~nectar~~ still reddens our cups as they flow?
   decoction
Pour out the ~~rich juices~~ still bright with the sun,
     dye-stuff
Till o'er the brimmed crystal the ~~rubies~~ shall run.
  half-ripened apples
The ~~purple-globed clusters~~ their life-dews have bled;
    taste   sugar of lead
How sweet is the ~~breath~~ of the ~~fragrance they shed~~!
  rank poisons   wines!!!
For Summer's ~~last roses~~ lie hid in the ~~wines~~
    stable-boys smoking long-nines
That were garnered by ~~maidens who laughed through the~~
   ~~vines;~~
  scowl howl scoff sneer
Then a ~~smile~~, and a ~~glass~~, and a ~~toast~~, and a ~~cheer,~~
  strychnine and whiskey, and ratsbane and beer
For ~~all the good wine, and we've some of it here~~!
In cellar, in pantry, in attic, in hall,
Down, down with the tyrant that masters us all!
~~Long live the gay servant that laughs for us all!~~

Oliver Wendell Holmes

OUR NATIVE BIRDS

Alone I sit at eventide;
   The twilight glory pales,
And o'er the meadows far and wide
   I hear the bobolinks —
   (We have no nightingales!)

Song-sparrows warble on the tree,
   I hear the purling brook,

And from the old manse on the lea
  Flies slow the cawing crow —
  (In England 'twere a rook!)

The last faint golden beams of day
  Still glow on cottage panes,
And on their lingering homeward way
  Walk weary laboring men —
  (Alas! we have no swains!)

From farmyards, down fair rural glades
  Come sounds of tinkling bells,
And songs of merry brown milkmaids
  Sweeter than catbird's strains —
  (I should say Philomel's!)

I could sit here till morning came,
  All through the night hours dark,
Until I saw the sun's bright flame
  And heard the oriole —
  (Alas! we have no lark!)

We have no leas, no larks, no rooks,
  No swains, no nightingales,
No singing milkmaids (save in books)
  The poet does his best: —
  It is the rhyme that fails.

                        Nathan Haskell Dole

THE YOUNG GAZELLE

A MOORE - ISH TALE

In early youth, as you may guess,
  I revelled in poetic lore,
And while my schoolmates studied less,
  I resolutely studied *Moore.*

Those touching lines from "Lalla Rookh," —
  "Ah, ever thus —" you know them well,
Such root within my bosom took,
  I wished *I* had a young Gazelle.

Oh, yes! a sweet, a sweet Gazelle,
" To charm me with its soft black eye,"
So soft, so liquid, that a spell
   Seems in that gem-like orb to lie.

Years, childhood passed, youth fled away,
   My vain desire I'd learned to quell,
Till came that most auspicious day
   When *some one gave me a Gazelle.*

With care, and trouble, and expense,
   'Twas brought from Afric's northern cape;
It seemed of great intelligence,
   And oh! so beautiful a shape.

Its lustrous, liquid eye was bent
   With special lovingness on me;
No gift that mortal could present
   More welcome to my heart could be.

I brought him food with fond caress,
   Built him a hut, snug, neat, and warm;
I called him " Selim," to express
   The marked *s(e)lim*ness of his form.

The little creature grew so tame,
   He "learned to know (the neighbors) well;"
And then the ladies, when they came,
   Oh! how they "nursed that dear Gazelle."

But, woe is me! on earthly ground
   Some ill with every blessing dwells;
And soon to my dismay I found
   That this applies to young Gazelles.

When free allowed to roam indoors,
   The mischief that he did was great;
The walls, the furniture, the floors,
   He made in a terrific state.

He nibbled at the table-cloth,
   And trod the carpet into holes,
And in his gambols, nothing loth,
   Kicked over scuttles full of coals.

To view his image in the glass,
  He reared upon his hinder legs;
And thus one morn I found, alas!
  Two porcelain vases smashed like eggs.

Whatever did his fancy catch
  By way of food, he would not wait
To be invited, but would snatch
  It from one's table, hand, or plate.

He riled the dog, annoyed the cat,
  And scared the goldfish into fits;
He butted through my newest hat,
  And tore my manuscript to bits.

'Twas strange, so light his hooflets weighed,
  His limbs as slender as a hare's,
The noise my little Selim made
  In trotting up and down the stairs.

To tie him up I thought was wise,
  But loss of freedom gave him pain;
I could not stand those pleading eyes,
  And so I let him go again.

How sweet to see him skip and prance
  Upon the gravel or the lawn;
More light in step than fairies' dance,
  More graceful than an English fawn.

But then he spoilt the garden so,
  Trod down the beds, raked up the seeds,
And ate the plants — nor did he show
  The least compunction for his deeds.

He trespassed on the neighbors' ground,
  And broke two costly melon frames,
With other damages — a pound
  To pay, resulted from his games.

In short, the mischief was immense
  That from his gamesome pranks befel,
And, truly, in a double sense,
  He proved a *very* " dear Gazelle."

At length I sighed — "Ah, ever thus
  Doth disappointment mock each hope;
But 'tis in vain to make a fuss;
  You'll have to go, my antelope."

The chance I wished for did occur;
  A lady going to the East
Was willing; so I gave to her
  That little antelopian beast.

I said, "This antler'd desert child
  In Turkish palaces may roam,
But he is much too free and wild
  To keep in any English home."

Yes, tho' I gave him up with tears,
  Experience had broke the spell,
And if I live a thousand years,
  I'll never have a young Gazelle.

Walter Parke

THE POETS AT TEA

I. — (MACAULAY)

Pour, varlet, pour the water,
  The water steaming hot!
A spoonful for each man of us,
  Another for the pot!
We shall not drink from amber,
  No Capuan slave shall mix
For us the snows of Athos
  With port at thirty-six;
Whiter than snow the crystals
  Grown sweet 'neath tropic fires,
More rich the herb of China's field,
The pasture-lands more fragrance yield;
For ever let Britannia wield
  The teapot of her sires!

II. — (TENNYSON)

I think that I am drawing to an end:
For on a sudden came a gasp for breath,
And stretching of the hands, and blinded eyes,
And a great darkness falling on my soul.
O Hallelujah! . . . Kindly pass the milk.

III. — (SWINBURNE)

As the sin that was sweet in the sinning
  Is foul in the ending thereof,
As the heat of the summer's beginning
  Is past in the winter of love:
O purity, painful and pleading!
  O coldness, ineffably gray!
O hear us, our handmaid unheeding,
  And take it away!

IV. — (COWPER)

The cosy fire is bright and gay,
The merry kettle boils away
        And hums a cheerful song.
I sing the saucer and the cup;
Pray, Mary, fill the teapot up,
        And do not make it strong.

V. — (BROWNING)

Tut! Bah! We take as another case —
  Pass the bills on the pills on the window-sill; notice the
    capsule
(A sick man's fancy, no doubt, but I place
  Reliance on trade-marks, Sir) — so perhaps you'll
Excuse the digression — this cup which I hold
  Light-poised — Bah! it's spilt in the bed! — well, let's on
    go —
Hold Bohea and sugar, Sir; if you were told
  The sugar was salt, would the Bohea be Congo?

VI. — (WORDSWORTH)

" Come, little cottage girl, you seem
　　To want my cup of tea;
And will you take a little cream?
　　Now tell the truth to me."

She had a rustic, woodland grin,
　　Her cheek was soft as silk,
And she replied, " Sir, please put in
　　A little drop of milk."

" Why, what put milk into your head?
　　'Tis cream my cows supply; "
And five times to the child I said,
" Why, pig-head, tell me, why? "

" You call me pig-head," she replied;
　　" My proper name is Ruth.
I called that milk " — she blushed with pride —
　　" You bade me speak the truth."

VII. — (ROSSETTI)

The lilies lie in my lady's bower,
(O weary mother, drive the cows to roost),
They faintly droop for a little hour;
My lady's head droops like a flower.

She took the porcelain in her hand
(O weary mother, drive the cows to roost);
She poured; I drank at her command;
Drank deep, and now — you understand!
(O weary mother, drive the cows to roost).

VIII. — (BURNS)

Weel, gin ye speir, I'm no inclined,
Whusky or tay — to state my mind
　　Fore ane or ither;
For, gin I tak the first, I'm fou,
And gin the next, I'm dull as you,
　　Mix a' thegither.

IX. — (WALT WHITMAN)

One cup for my self-hood,
Many for you. Allons, camerados, we will drink together,
O hand-in-hand! That teaspoon, please, when you've done
  with it.
What butter-color'd hair you've got. I don't want to be
  personal.
All right, then, you needn't. You're a stale-cadaver.
Eighteen-pence if the bottles are returned.
Allons, from all bat-eyed formules.

Barry Pain

ELLEN McJONES ABERDEEN

Macphairson Clonglocketty Angus McClan
Was the son of an elderly laboring man;
You've guessed him a Scotchman, shrewd reader, at sight,
And p'r'aps altogether, shrewd reader, you're right.

From the bonnie blue Forth to the beastly Deeside,
Round by Dingwall and Wrath to the mouth of the Clyde,
There wasn't a child or a woman or man
Who could pipe with Clonglocketty Angus McClan.

No other could wake such detestable groans,
With reed and with chaunter — with bag and with drones:
All day and all night he delighted the chiels
With sniggering pibrochs and jiggety reels.

He'd clamber a mountain and squat on the ground,
And the neighboring maidens would gather around
To list to his pipes and to gaze in his een,
Especially Ellen McJones Aberdeen.

All loved their McClan, save a Sassenach brute,
Who came to the Highlands to fish and to shoot;
He dressed himself up in a Highlander way;
Tho' his name it was Pattison Corby Torbay.

Torbay had incurred a good deal of expense
To make him a Scotchman in every sense;
But this is a matter, you'll readily own,
That isn't a question of tailors alone.

A Sassenach chief may be bonily built,
He may purchase a sporran, a bonnet, and kilt;
Stick a skeän in his hose — wear an acre of stripes —
But he cannot assume an affection for pipes.

Clonglocketty's pipings all night and all day
Quite frenzied poor Pattison Corby Torbay;
The girls were amused at his singular spleen,
Especially Ellen McJones Aberdeen.

" Macphairson Clonglocketty Angus, my lad,
With pibrochs and reels you are driving me mad.
If you really must play on that cursed affair,
My goodness! play something resembling an air."

Boiled over the blood of Macphairson McClan —
The Clan of Clonglocketty rose as one man;
For all were enraged at the insult, I ween —
Especially Ellen McJones Aberdeen.

" Let's show," said McClan, " to this Sassenach loon
That the bagpipes can play him a regular tune.
" Let's see," said McClan, as he thoughtfully sat,
" ' *In my Cottage* ' is easy — I'll practise at that."

He blew at his " Cottage," and blew with a will,
For a year, seven months, and a fortnight, until
(You'll hardly believe it) McClan, I declare,
Elicited something resembling an air.

It was wild — it was fitful — as wild as the breeze —
It wandered about into several keys;
It was jerky, spasmodic, and harsh, I'm aware;
But still it distinctly suggested an air.

The Sassenach screamed, and the Sassenach danced;
He shrieked in his agony — bellowed and pranced;
And the maidens who gathered rejoiced at the scene,
Especially Ellen McJones Aberdeen.

" Hech gather, hech gather, hech gather around;
And fill a' ye lugs wi' the exquisite sound.
An air fra' the bagpipes — beat that if ye can:
Hurrah for Clonglocketty Angus McClan! "

The fame of his piping spread over the land:
Respectable widows proposed for his hand,
And maidens came flocking to sit on the green —
Especially Ellen McJones Aberdeen.

One morning the fidgety Sassenach swore
He'd stand it no longer — he drew his claymore,
And (this was, I think, extremely bad taste)
Divided Clonglocketty close to the waist.

Oh! loud were the wailings for Angus McClan,
Oh! deep was the grief for that excellent man —
The maids stood aghast at the horrible scene,
Especially Ellen McJones Aberdeen.

It sorrowed poor Pattison Corby Torbay
To find them " take on " in this serious way;
He pitied the poor little fluttering birds,
And solaced their souls with the following words: —

" Oh, maidens," said Pattison, touching his hat,
" Don't blubber, my dears, for a fellow like that;
Observe, I'm a very superior man,
A much better fellow than Angus McClan."

They smiled when he winked and addressed them as
    " dears,"
And they all of them vowed, as they dried up their tears,
A pleasanter gentleman never was seen —
Especially Ellen McJones Aberdeen.

William S. Gilbert

THE RULING PASSION

FROM " MORAL ESSAYS," EPISTLE I.

The frugal crone, whom praying priests attend,
Still tries to save the hallowed taper's end,
Collects her breath, as ebbing life retires,
For one puff more, and in that puff expires.
  "Odious! in woollen! 'twould a saint provoke,"
Were the last words that poor Narcissa spoke;
" No, let a charming chintz and Brussels lace
Wrap my cold limbs, and shade my lifeless face:
One would not, sure, be frightful when one's dead, —
And — Betty — give this cheek a little red."
  The courtier smooth, who forty years had shined
An humble servant to all humankind,
Just brought out this, when scarce his tongue could stir,
" If — where I'm going — I could serve you, sir? "
  "I give and I devise " (old Euclio said,
And sighed) " my lands and tenements to Ned."
Your money, sir? " My money, sir! What, all?
Why — if I must " (then wept) — " I give it Paul."
The manor, sir? " The manor, hold! " he cried,
" Not that, — I cannot part with that," — and died.

Alexander Pope

TO PHŒBE

" Gentle, modest little flower,
    Sweet epitome of May,
Love me but for half an hour,
    Love me, love me, little fay."
Sentences so fiercely flaming
    In your tiny, shell-like ear,
I should always be exclaiming
    If I loved you, Phœbe dear.

" Smiles that thrill from any distance
    Shed upon me while I sing!

Please ecstaticize existence,
  Love me, oh, thou fairy thing!"
Words like these, outpouring sadly,
  You'd perpetually hear,
If I loved you fondly, madly; —
  But I do not, Phœbe dear.

William S. Gilbert

MATRONS AND MAIDS

I.

There's doubtless something in domestic doings
  Which forms, in fact, true love's antithesis;
Romances paint at full length people's wooings,
  But only give a bust of marriages;
For no one cares for matrimonial cooings,
  There's nothing wrong in a connubial kiss;
Think you, if Laura had been Petrarch's wife,
He would have written sonnets all his life?

Don Juan, III. st. 8

II.

However, I still think, with all due deference
  To the fair *single* part of the Creation,
That married ladies should preserve the preference
  In *tête-à-tête* or general conversation —
And this I say without peculiar reference
  To England, France, or any other nation —
Because they know the world, and are at ease,
And being natural, naturally please.

'Tis true, your budding Miss is very charming,
  But shy and awkward at first coming out,
So much alarm'd that she is quite alarming,
  All giggle, blush; half pertness and half pout;
And glancing at Mamma, for fear there's harm in
  What you, she, it, or they may be about;
The Nursery still lisps out in all they utter —
Besides, they always smell of bread and butter.

Beppo, stanzas 38-39
Lord Byron

TO THE PLIOCENE SKULL

A GEOLOGICAL ADDRESS

" Speak, O man, less recent! Fragmentary fossil!
    Primal pioneer of pliocene formation,
    Hid in lowest drifts below the earliest stratum
                Of volcanic tufa!

" Older than the beasts, the oldest Palæotherium;
    Older than the trees, the oldest Cryptogami;
    Older than the hills, those infantile eruptions
                Of earth's epidermis!

" Eo — Mio — Plio — whatsoe'er the ' cene' was
    That those vacant sockets filled with awe and wonder, —
    Whether shores Devonian or Silurian beaches, —
                Tell us thy strange story!

" Or has the professor slightly antedated
    By some thousand years thy advent on this planet,
    Giving thee an air that's somewhat better fitted
                For cold-blooded creatures?

" Wert thou true spectator of that mighty forest
    When above thy head the stately Sigillaria
    Reared its columned trunks in that remote and distant
                Carboniferous epoch?

" Tell us of that scene, — the dim and watery woodland
    Songless, silent, hushed, with never bird or insect
    Veiled with spreading fronds and screened with tall
        club-mosses,
                Lycopodiacea, —

" When beside thee walked the solemn Plesiosaurus,
    And around thee crept the festive Ichthyosaurus,
    While from time to time above thee flew and circled
                Cheerful Pterodactyls.

"Tell us of thy food, — those half-marine refections,
Crinoids on the shell and Brachipods *au naturel*, —
Cuttle-fish to which the *pieuvre* of Victor Hugo
Seems a periwinkle.

"Speak, thou awful vestige of the Earth's creation, —
Solitary fragment of remains organic!
Tell the wondrous secret of thy past existence, —
Speak! thou oldest primate!"

Even as I gazed, a thrill of the maxilla,
And a lateral movement of the condyloid process,
With post-pliocene sounds of healthy mastication,
Ground the teeth together.

And, from that imperfect dental exhibition,
Stained with expressed juices of the weed Nicotian,
Came these hollow accents, blent with softer murmurs
Of expectoration:

"Which my name is Bowers, and my crust was busted
Falling down a shaft in Calaveras County,
But I'd take it kindly if you'd send the pieces
Home to old Missouri!"

Bret Harte

THE POPE AND THE NET

What, he on whom our voices unanimously ran,
Made Pope at our last Conclave? Full low his life began:
His father earned the daily bread as just a fisherman.

So much the more his boy minds book, gives proof of
     mother-wit,
Becomes first Deacon, and then Priest, then Bishop: see
     him sit
No less than Cardinal ere long, while no one cries "Unfit!"

But some one smirks, some other smiles, jogs elbow and
    nods head;
Each winks at each: "I' faith, a rise! Saint Peter's net,
    instead
Of sword and keys, is come in vogue!" You think he
    blushes red?

Not he, of humble holy heart! "Unworthy me!" he sighs:
"From fisher's drudge to Church's prince — it is indeed
    a rise:
So, here's my way to keep the fact forever in my eyes!"

And straightway in his palace-hall, where commonly is set
Some coat-of-arms, some portraiture ancestral, lo, we met
His mean estate's reminder in his fisher-father's net!

Which step conciliates all and some, stops cavil in a trice:
"The humble holy heart that holds of new-born pride no
    spice!
He's just the saint to choose for Pope!" Each adds,
    "'Tis my advice."

So Pope he was: and when we flocked — its sacred slipper
    on —
To kiss his foot, we lifted eyes, alack, the thing was gone —
That guarantee of lowlihead, — eclipsed that star which
    shone!

Each eyed his fellow, one and all kept silence. I cried
    "Pish!
I'll make me spokesman for the rest, express the common
    wish.
Why, Father, is the net removed?" "Son, it hath caught
    the fish."

Robert Browning

RESIGNATION

I could resign that eye of blue,
    Howe'er it's splendor used to thrill me;
And e'en that cheek of roseate hue —
    To lose it, Chloe, scarce would kill me.

That snowy neck I ne'er should miss,
   However much I raved about it;
And sweetly as that lip can kiss,
   I think I could exist without it.

In short, so well I've learn'd to fast,
   That, sooth, my love, I know not whether
I might not bring myself at last
   To do without you altogether.

Thomas Moore

HOW TO ASK AND HAVE

"Oh, 'tis time I should talk to your mother,
   Sweet Mary," says I;
"Oh, don't talk to my mother," says Mary,
   Beginning to cry:
"For my mother says men are decaivers,
   And never, I know, will consent;
She says girls in a hurry to marry,
   At leisure repent."

"Then, suppose I should talk to your father,
   Sweet Mary," says I;
"Oh, don't talk to my father," says Mary,
   Beginning to cry:
"For my father he loves me so dearly,
   He'll never consent I should go; —
If you talk to my father," says Mary,
   "He'll surely say ' No.'"

"Then how shall I get you, my jewel,
   Sweet Mary?" says I;
"If your father and mother's so cruel,
   Most surely I'll die!"
"Oh, never say die, dear," says Mary;
   "A way now to save you I see:
Since my parents are both so conthrairy,
   You'd better ask *me*."

Samuel Lover

THE PLAIDIE

Upon ane stormy Sunday,
   Coming adoon the lane,
Were a score of bonnie lassies —
   And the sweetest I maintain
     Was Caddie,
That I took unneath my plaidie,
   To shield her from the rain.

She said that the daisies blushed
   For the kiss that I had ta'en;
I wadna hae thought the lassie
   Wad sae of a kiss complain:
     "Now, laddie!
I winna stay under your plaidie,
   If I gang hame in the rain!"

But, on an after Sunday,
   When cloud there was not ane,
This selfsame winsome lassie
   (We chanced to meet in the lane),
     Said, "Laddie,
Why dinna ye wear your plaidie?
   Wha kens but it may rain?"

Charles Sibley

AN IDYL

I saw her first on a day in Spring,
   By the side of a stream, as I fished along,
And loitered to hear the robins sing,
   And guessed at the secret they told in song.

The apple-blossoms, so white and red,
   Were mirrored beneath in the streamlet's flow;
And the sky was blue far overhead,
   And far in the depths of the brook below.

" I wadna hae thought the lassie
Wad sae of a kiss complain."

I lay half hid by a mossy stone,
   And looked in the water for flower and sky.
I heard a step — I was not alone:
   And a vision of loveliness met my eye.

I saw her come to the other side,
   The apple-blossoms were not more fair;
She stooped to gaze in the sunlit tide —
   Her eyes met mine in the water there.

She stopped in timid and mute surprise,
   And that look might have lasted till now, I ween,
But modestly dropping her dove-like eyes,
   She turned her away to the meadow green.

I lay in wonder and rapture lost
   At her slender form and her step so free,
At her raven locks by the breezes tossed,
   As she kicked up her heels in the air for glee.

The apple-blossoms are withered now,
   But the sky, and the meadow, and stream are there;
And whenever I wander that way I vow
   That some day I'll buy me that little black mare.
                      Charles Gurdon Buck

THE END

NOTES

Page 1. *Plain Language from Truthful James.* This poem, popularly known as "The Heathen Chinee," together with the brilliant story, "The Luck of Roaring Camp," established Harte's reputation. The poem was copied everywhere, and created a sensation, both in England and America.

5. *The Ahkoond of Swat.* The author of this capital burlesque was born in Canada, in 1845, and died in Philadelphia in 1886. Lanigan held responsible positions on the Chicago *Times,* St. Louis *Democrat,* New York *World,* and Philadelphia *Record.* Edward Lear has a comic poem on the same oriental potentate, entitled, "The Akond (*sic*) of Swat." It is included in Lear's *Laughable Lyrics: A Fourth Book of Nonsense Poems.*

9. *Widow MacShane.* Newell was born in New York City. Under the *nom de plume* of "Orpheus C. Kerr" (Office Seeker), he published a series of humorous and satirical papers on the Civil War, which met with great success. "Versatilities," 1871, contains most of his humorous verse.

13. *Robinson Crusoe.* The author of this poem is a broker and member of the New York Stock Exchange, who has made several successful excursions into the fields of children's, humorous, and fanciful literature. His books are published by the Harpers, Century, and Houghton, Mifflin companies.

16. *Only Seven.* This delicious parody on Wordsworth's "We are Seven" is taken from Mr. Leigh's "Carols of Cockayne," a volume of humorous verse which, in the judgment of Mr. W. Davenport Adams, "deserves to be put by the side of 'The Bab Ballads.'" Mr. Leigh was an early contributor to *Fun,* and has published several books of very clever verse. Line 34, *Ache-inside,* a pun on the name of the English poet, Mark Akenside, 1721 — 1770.

379

18. *An Actor.* The concluding lines of Ode X. of the " Farewell Odes for the Year 1786," by " Peter Pindar," beginning,

> " A modest love of praise I do not blame —
> But I abhor a rape on Mistress Fame."

19. *The Biter Bit.* This clever burlesque on Tennyson's " May Queen " is from the " Bon Gaultier Ballads," a series of parodies of modern poetry, collaborated by W. E. Aytoun and Theodore Martin.

20. *Ode to Tobacco.* The late Mr. Calverley was as truly a master in the field of lightly touched and refined comic poetry as either Locker-Lampson or Praed. An educator, lecturer, and lawyer, he was educated at Balliol College, Oxford, and Christ's College, Cambridge, and published " Verses and Translations," 1862, " Fly Leaves," 1872, etc. He carried the art of parody to a perfection never before attained.

26. *Captain Reece.* Gilbert is admittedly the greatest comic dramatist of our time. He collaborated with Sir Arthur Sullivan in producing numerous light operas, which still enjoy wide popularity. All of his poems in this book are taken from the inimitable " Bab Ballads." In *Captain Reece* may be discovered the germ of " H. M. S. Pinafore," and " The Pirates of Penzance."

36. *The Lawyer's Invocation to Spring.* There has been considerable discussion over the authorship of this poem. Rossiter Johnson assigns it to a Mr. H. P. H. Brownell, about whom little can be learned, but Bryant's " Library of Poetry and Song" attributes the authorship to Henry Howard Brownell. It is not contained among the latter's collected works.

38. *Rhymes of Ironquill.* The " Rhymes of Ironquill " were published in 1889, in Topeka, Kansas. Ten editions have been exhausted in this country, and several in London, and a new revised edition has just been published in New York by G. P. Putnam's Sons. The author is a prominent lawyer who has been appointed this year (1902) United States Pension Commissioner by President Roosevelt.

41. *The Baby's Début.* James Smith and his brother Horace were the co-authors of the celebrated " Rejected Addresses," 1812, a series of burlesques upon the style of famous contemporary poets, including Byron, Scott, and

Wordsworth. This book, which went through more than twenty editions within the first half-century after its publication, was pronounced by Parton "the most successful *jeu d'esprit* of modern times."

43. *Larrie O'Dee.* First appeared in *The Independent,* and has been widely copied.

53. *Salad.* An imitation of the style of Swinburne. Mr. Collins has produced many other successful examples of parody and genial persiflage.

53. *The Origin of the Banjo.* Irwin Russell was born in Mississippi in 1853, and died at New Orleans in 1879, at the early age of twenty-six. A posthumous volume of his poems was published by the Century Co. in 1888, with an introduction by Joel Chandler Harris. Mr. Harris pronounces Russell's "Christmas Night in the Quarters," from which our selection is taken, to be "inimitable," and adds that Russell's studies of negro and plantation life have never been surpassed.

55. *Wanderers.* This parody on Tennyson's "Brook" is as truly a masterpiece as its original.

60. *The Romance of the Carpet.* Burdette is a native of Pennsylvania, and served as a private during the Civil War. He entered journalism, and made his reputation as a humorist in the columns of the Burlington *Hawkeye.* In 1887 he entered the Baptist ministry. Author of numerous books. A few examples in this poem of assonance instead of perfect rhyme must be pardoned in view of its general effectiveness.

62. *The Friend of Humanity and the Knife-grinder.* From "The Anti-Jacobin," the famous collection of political satires, originated by Canning in 1797, and designed to expose the doctrines of the French Revolution. It appeared as a weekly newspaper containing both prose and verse, and edited by William Gifford. The "Friend of Humanity" was intended for Mr. Tierney, M. P., an aggressive reformer, and a member of the "Society of Friends of the People." The poem was written to ridicule the early poetry of Southey, being a parody of Southey's "The Widow." Canning's poem "is said to have annihilated English Sapphics." (L'Estrange's "History of English Humour," Vol. II.)

63. *Leedle Yawcob Strauss.* First published in the Detroit *Free Press* in 1876, these lines have been widely

popular. "Leedle Yawcob Strauss and Other Poems" was published in 1877 from the press of Lee and Shepard, Boston. "Dialect Ballads," Harper & Brothers, followed in 1888. Mr. Adams lives in Roxbury, Mass., and is well known as a public reader and entertainer.

65. *Jones at the Barber Shop. Punch* was founded in July, 1841. Among its most famous artists have been John Leech, John Tenniel, Gilbert, H. K. Browne, and George Du Maurier. The literary staff has included such names as Douglas Jerrold, Doctor Maginn, Thackeray, Tom Taylor, Mortimer Collins, and F. C. Burnand.

66. *Wedded Bliss.* Mrs. Gilman is prominent as a lecturer upon social reforms and woman's suffrage. Her most widely known poem is "Similar Cases," a vigorous satire which nothing except its length has crowded out of this anthology.

68. *Address to the Toothache.* Line 3, *lug,* ear; 15, *giglets keckle,* youngsters giggle; 16, *loup,* leap; 17, *heckle,* flax-comb; 18, *doup,* bottom; 19, *dools,* sorrows, woes; 20, *hairsts,* harvests; 20, *cutty-stools,* stools of repentance (*cutty,* short or small). This cutty-stool was "conspicuously placed in front of the pulpit, and the penitent, the opening prayer being done, was conducted to it by the beadle, sat on it through the service, and at the close arose from it to receive the rebuke." 21, *mools,* mould, grave; 23, *fash,* annoyance; 24, *gree,* prize; 28, *raw,* a row; 32, *gars,* makes, causes; 36, *towmond,* twelve-month.

77. *True to Poll.* A song from the famous extravaganza, "Poll and Partner Joe." Burnand was educated at Eton and Cambridge, became editor of *Punch,* and is the author of numerous successful plays, farces, and burlesques. He was knighted by King Edward in 1902.

87. *The V-A-S-E.* Mr. Roche, editor of *The Pilot,* since 1890, is a native of Ireland. He has published a biography of his friend, John Boyle O'Reilly, three volumes of successful verse, and several other books.

92. *Cure for Homesickness.* The author is a journalist of Auburn, Maine, whose writings for the Lewiston *Journal* and *Saturday Evening Post* of Philadelphia have been widely popular. Of the selections in this book, "Uncle Tascus and the Deed" is from "Pine Tree Ballads," 1902; the other poems are from "Up in Maine," 1900.

94. *To the Lord of Potsdam.* Mr. Seaman's "Cap and

Bells" and "The Battle of the Bays," published by John Lane, are filled with admirably witty verse, and prove the author to be, since Calverley, the foremost among English parodists and wits.

100. *Dibdin's Ghost.* Field has been happily characterized by Mr. Stedman as "the Yorick of American Poetry." The Dibdin referred to in this poem is Thomas Frognall Dibdin, D. D., the distinguished English bibliographer, 1776 — 1847.

104. *My Other Chinee Cook.* The author of this ballad was born and educated in Scotland, but has passed most of his life in Australia. Of his volumes of verse, "Convict Once," Macmillan, 1885, is the best known.

106. *Prehistoric Smith.* Proudfit printed most of his verse in the New York *Daily Graphic* under the *nom de plume* of "Peleg Arkwright," a pseudonym which was accidentally attached to his first publication, and which he finally discarded. His "Love Among the Gamins, and Other Poems," was published by Dick & Fitzgerald, of New York, in 1877, his "Mask and Domino" by Porter & Coates, Philadelphia, in 1888. The verses quoted are from the latter volume.

108. *The Irish Schoolmaster.* Doctor Sidey, an Edinburgh surgeon, published a book of verses for private circulation, entitled, "Mistura Curiosa," from which this poem is taken. "The Irish Schoolmaster" has been set to music and sung all over Great Britain.

113. *Mr. Barney Maguire's Account of the Coronation.* We are told by Barham's biographer that this poem was composed as a pure improvisation, and published with but few changes. The Irishman is supposed to be relating the result of his observations at the coronation of Victoria (June 28, 1838), to his associates in the Servants' Hall upon his return from the ceremony. How he managed to insinuate himself into the Abbey is not explained. For exhaustive notes on this poem, explaining all the historical allusions, see the (London) *Academy and Literature* for August 9, 1902.

117. *Feminine Arithmetic.* From "Lyrics by the Letter H," published in New York by J. C. Derby in 1854. Charles G. Halpine, the author, born in Ireland, was graduated at Trinity College, Dublin, spent several years in London, and, after emigrating to the United States, engaged in

journalism, first in Boston, and afterward in New York. During the Civil War he was an officer in the Northern army. He assumed, in 1862, the pseudonym of "Miles O'Reilly," a "private in the Forty-seventh New York," which at once became a household word in all parts of the North.

117. *Sky-making.* "An admirable *reductio ad absurdum* of a pet theory of Professor Tyndall's." W. D. Adams.

123. *A Piazza Tragedy.* First published in the Denver *Tribune,* and included in "A Little Book of Tribune Verse."

129. *A Kiss in the Rain.* Doctor Peck is a physician of Tuscaloosa, Alabama, who has written much graceful verse. This selection is from "Cap and Bells," 1886.

131. *Vat You Please.* The author, J. R. Planché, was a native of London, and produced about two hundred plays and extravaganzas, besides books of travel, biography, heraldry, fairy tales, and verse.

134. *Tam O'Shanter.* Line 1, *chapman billies,* peddlers or small tradesmen; 2, *drouthy,* thirsty; 4, *gate,* road; 5, *nappy,* ale; 8, *slaps,* breaches in hedges or walls; 19, *skellum,* a worthless fellow; 20, *blellum,* a babbler; 23, *melder,* a quantity of corn sent to the mill to be ground; 25, *naig,* horse, nag; 31, *mirk,* dark; 33, *gars me greet,* makes me weep; 38, *unco,* unusually; 39, *ingle,* fire; 40, *reaming swats,* foaming ale; 81, *skelpit,* hastened; 86, *bogles,* hobgoblins, bogies; 90, *smoor'd,* was smothered; 103, *ilka bore,* every chink; 108, *usquabae,* whisky; 109, *the swats,* etc., the ale so wrought in Tammie's head; 110, *boddle,* a farthing; 119, *winnock-bunker,* window-seat; 121, *tousie tyke,* a shaggy dog; 123, *gart,* made; 123, *skirl,* scream; 124, *dirl,* ring; 127, *cantraip,* spell; 131, *airns,* irons; 134, *gab,* mouth; 148, *till ilka carlin,* etc., till each old beldam smoked with sweat; 149, *coost,* stript; 149, *duddies,* rags, clothes; 150, *linket,* tripped, danced; 150, *sark,* shirt; 151, *queans,* young girls; 153, *creeshie flannen,* greasy flannel; 154, *Seventeen hunder linen,* woven in a reed of seventeen hundred divisions; 155, *thir breeks,* these breeches; 157, *hurdies,* thighs; 158, *burdies,* lassies; 160, *rigwoodie,* lean or ancient; 160, *spean,* wean; 161, *crummock,* crooked staff; 163, *brawlie,* full well; 164, *wawlie,* hearty, robust; 171, *cutty,* short; 171, *harn,* a coarse cloth; 174, *vauntie,* proud of it; 176, *coft,* bought; 179, *cour,*

lower; 181, *lap and fling*, jumped and kicked; 185, *fidg'd*, fidgeted; 186, *hotch'd*, hitched; 188, *tint*, lost; 193, *fyke*, fuss; 194, *byke*, hive; 201, *fairin*, deserts; 210, *fient*, fiend (petty oath), *fient a*, not a; 213, *ettle*, design, aim.

140. *The Latest Decalogue.* No one at all acquainted with Clough's poetry will need to be assured that the flippancy which may be suspected to exist in this and the following poem is only apparent. Clough was as reverent, truth-loving a soul as ever lived. His invectives against Phariseeism, religious or social, are no less fierce because so often couched in the language of irony, but they are always manly and sincere.

152. *The American Traveller.* Originally appeared in the " Orpheus C. Kerr Papers," First Series, Letter Third. Republished in " Versatilities " (poems), Boston: Lee and Shepard, 1871. Newell introduces the poem by the facetious explanation that he wrote it in reply to an article in a British journal, affirming that all our writers are but weak imitators of English authors, and that such a thing as a distinctively American poem *sui generis* had not been produced.

155. *Song of One Eleven Years in Prison.* From the " Anti-Jacobin," 1798. Sung by Rogero in the burlesque play of " The Rover." The first five stanzas are by Canning; the last stanza is said to have been added by Mr. Pitt.

156. *Mary the Cook-maid's Letter.* " Doctor Sheridan, one of Swift's friends and butts, was a schoolmaster of considerable wit and scholarship, and progenitor of a distinguished family, in which genius is hereditary. . . . Swift delighted in showing his knowledge of servants — their phraseology, and ways of thinking." Leigh Hunt: *Wit and Humour.*

162. *Holy Willie's Prayer.* Line 32, *fash'd*, troubled, annoyed; 56, *splore*, a row; 60, *kail*, cabbage; 70, *pish'd wi' dread*, filled with dread; 71, *snakin*, sneering; 81, *gear*, goods, wealth. " Holy Willie" was a certain William Fisher, an elder in the parish church of Mauchline, who was active in the prosecution of Mr. Gavin Hamilton, a friend of Burns, on the charge of violation of the Sabbath and neglect of ordinances. Robert Aiken was Hamilton's counsel. Henley calls the poem an " amazing achievement in satire . . . so nice, so exquisite in detail, so overwhelming in effect."

164. *What Mr. Robinson Thinks.* This selection, like *The Courtin'*, p. 29, is from "The Biglow Papers." It is Number III. of the First Series. "This satire was directed against the Mexican War, which was forced upon the country in 1845 by the South, in conformity with their policy of an extension of slave territory." H. C. Lodge.

166. *John Gilpin.* The editor has taken the liberty of printing the stanzas (written as quatrains) in the form of couplets, for the sake of economizing space. He believes that little is lost by this merely formal alteration. *John Gilpin* was first published anonymously in *The Public Advertiser* in 1782. "The story was related to Cowper by Mrs. Austen, and is supposed to refer to a Mr. Bayer, 'an eminent linen draper,' whose shop was situated at the corner of Cheapside, London." Adams's "Dictionary of English Literature."

173. *The Irishman and the Lady.* William Maginn, born at Cork, was educated at Trinity College, Dublin, and was on the staff of *Blackwood's* and *Fraser's*.

177. *He Came to Pay.* Mr. Kelley was born in New York, and contributed humorous verse, 1870 — 1880, to the *Century* and the Detroit *Free Press*. This poem was imitated from "The Aged Stranger" of Bret Harte.

181. *The Wife.* From "Poems and Parodies," Boston: Ticknor, Reed & Fields, 1854. A parody on James Aldrich's "A Death-bed" ("Her suffering ended with the day," etc.). See Stedman's "American Anthology," p. 197.

186. *The Poster-Girl.* This clever parody on Rossetti's "Blessed Damozel" first appeared in the *Century*. Miss Wells lives in Rahway, N. J. She has published "The Jingle Book," 1899, "Idle Idyls," 1900, and several other books.

188. *The Prayer of Cyrus Brown.* Mr. Foss has published four volumes of humorous and dialect verse, which have had an extensive sale. He is librarian of the Somerville, Mass., City Library, a member of the Boston Authors' Club, and a popular public reader and lecturer.

191. *The Chimpanzor and the Chimpanzee.* Hamilton received his education at Trinity College, Dublin. Wrote "Dublin Doggerels," 1877, and "The Moderate Man," 1888. A member of the Royal Irish Academy.

194. *A Rhyme for Priscilla.* An admirable example of delicately turned society verse. Included in " Madrigals and

Catches," 1887 (Stokes), and quoted by kind permission of the author. Mr. Sherman is adjunct professor of architecture at Columbia University.

200. *The Usual Way.* Mr. Weatherley, born in 1848, was graduated at Brasenose College, Oxford, 1871, and called to the bar in 1887. Lyrics, librettos, children's books.

212. *Jabberwocky.* The clergyman, mathematician, and laureate of the nursery, who wrote under the pen name of " Lewis Carroll," was one of the most rare and versatile geniuses of modern times. This selection is from " Through the Looking Glass," the sequel to " Alice in Wonderland," and has been well called " an inimitable satire upon the unintelligible school in modern poetry." Some prefer to consider it a piece of pure fun without any deeper meaning. In either case, it must be regarded, as Mr. Davenport Adams says, " a miracle of ingenuity."

213. *Little Mamma.* Mr. Webb lives in Nantucket, Mass. His best known books are " Vagrom Verse," 1889, and " With Lead and Line," 1901. He founded *The Californian* (1864), to which Mark Twain and Bret Harte contributed.

218. *Father William.* Parody on a well-known didactic poem by Robert Southey, beginning

> "'You are old, Father William,' the young man cried,
>   'The few locks which are left you are gray,'"

and entitled in Southey's works, " The Old Man's Comforts, and How He Gained Them." Another capital parody on this original is " You are young, Kaiser William," by Mostyn T. Pigott, contained in T. A. Cook's " Anthology of Humorous Verse," London : H. Virtue and Co. The opening stanzas are too good not to quote :

> " 'You are young, Kaiser William,' the old man exclaimed,
>   'And your wisdom-teeth barely are through,
> And yet by your deeds the whole world is inflamed —
>   Do you think this is proper of you ?'
> 'As a baby I doted on playing with fire,'
>   Replied the irascible prince,
> 'And though I was spanked by my excellent sire,
>   I've been doing the same ever since.'
>
> " 'You are young,' said the Sage, 'and your juvenile legs
>   Are not what one would call fully grown ;
> Yet you point out to Grandmamma how to suck eggs —
>   Why adopt this preposterous tone ?'
> 'As a child,' said the youth, 'I perceived that my head
>   Wouldn't ever allow me to learn,
> So I made up my mind to start teaching instead,
>   And I've taught everybody in turn.'"

224. *Elegy on the Death of a Mad Dog.* From "The Vicar of Wakefield," Chapter 17. Goldsmith had severely attacked the popular "plaintive elegies" of his day in the "Enquiry into the Present State of Polite Learning in Europe," 1759. The ironical purpose of his own burlesque elegies is apparent. The epigrammatic conclusion of the stanzas in this and the "Mary Blaize" elegy (p. 291), was imitated from the French. Goldsmith's model was "Le fameux La Galisse," each stanza of which "ends with a ludicrous truism."

225. *Woman's Will.* The same conceit is embodied in a couplet included in Adams's "English Epigrams." It is by one R. Hugman, and dates from about 1628. Is this a case of unconscious reminiscence on the part of the American humorist, or is it a pure coincidence? Here is the couplet:

> " WHY WIVES CAN MAKE NO WILLS.
> " Men dying make their wills, why cannot wives?
> Because wives have their wills during their lives."

Probably the jest is much older even than the seventeenth century.

225. *A Lawyer's Daughter.* This clever quatrain appeared some years ago in *Life*. The editor has been unable to learn anything regarding the author.

226. *My Lord Tomnoddy.* Robert B. Brough wrote successful comedies, which were produced at the Olympic and other theatres, and published "Songs of the Governing Classes," in 1855.

240. *Ould Doctor Mack.* Appeared in the *Spectator* for November 9, 1889. Graves is an Irish writer, whose "Songs of Killarney," 1873, and other books of verse have been popular.

242. *The White Squall.* "Surely one of the most graphic descriptions ever put into verse. Nothing written by Thackeray shows more plainly his power over words and rhymes. He draws his picture without a line omitted or a line too much, saying with apparent facility all that he has to say, and so saying it that every word conveys its natural meaning." Anthony Trollope, in "Thackeray," Chapter 8 (English Men of Letters Series).

247. *The Banished Bejant.* Murray, the son of a Scotch clergyman, was born in New England, but was taken to Scotland in early boyhood. He lived in England and

Scotland, until his death in 1894. Educated at St. Andrews University. In 1890 published "The Scarlet Gown," a collection of clever parodies. This selection is, of course, a parody on Poe's "The Haunted Palace." *Bejant* (*i. e.* yellow-beak or fledgeling) is equivalent in the vernacular of St. Andrews and Aberdeen universities to *freshman.*

248. *The Smack in School.* Palmer was a graduate of Williams College, who studied medicine, but became a journalist. He wrote numerous poems, serious and comic, of which the rustic idyl which we quote seems to have the most tenacious lease of life.

251. *Sary "Fixes Up" Things.* Mr. Paine is one of the editors of *St. Nicholas.* He has contributed to *Scribner's, Century,* and other magazines, and has published numerous books, mostly for children.

254. *The Hunting of the Snark.* Part of "The Bellman's Speech," and "The Baker's Tale," divisions of Carroll's "The Hunting of the Snark: An Agony in Eight Fits." The entire poem, an extraordinary example of fanciful comicality, has 137 stanzas.

257. *Kentucky Philosophy.* The author of this popular poem, which has been widely copied in school readers and elsewhere, lives in Louisville, Kentucky.

259. *Bait of the Average Fisherman.* Mr. Dodge is a facile writer of newspaper verse, much of which has seen the light in the Detroit *Free Press.*

260. *On the Death of a Favorite Cat.* These lines were sent by Gray in a letter to Horace Walpole, who had written to the poet that his "handsome cat" had been drowned in a bowl of goldfishes. Gray's letter is delightfully humorous.

261. *Here She Goes, and There She Goes.* James Nack, a native of New York City, met with an accident in his ninth year which deprived him of speech and hearing. He was placed in the Institution for the Deaf and Dumb in New York, where he showed great aptitude in the mastery of languages. He published four volumes of original verse.

265. *In the Catacombs.* Mr. Ballard was born in Ohio, is a graduate of Williams, and lives in Pittsfield, Mass. He is librarian of the Berkshire Athenæum, and president of the Agassiz Association, and has written several books. This poem has long been a favorite in reading

and declamation books. A few alterations from the
commonly known version have been made by the author, at
his personal request, for the present compilation.

274. *Mr. Molony's Account of the Ball.* This poem " is
so like Barham's ' Coronation ' in the account it gives of
the guests that one would fancy it must be by the same
hand." Trollope. " Thackeray has made for himself a
reputation by his writing of Irish. In this he has been
so entirely successful that for many English readers he has
established a new language which may not improperly be
called Hybernico-Thackerayan." *Ibid.* Line 43, *troat.* No
Irishman would naturally use such a word, but, as Trollope
points out, the visitor from Erin on coming to London finds
that he is wrong with his " dhrink," etc., and thus begins
to leave out h's wherever he can.

276. *Kitty of Coleraine.* Lysaght was graduated at
Trinity College, Dublin, in 1782, and took his M. A. at
Oxford in 1784. Practised law for many years at the
English and Irish bars. Some compilations give this poem
as anonymous, but there is small ground for doubting
Lysaght's authorship.

277. *Reasons for Drinking.* Henry Aldrich, D. D., was
dean of Christ Church, Oxford, and wrote several works
on architecture, logic, etc.

282. *False Love and True Logic.* Laman Blanchard
was an English *littérateur* who was associated with Bulwer
as editor of *The New Monthly Magazine,* in 1831, and
subsequently assisted in editing several other prominent
journals. His poetical works were published with a memoir
in 1876.

291. *An Elegy on Mrs. Mary Blaize.* From *The Bee,*
1759; Number 4. Gray's " Elegy " (1751) gave rise to a
mass of imitations, and it was apparently Goldsmith's
purpose in his different satirical elegies to ridicule this
fashionable kind of sentimentalism.

297. *Casey at the Bat.* This lively ballad, a masterpiece
of its kind, was a great favorite with the late Charles A.
Dana, of the New York *Sun.* Few American poems have
been so widely copied in the press. The author recently
died at his home in St. Louis.

301. *Old Grimes.* Judge Greene was one of the founders
of the Providence Athenæum, and was president of the
Rhode Island Historical Society, 1854 — 1868. He was

a graduate of Brown University. His poems have never been collected.

303. *Widow Bedott to Elder Sniffles.* "The Widow Bedott Papers," by Mrs. Frances Miriam (Berry) Whitcher, were introduced to public notice through *Neal's Saturday Gazette,* edited by Joseph C. Neal, author of "Charcoal Sketches," and were subsequently published in New York by Mason, Baker, & Pratt, with an introduction by Mrs. Alice B. Neal. The lines quoted are from the thirteenth chapter of the "Papers."

305. *Home They Brought Her Lap-dog Dead.* This and the following poem are parodies on Tennyson's "Home They Brought Her Warrior Dead." Mr. Brooks was editor of *Punch,* 1870 — 1874.

306. *The Recognition.* Mr. Sawyer is an English versifier who has written much successful comic poetry for the pages of *Funny Folks* and other periodicals.

312. *The Jumblies.* "'I shall place Mr. Edward Lear first of my hundred authors' — so Mr. Ruskin has said, and the saying is by no means the least wise of his literary judgments. To write inspired nonsense is a gift vouchsafed to few, and to no man was it given in more lavish measure than to Edward Lear. . . . Lear is in his way as consummate an artist as Shelley or Coleridge are in theirs." Walter Whyte, in "The Poets and Poetry of the Century," Vol. ix.

314. *My Angeline.* Mr. Smith is the author of librettos for numerous successful comic operas, among others "Robin Hood," "Rob Roy," "The Fencing Master," etc. He published "Lyrics and Sonnets" in 1894, and "Stage Lyrics," 1901.

317. *The Ideal Husband to His Wife.* The two last stanzas are omitted.

319. *The Confession.* Barham's original reads, in last line :

"I've eat, and can't digest."

320. *The Editor's Wooing.* Appeared in the "Orpheus C. Kerr Papers," 1862, Series I., Letter 15.

321. *Our Traveller.* Mr. Pennell entered the public service (of Great Britain) in 1853, has been Inspector of Fisheries, and has held other official appointments. He has written numerous works on angling, as well as "Puck

on Pegasus," and several other books of successful *vers de société*.

326. *Epitaph Intended for His Wife.* This epigram has been frequently paraphrased. The following, for example, is cited in Adams's "English Epigrams":

> "Here lies my wife, poor Molly: let her lie,
> She's found repose at last, and so have I."

326. *A Farewell to Tobacco.* Sent in a letter to Wordsworth and his sister in September, 1805. Published in *The Reflector*, No. iv., 1811. The metre was Lamb's favorite, as well as that of George Wither, whom Lamb admired and imitated. The poet's "alternate praise and abuse of his theme is borrowed from the 'Author's Abstract of Melancholy,' prefixed to Burton's 'Anatomy'" (Ainger).

326. *On Hearing a Lady,* etc. George Outram was a Scotch lawyer and journalist. Author of "Lyrics, Legal and Miscellaneous."

326. *Dido.* Doctor Porson was a graduate of Trinity, Cambridge, and was elected Greek professor in that university in 1785. He wrote this epigram on the Latin gerunds in proof of the assertion that he could rhyme upon anything suggested. See his Life by Watson (1861), also Adams's "English Epigrams."

330. *If I Should Die To-night.* These clever lines are a parody on "If I Should Die To-night," by Belle E. Smith, to be found in Warner's "Library of the World's Best Literature," Volume xxviii. The parody is from "Ben King's Verse," Boston: Forbes & Co.

333. *The Walrus and the Carpenter.* From "Through the Looking Glass." Mr. W. D. Adams, in his "Witty and Humorous Side of the English Poets," calls this poem "the best possible subject that could be chosen as the test of any person's humorous capacity. If this did not excite his risible faculties, then he would be in a bad way."

339. *Sympathy.* Almost the only excursion into the province of humorous composition of this distinguished English prelate and hymnist.

340. *The Millennium.* Mr. Stephen (not to be confounded with J. B. Stephens) was born in London, and educated at Eton and Cambridge. Athlete, tutor, journalist, poet, public official, his short career was one of brilliant promise. He published two volumes of verse. This selection is from "Lapsus Calami, and Other Verses," Cambridge, 1896. It first appeared in the *Cambridge Review*, February, 1891.

341. *Clam-soup.* Mr. Croffut served in the Civil War, and has travelled widely. He has been engaged in newspaper work since 1854. Has published many books, including "Poems," 1895. In 1899 he organized the Anti-Imperialist League.

341. *On Taking a Wife.* "The story is told of R. B. Sheridan and his son." "English Epigrams."

341. *The Remedy Worse than the Disease.* The Doctor Radcliffe satirized by Prior was born in 1650, and died in 1714. He founded the Radcliffe Library at Oxford.

347. *That Gentle Man from Boston Town.* From "In Classic Shades, and Other Poems," Belford - Clarke Company, Chicago, 1890. Mr. Miller's collected works are now published by The Whitaker & Ray Company, San Francisco.

354. *The Rejected National Hymns.* Appeared in the First Series of "Orpheus C. Kerr Papers," Letter 8, and included a running commentary in humorous prose. The hymns attributed to Edward Everett, George P. Morris, and R. H. Stoddard are omitted. In Newell's "Versatilities," 1871, the Everett hymn is assigned to Charles Sumner.

356. *Earth.* From "The Bashful Earthquake, and Other Fables and Verses" (Scribner's). Included, together with "Gold," p. 342, by personal permission of the author.

360. *Our Native Birds.* Included under the title of "Larks and Nightingales," in Doles's "The Hawthorn Tree, and Other Poems," New York: Crowell, 1895. The change in title is made at the personal request of the author.

361. *The Young Gazelle.* From "Songs of Singularity," by Walter Parke, an English comic poet, sometimes known as the "London Hermit." He has written a great deal of clever nonsense verse.

364. *The Poets at Tea.* The stanza parodying the style of Poe is omitted. Barry Pain has been the editor of *To-day* since 1897. On staff of London *Daily Chronicle* and *Black and White.* Lives in London.

376. *An Idyl.* Published in *The Manhattan Magazine* for March, 1884. Quoted in "Humorous Masterpieces from American Literature," Putnam.

INDEX OF FIRST LINES

INDEX OF TITLES